The Preacher's Treasury: Being One Hundred Outlines of Sermons, Selected from "The American National Preacher."
by Rev. John Morgan

Copyright © 2019 by HardPress

Address:
HardPress
8345 NW 66TH ST #2561
MIAMI FL 33166-2626
USA
Email: info@hardpress.net

THE
𝔓reachers' 𝔗reasury:

BEING

ONE HUNDRED OUTLINES OF SERMONS,

SELECTED FROM

"THE AMERICAN NATIONAL PREACHER."

BY

REV. JOHN MORGAN.

THIRD SERIES.

A NEW EDITION

London:
R. D. DICKINSON,
73 (LATE 92), FARRINGDON STREET.
1871.

INDEX OF TEXTS.

	Page.		Page.
Gen. v. 26	255	Isa. v. 20	59
vii. 1	270	xi. 1—4	308
Exod. v. 2	80	xxxviii. 16	209
xx. 12	212	xlv. 1—6	312
14	217	l. 10	71
Num. xiv. 20, 1	175	lx. 22	1
Deut. xxxii. 47	268	lxii. 6, 7	74
2 Sam. ix. 3	237	Jer. iii. 5	186
2 Kings iv. 13	196	ix. 4	150
viii. 13	206	Lam. i. 9	124
Neh. vi. 3	273	Dan. vii. 27	26
Job v. 24	160	ix. 3	111
24	163	Zech. iv. 6	132
vii. 2, 3	37	xiii. 6	64
xi. 20	32	Mal. iii. 11	104
xxii. 21	234	Matt. v. 44—7	148
Psalm xxvi. 9	188	vi. 10	200
xlix. 8	224	30	45
lxvi. 18	81	vii. 13	90
xc. 12	294	16	220
cxxii. 7	157	ix. 37, 8	94
cxxxix. 7	293	x. 35	260
Prov. iv. 18, 19	131	xiii. 3	214
xv. 24	140	33	201
Eccles. vi. 3	153	xxvi. 13	33
		24	21

	Page
Mark iii. 17	42
ix. 2	290
x. 23	85
Luke ii. 37	199
xvi. 22	296
25	15
xix. 8	144
8, 9	159
xxii. 32	104
John v. 28, 9	227
xii. 32	283
xiii. 23	42
Acts ii. 33	166
33	169
33	173
xvi. 13—15	245
29—34	143
xvii. 30	104
xx. 32	184
xxiv. 25—7	143
Rom. vi. 21	311
vii. 19	106
viii. 6	77
28	306
1 Cor. ii. 2	231
xv. 17	242
2 Cor. i. 5	49

	Page
2 Cor. iii. 2	100
iv. 3	286
v. 20	136
vii. 10	53
x. 5	252
xii. 1—4	248
Eph. i. 22, 3	240
vi. 10	291
Philip. i. 28	276
ii. 5	194
1 Thes. v. 22	68
1 Tim. i. 15	250
ii. 1, 2	128
5	302
vi. 19	309
2 Tim. ii. 15	180
Heb. ix. 13, 14	96
xii. 22—4	229
James iv. 17	104
1 Peter ii. 17	54
iv. 13	49
1 John iv. 10	319
Jude 14, 15	115
Rev. iii. 8	289
xx. 11	119
13	265
xxii. 13	299

The Ministries of Time.

By the Rev. A. L. STONE, D.D., Boston.

"I the Lord will hasten it in his time."—Isaiah lx. 22.

GOD is sovereign and omnipotent, but He waits the ministration of time. He could force seasons and laws, but it is His way rather to work through them and by them. Time is the prime minister of providence, and brings to pass in due order, at their full periods, and at the appointed juncture, the patient counsels of the Most High. There is no hurrying and no sickness of deferred hope on that eternal and tranquil mind. "One day is with the Lord as a thousand years, and a thousand years as one day."

Man is strong, and works great changes upon the earth, and his fellow-man. Art is strong, and produces its rapid marvels. The forces serving the human will are nimble and muscular. Heat and frost lift up monuments of their might and magic. The fires of earth's centre, the winds that sweep over her surface, the seas that thunder along her shores, these have their power and their trophies. But time is the great magician. All these latter forces are sinews of its own arm. The changes, the revolutions, the histories of this world are only chronicles of the vice-regency of time.

It is fitting, as the swift shuttle glances past again, drawing another thread into the woven fabric of God's scheme for earth and man, bringing out yet more clearly the parts in the pattern for the whole, that we pause to consider this ministry of time in accomplishing the divine pleasure. If the whole scope of the supreme administration may not be known thus, we may gather at least some of the principles and particulars that unite at last to perfect that consummate whole. We shall see that time is among men the revealer, the attester, the vindicator, the rectifier, the fulfiller.

I. *Time tests the principles of human conduct.*

I speak here of avowed principles, consciously, perhaps boldly proceeded upon, set in contrast or antagonism with one another. There is a difference among men, both in theory and in practice, in respect to these principles. The diversity and the divergence illustrate themselves in innumerable ways. Look in upon two scenes of family training. In one of them the idea is, with the controlling head, that the true end of domestic nurture is *social success ;* and all the care and painstaking converge to this issue. In the other the commanding object is the *formation of a right character.* The interior life of gentle manners must be gentle thoughts. The only external polish that will never grow coarse is the outshining of inward purity and kindness.

You shall hear now the first of these two systems remonstrating with the other—predicting social isolation, social failure, urging the demonstrative and forcing culture, adopting it for the sons and daughters under its guardianship, and resting cheerfully and complacently in its superior discernment and wisdom. And, to be sure, the sober, puritanical portion of the rising generation were left quite outside this conventional society. And so the issue was made, and the trial of the two systems entered upon. And in the one circle doors stood wide open to social settlement and domestic alliances. And sometimes it was felt, I know, on the other side, that all such doors were shut against them. They seemed isolated from those of their own age; their seclusion was uninvaded, they could improve their minds, cultivate their taste, study the secrets of happy, dignified, and well-ordered homes, quite to themselves; and the more worldly policy looked like a success. There all was bright and glittering,—here lay a shadow. There, there was mating and marrying, and giving in marriage—here all relations were undisturbed. Taking life as it is, this more select discipline promised to be barren of results. But principles are everlasting verities; they change not,—they are of slow development often,—their seed lies cold and motionless long,—their harvest comes late,— but it comes. Such issues are not to be settled in a day. Their trial takes in, in its progress, more elements than are at first seen to be included. The earlier appearances are not reliable exponents of the final consummation. Across the breadth of years I look and read the story truer. The paths of life from those two circles, the streams from those separate fountains, are visible before me. The gay, brilliant type quickly darkened and degenerated. There were early excesses—there were early and dishonoured graves—there were floating wrecks of vice and dissipation—there were sad, sad tales of shame and anguish—there were miserable disappointments. The glittering bubble burst, and there was nothing in the hand but the stain of defiling moisture.

On the other side, there was always a wealth of personal resources—there was a growing but unconscious refinement—there was fostered a selecter and more discriminating taste; solid and abiding qualities grew with the passing youthful season, and when more difficult and fastidious minds came searching for fresh, unsoiled natures, and an outfit for wider and higher spheres, they found the golden fruit hidden beneath the overshadowing leaves, and gathered it with pride and joy. Time is the slow scribe, the sure expounder.

One man argues that,—"Take the world as it goes, and you must practice upon it to gain your ends." Another man plants his foot immovably upon the conviction that honesty is the best policy; and the two procedures start together on the track. The first success is almost always on the side of cunning. Slow moving, downright honesty is speedily distanced. Ah! wait a little. Principles have had their development, and each after its kind borne their fruit. Time has ripened and gathered it— apples of Sodom for the one, apples of gold, nay, golden-globed sweetness from the tree of life for the other. This is the demonstration of principle that cannot be set aside—the demonstration of time.

II. *Time is the test of friendships.*

Where is the love that never grows cold,—that outlives youth and bloom,—that was founded on deeper and more vital attractions than those that pass away with life's roseate morning? Where are the hands that used to clasp ours? Have they warm and welcoming palms for us still? Where are the lips that smiled upon us once? Do they keep smiles or sternness for us now? How many of our later associations have kept their first gushing promises in truth and faithfulness? And yet we must not judge harshly. We have been deceived and betrayed, but we must not generalize from that instance. We have broken through the ice here and there, but there may be yet broad fields of it as firm as a marble floor. The very hearts that we pronounce alienated and estranged may rather have become wearied than chilled. Dislocated from one side, the broken fibres of social affection must cling somewhere. Thrown upon other fellowships, the tendrils have caught and twined about fresh objects. Once they were all free to turn and choose as they listed, but they have been pressed long since into new alliances, and have responded to the new appeals as once they responded to ours. But in this very fact they show that their nature is unchanged. To human love, if not to our personal memory, they are still true; yes, and bring back the old relations, and we, it may be, should not find them wanting. This is what time teaches.

III. *Time tries his tests upon character.*

Sorrowful, often, we are made to watch this process. All seems fair outwardly. We have unbounded confidence. We surrender our gravest trusts. We rest upon this tried and approved integrity. It becomes a standard-bearer in the most salient advances of Christianity. It wins a good report. It stands a pillar, straight, strong, and upright. Lay your weight there, build thereon; and we build, and feel secure for solid years. And, one day, there is a crash. It was only the shell of a pillar; either within it was all rottenness and hollowness, or a sudden and violent wrench twisted it out of place, and down it came, fallen and broken. It is a mournful lesson time has read us. Whom shall we trust? What shall we build with? Character that has stood seemingly all severer tests, passed unsullied amid youthful passions and summer temptations, met the hour and call of solemn duties, took on the sober livery of its autumn staidness and ripeness—can not this be confided in? Are life-long victories over manifold forces of evil no security? Ah! one test remains. It is a silent, patient, long-waiting detective. At last it gives in its report, and we are stricken dumb with surprise and grief. Hastily, perhaps, we say,—"All is over; this is the end; there is nothing left there; here shuts down the gate of life and hope." And time may yet correct this too hasty conclusion, and read us an unpublished story that would draw deep upon our tenderest sympathies, and forbid us to pass capital sentence upon our brother on one indictment only, when we are impeachable in many points, and lead up out of the valley of humiliation a chastened penitent,— a restored wanderer,—whose lore in divine grace and infinite compassion shall surpass all that we have known, whose fitness for rare and special service shall be tempered in this fiery furnace, and whose evening of life shall yet show a serene and glowing west.

Is there a ghost in every house, a phantom dogging every

man's footsteps, a secret in every bosom? Time becomes the minister of justice; and the last words of every dying year wake in guilty breasts this dreary echo,—"There is nothing covered that shall not be revealed, and hid, that shall not be known."

And yet there are those to whom this word is not dreary, but animating; not a menace, but a long-sustaining promise. They have been under a cloud. Their character has been unrighteously aspersed. Men have believed evil of them. They have been the victims of mistakes, or of circumstances, or of malignant conspiracy. Many a hand has been withdrawn from them; many a face has turned away. Friends, once trustful and beloved, have passed by on the other side. So they have walked on in the cold shadows of the long night, waiting for the dawn; and the slow hours rolled away. They had no hope but in God, and God sent to them this championship of time. It is seen that character is not committed to human keeping. No enemy can take it from us; and when girt about with hissing serpents, who boast that they have us in their own den and power, we can stand in the heroism of this single truth,—"The Lord is on my side, I will not fear; what can man do unto me?" Observe:—

1. The real struggle of a man's life, the crisis of his moral history, time often holds in reserve. It comes not in his sheltered boyhood, over which bend only bright and genial skies. His youth glides past him, a peaceful stream flowing on through gentle meadows. Manhood takes him by the hand, and there has been as yet no faltering in his step. He seems to have conquered in the fields of life, to have mastered his passions without a conflict. He knows not, and no man knows, the strength of his propensities. The hour of trial has never fairly fronted him. It may happen to him to know better by and by. The ripe hour hurries on. The train is fired, and the tumult begins. Let him gird himself like a man. The combat rages. What a fearful strife! Forward and backward the tide ebbs and flows. No such strain as this has ever tested the might of his arm. He has called himself a soldier, but he has never had a field-day till now. What if it should go against him? He pants, and bleeds, and falters. Oh! woe the day, if he have not a Divine Helper, or if he forget to look up for heavenly succour! Let no man speak harshly of the fallen,—let no man plume himself upon his own immaculateness. Our day may come.

2. God even commits His own vindication to time. He delays, both to visit for daring wrong, and to reward patient faith.

His threatenings and His promises seem laid aside, forgotten. The impious cry derisively,—"Where is the promise of His coming?" and the believer,—"Lord, how long?" But there is no demonstration from the silent heavens. That sovereign hand begins its work afar off. It rolls up, not a single event, but an ordered and massive system. The good die while yet the consummation hoped for lingers. The vile triumph, and their seed seems established in the earth. Then on the vast, dim dial, the index points to the appointed hour, and vengeance and deliverance do their work; and, amid blasphemy confounded and righteousness exultant, sounds the blessed voice,—"I the Lord will hasten it in his time."

3. In the individual life, the grandest spiritual truths are learned late. Here, as in all learning, there is an alphabet first, and more wondrous revelations afterward. For these deeper and more radiant mysteries there must be often a peculiar preparation.

4. But these ministries of time touch heart-nerves in passing. There are weeping kindreds here, who dreamed not a year ago, in their glad security, what time had in store for them; that he should lead their best-beloved away from their circle; that he was weaving ever, while they smiled and slept, a winding-sheet for tender, fair, and manly forms; that, in the silence and in the darkness, he was digging a grave, and lettering some sweet household name in marble.

5. Yet time has a ministry of consolation too. It is of God that his touch has such a balm in it. He wipes away tears; he unknits the furrowed brow; he brings back the smile to the quivering lips; he leads the captive forth into the sunshine; he gathers upon the bereaved the tender and soothing spell of memory; he plants flowers in the path where bleeding feet have walked, pierced by the thorns.

O time! what dost thou yet keep back from us? No voice answers. Into the mist opens no vista of light. But this we know, time is a creature of God. It waits upon that sovereign will. It comes to us, a guide sent from heaven, to conduct us onward into the good-pleasure of One whom, in life and in death, we can trust with our mortal and immortal hopes.

The Retributive Power of Memory.
By Rev. SAMUEL T. SPEAR, D.D., Brooklyn.

"But Abraham said, Son, remember that thou in thy lifetime receivedst thy good things, and likewise Lazarus evil things: but now he is comforted, and thou art tormented."—Luke xvi. 25.

WHEN the life that now is shall be past, and that which is to come shall be present, it will be the office of memory to establish and perpetuate the connection of knowledge between these two periods of our conscious being. Without such a connection, the religion of the Bible, considered as expounding the relations between time and eternity, would seem to be a failure. The theory of probation here, followed by judgment and retribution hereafter, in order to be consciously realized in the future life, supposes that we shall be able in that life to return our thoughts to the scene through which we are now passing, reproducing it in the eye of the mind. This we must do, or we could not identify ourselves as the same beings, in the two states; nor could we see the relation between what we *are* in the one life, and what we have *done* in the other. The rich man who lifted up his eyes in the world of woe, was told to recur in thought to the facts of his former lifetime. True, his body had died; but his memory was still living and active, fully able to go back to the world he had left, and recall its scenes. Those, moreover, who believe in the immortality of the soul, whether on the ground of reason, or revelation, or both, must also believe in the immortality of its faculties. Reason, memory, and conscience belong to this class of mental powers. We see not in what way death can wield any agency, either to destroy these powers or impair their activity. How shall we be affected by this return of thought to the scenes of an earthly life? To this solemn and deeply interesting question, 1 propose in the present sermon to seek an answer, using our present knowledge of memory, as the medium of ascending to the sight of things future and eternal.

I. *What, then, is memory ? Let us first define the faculty.*

Every one is aware of the fact, that the knowledge which we have once acquired, the things we have seen and done, the experiences that we have had, though not always present to the mind, are nevertheless so *retained*, that these same things may be, and often are, recalled to our mental notice. Every one is fully conscious of such a fact in his own history. We designate this fact by the term memory. Memory is, therefore, the mind's power of preserving and knowing its own past history. This is memory here : it is the kind of mental activity to which we apply the term ; and if the faculty be immortal, it will be memory hereafter. A change of worlds will not alter the nature of the power. It is the same in both worlds. We are, moreover, so constructed, that we cannot discredit the knowledge given by memory. I am as certain of what I distinctly remember, as I can be of anything.

From this definition we see at a glance the immense importance of memory in the constitution of man. Without it he would be nothing as a spiritual being, either here or hereafter. The absolute loss of memory would destroy the whole framework of his mental existence, by limiting his intellectual life to the impressions of the passing moment. He would know nothing of the past, and could rise to no view of the future. He could neither love nor hate, hope nor fear. Observe what the faculty now does, how it traverses the silent chambers of the past, preserving our knowledge, and diffusing light and life, health and force, through the complicated energies of our mental nature; we are lost in the contemplation of what it will do, when the hindrances of flesh and blood are gone, and the ever-increasing ages of the past shall be the field of its endless action.

II. *Let me say that memory operates in obedience to established and permanent laws.*

No one can have failed to see, at least in a general sense, that our ideas are in some way so connected together that they are mutually suggestive of each other, and hence proceed in companies or regular trains. The object present to the eye of thought brings up one that is absent, in virtue of some relation between the two ; and thus we advance from thought to thought with the utmost celerity, precision, and certainty of movement.

> "Lulled in the countless chambers of the brain,
> Our thoughts are linked by many a hidden chain :
> Awake but one, and lo ! what myriads rise !
> Each stamps its image as the other flies."

Thus, according to this law of similars, you see a portrait, and you instantly think of the person whom it represents. You meet a man whom you never saw before, passing him without saying a word, and that man suggests to you an absent friend, perhaps long since dead, owing to some resemblance, very slight, it may be, between the two persons. According to the law of opposites, vice will suggest virtue, and wealth poverty. Again, things that have been contemplated together in either time or place, are for this reason so connected that they are suggestive of each other ; and this general fact is called the law of proximity or nearness. Thus the man of three-score years and ten has no sooner fixed his mind upon some item of his childhood, than a whole army of other items passes under his review. He can talk for hours together, reproducing with great vividness the by-gone scenes of early life, separated from them in time but not in thought. Still further, things that hold to each other the relation of dependence expressed by the term cause and effect, have the same power of mutual suggestion.

Such, then, are the hidden chains or laws of mental association, by which our thoughts are linked together, and hence have the power of rescuing each other from the grave of oblivion. By them we conduct the process of memory. We do it without labour, yea, by necessity, having no power not to do it. We can neither change the laws, nor refuse to accept the results of their action. The truth is, we must remember ; we must converse with the past. By a force wholly within itself, by a necessary energy in its own nature, alike inscrutable and irresistible, the mind makes the connection, in virtue of which our thoughts reproduce and follow each other in regular trains. It is so constructed by its great Author, that it must think in this way. And if such be its present constitution, —if the laws of memory be inherent in the very nature of man's soul,—if our intellectual reproduction and recognition of the past be thus an absolute necessity in the present life, think you that a transfer of the mind to other scenes will be the end of these facts? Exactly the opposite is the probability to be gathered from what we now know of man. Thus we think of ourselves as intelligent, conscious, voluntary, in both worlds, in both exercising memory according to fixed laws, some of which at least rule our present life.

III. *I wish to call your attention to the extent of its retentive and reproductive power.*

In the amazing greatness of this power, as we observe it in time, we shall perhaps find the condition of at least conjecturing what it will be in eternity. It was the opinion of Lord Bacon that nothing in one's antecedent history is ever irrecoverably forgotten. Coleridge held the same view. We know, as a matter of positive experience, that the prominent and leading facts of life past are safely retained in the bosom of memory. The available contents of this faculty, those to which we have constant access, and which, because they are so common, excite but little attention, evince the marvellous scope of its power. They show the breadth, extent, and force of this grasp upon the past. Even the most common man may well be astonished at the vast resources of his own memory. The laws of memory, alike irresistible and infallible, contain a most wonderful arrangement to transmit the soul along the corridors of the past, even to the remotest period. They are suited to lay open the broad field of its realities, and bring them under present view. One knows not where to fix the boundary of a process conducted and facilitated by such powerful laws.

The many instances of remarkable memory that we gather from history, are an instructive commentary upon the greatness of this power. Themistocles, we are told, could call by their names the twenty thousand citizens of Athens. It is said of Cyrus, that he could repeat the name of every soldier in his army. Hortensius, one of the orators of Rome, after sitting a whole day at a public sale, could enumerate from memory all the things sold, their prices, and the names of their purchasers. Ben Jonson could repeat all that he had ever written, and whole books that he had simply read. Seneca, the rhetorician, was able to repeat two thousand names read to him in the order in which they had been spoken; and on one occasion, two hundred unconnected verses having been pronounced in his hearing, he at once repeated the whole of them in a reversed order. Sir Wm. Hamilton, who states these facts, also mentions the case of a young Corsican who could, without the slightest hesitation, repeat "thirty-six thousand names in the order in which he had heard them, and then reverse the order, and proceed backward to the first," and this, too, after the lapse of a whole year. It is said of Pascal, that he " forgot nothing of what he had read, or heard, or seen." There are persons who can recite every word of a lengthy discourse upon simply hearing it once.

There are also many striking and peculiar cases of resuscitated knowledge, in which apparently extinct memories are suddenly restored. Numerous instances of quickened memory, under the influence of physical causes, show what the mind may do under special and extraordinary exaltations of its activity. Persons on the brink of death by drowning are said to have unusually vivid visions of the past.

If such be memory here, in this nascent state of our being,—this mere infancy of our intellectual life,—what may it not be, and what may it not do, when, with our other faculties, freed from a body of flesh and blood, it shall soar in progressive expansion and enlargement through the ages of a coming eternity? We cannot well avoid the inference that this faculty will rise to a scope, a compass, a certainty, precision and fulness of action, that will throw the most vivid light of thought back upon our anterior being. We shall doubtless more perfectly recollect the life that now is, looking at it from eternity, than we can now recollect it, looking at it from time.

> "Each fainter trace that memory holds
> So darkly of departed years,
> In one broad glance the soul beholds,
> And all that *was* at once appears."

The Bible regards the present and the future as merely two stages in the history of one and the same being, linking them together in the relation of time, and in that of moral dependence, implying, too, the continuance of the same mental faculties; and analogy, coinciding with this Bible view, and studying memory in the light of those impressive facts which are earthly, passes onward and upward to those greater facts which are future and eternal. Beginning thus with the data of experience, reason flies to the land of spirits, and there beholds the immortal Memorist in the full vigour and vastness of His endless career. "Remember," says the word of God,—"Remember," echoes the responding voice of reason.

IV. *What is to be the impression of memory upon our happiness or misery in the future world?*

That so great a power will make an impression upon the soul, pleasant or painful, according to the character of the facts embraced in the exercise, is an inference derivable not only from the greatness of the power, but equally from the ample materials of our present experience.

Those who, in their conduct towards God and man, have been governed by the principle of virtue, ordinarily enjoy the rich blessing of very pleasant memory. [Instance Paul.]

Just the opposite experience, even on earth, will sooner or later flow from a life distinguished by opposite qualities.

> "Sometimes the universal air
> Seems lit with ghastly flame;
> Ten thousand thousand dreadful eyes
> Are looking down in blame."

Facts, to almost any extent, some of them of the most startling character, are ready to testify to the truth of this picture. The disquietude, bitterness, and despair felt by every sinner in the hour of his conviction, his dissatisfaction with himself, his fears for the future, his universal wretchedness of feeling, grow out of the elements of his own life, as rehearsed to him by the faithful voice of memory. [Instance Voltaire, Newport, and Altamont.] The lines of Lord Byron, penning and publishing the retrospective griefs of his own spirit, seem pertinent to this entire class of cases,—

> "My days are in the yellow leaf;
> The flowers, the fruits of love are gone;
> The worm, the canker, and the grief
> Are mine alone.
> The fire that on my bosom preys
> Is lone as some volcanic isle;
> No torch is lighted at its blaze—
> A funeral pile."

In respect, then, to the dead who die in the Lord, the Bible assures us that they are blessed, not only in the fact that they rest from their labours, but also in the further fact that their works do follow them. As Christians, they could hardly understand themselves in the skies without recurrence to these antecedents of preparation for and progress towards their heavenly home.

What shall we say of memory in the experience of those whom God's decree for life's misdeeds has consigned to penal woe? In whatever this woe may consist, whether in the natural effects of sin, or in special inflictions, or in both combined, it is, in relation to the consciousness of the subject and the sufferer, an experience, something which he feels, and the reasons of which he cannot but know,—memory for ever keeping up the connection of thought between what he is and what he was. I have no desire to speak in terms of extravagance or severity; yet I cannot but think that it will be a dreadful thing to remember in hell. What is there in a life that breaks the law of duty, incurs the frown of heaven, and ruins the soul, of which one can ever think with pleasure? It is a clear doctrine of both reason and revelation, that the more light one has, making a bad use thereof, the more guilt he incurs, and proportionately the darker his prospects for the world to come. My prayer to God is, that we may so act in this life, that when we review it in the next, memory will be our blessing, and not the minister of endless woe.

Lessons from the Life and End of Judas Iscariot.

By Rev. W. S. PLUMER, DD., LL.D., Allegheny, Pa.

"It had been good for that man if he had not been born."—Matt. xxvi. 24.

SUCH is the alarming and astounding language of the Lord Jesus Christ respecting one of his disciples and apostles. The person here spoken of is Judas, whose surname is Iscariot. Judas, Juda, Judah, Jehudah, and Jude are all the same word, varied only in unimportant particulars. One of Jacob's sons was called Judah. From him descended the tribe, within whose territory was Jerusalem, and from which arose the name of Jews. After the ten tribes broke off, Judah designated the tribes of Judah and Benjamin, while the rest were called Israel. One of the Maccabees, very renowned in history, was called Judas. Another of them, who bore the same name, suffered martyrdom under Antiochus Epiphanes. Besides these, there are several other persons of the same name, more or less noticed in Jewish history before the coming of Christ. After that we have an account of four men called Judas. The word Iscariot is variously derived. Some say it is an abbreviation of Issachariothes, and simply declares that he was of the tribe of Issachar. Others derive it from two Hebrew words that unitedly signify a man of murder. Others suppose that his surname simply shows that he was of the place called Carioth, or Kerioth. This is probably the true explanation. Ish-Carioth, or Iscariot, is literally a man of Carioth.

Of this man the fearful sentence is uttered by the Lord,—"It had been good for that man if he had not been born." What language of terror! Well might any ears tingle at the sound. What heart can conceive the awful and tremendous import of those words? Let us consider the life and end of him of whom they were spoken. But before entering into the particulars of his history, a few general remarks are pertinent.

1. There is no evidence that Judas Iscariot was a man of bad countenance. Most men are much influenced by looks, and many think they can tell a man's character by the physiognomy. This may often be true, but there are many exceptions.

2. There is no evidence that, up to his betrayal of his Lord, his conduct was the subject of censure, complaint, jealousy, or of the slightest suspicion. His sins were all concealed from the eyes of mortals. He was a thief, but that was known only to Omniscience.

3. There is no evidence that, during his continuance with Christ, he regarded himself as a hypocrite. Doubtless he thought himself honest.

4. Let it not be supposed that Judas ought not to have known his character. He shut his eyes to the truth respecting himself.

The first mention made of this man is entirely creditable to him. He is introduced to us as one of the twelve, whom Christ chose as disciples and confidential friends, to be with Him, and hear His instructions, both public and private. Having for some time been a disciple, the Lord ordained him with the other eleven to the office and work of an apostle. (Matt. x. 2-4; Mark iii. 13; Luke vi. 12.) Since the birth of Christ, this is the highest office to which any mortal could attain. [Mention various incidents in his life, as given by the evangelists,—enlarge upon the betrayal of Christ.]

The aggravations of the sin of betraying Christ were many and great. The traitor was eminent in place, in gifts, in office, in profession; a guide to others, and

Lessons from the Life of Judas Iscariot.

one whose example was likely to influence many. The lessons taught us by the life and end of Judas are such as these:—

1. Though wicked men do not so intend, yet in all cases they shall certainly glorify God by all their misdeeds. "Surely the wrath of man shall praise thee: the remainder of wrath shalt thou restrain."—Ps. lxxvi. 10. The wickedness of Judas was by God over-ruled to bring about the most important event in man's salvation. The wicked now hate God, but they cannot defeat Him.

2. Nor shall God's unfailing purpose to bring good out of evil abate aught of the guilt of those who work iniquity. Judas' treason was all foretold, and of course it was predetermined. Yet his accountability for his wickedness was unimpaired; for he acted freely in all he did. Men may clamorously assert, but they never can prove, that the divine purpose so interferes with moral agency as to impair human obligation to do right. Judas acted with perfect freedom. He could not have had more liberty, therefore his guilt remained. That which was true of the betrayer, was also true of the murderers of our Lord.—Acts ii. 23, and iv. 27, 28.

3. From the history of Judas we also learn, that when a man is once fairly started in a career of wickedness, it is impossible to tell where he will stop. God's grace may arrest one in the maddest career, as it did Saul of Tarsus; but left to himself, man will dig into hell. The good providence of God mercifully restrains even the wicked, else existence on earth would not be desirable. Unrestrained, every heart would show its possessor a monster of wickedness. Natural affection, the voice of conscience, public opinion, regard to reputation, and fear of the law, are happily employed by providence to hold men back. Even in this life many a poor sinner has been affrighted at the lengths which he had gone in crime and debasement, and has cried out in sore amazement,—"And have I come to this! In the next world surprise awaits all the impenitent.

4. All men should especially beware of covetousness. "The love of money is the root of all evil: which while some coveted after, they have erred from the faith, and pierced themselves through with many sorrows."—1 Tim. vi. 10. Of the truth of this teaching Judas was a fearful witness. No tongue, no pen can describe the sorrows which rolled over his soul.

5. Did men but know how bitter would be the end of transgression, they would at least pause before they plunge into all evil. Oh! that men would hear the warning words of Richard

Baxter,—"Use sin as it will use you: spare it not, for it will not spare you; it is your murderer and the murderer of the world. Use it, therefore, as a murderer should be used."

6. In Judas' pretended regard for the poor, we see what foul wickedness may be covered with the most plausible pretences. The same thing is seen in every age. By false names, every virtue is depressed and every vice exalted.

7. Nor should we forget that character may as well be learned from small as from great things. Judas' petty larceny was as good an index to his character as his treason. A straw will show which way the wind blows. Human character is not made up of a few great acts, but of a multitude of little things. Everyday conduct shows the man.

8. It is also manifest that bad men may for a long time appear well. An honest blunderer is to be preferred before the most cunning knave on earth. A life of deception is full of hardship and uncertainty; and at its close, when amendment is impossible, the truth comes out; in a moment damnation flashes in the face, and the poor soul enters on an existence full of misery.

9. And yet bad men might know the truth concerning themselves if they did not hate it. Judas well knew his own theft, yet he refused to consider it a sin to be repented of.

10. How small a temptation to sin will at last prevail over a vicious mind. For less than twenty dollars, Judas sold his Lord and Master. Those temptations commonly esteemed great are not the most sure to prevail.

11. Nothing prepares a man for destruction faster than hypocrisy or formality in actions of a religious nature. The three years which Judas spent in the family of our Lord probably exceeded all the rest of his life in ripening him for destruction. So many, so solemn, so impressive truths were presented to his mind, that he must have become very rapidly hardened.

12. We should never forget that official character is one thing, and moral character another thing. *All* official characters may be sustained without any real grace in the heart. Balaam's prophecies were as true and as sublime as those of Moses or Isaiah. So far as we know, Judas' performance of the duties of his apostolic mission was as acceptable and as useful as that of the majority of his brethren. Even success in preaching is not proof of piety. It is the message, not the messenger,—the truth preached, and not the man who utters it, that converts the soul.

13. The history of Judas shows us how man will cling to false hopes. There is no evidence that during years of hypocrisy he ever seriously doubted his own piety.

14. If men thus self-confident forsake their profession, and

openly apostatize, we need not be surprised. It has been so from the beginning. Jesus had his Judas. Peter must deal with Ananias, Sapphira, and Simon Magus. Paul was in perils among false brethren, and Demas quite forsook him.

15. The case of Judas gives us the rule of admission to church-membership, and, so far as moral character is concerned, to church offices. We may require a credible profession of piety. Infallible evidence of love to Christ is not attainable. A profession of piety, accompanied by such evidence as a consistent life affords, is as much as we may demand. Our Saviour knew Judas from the beginning to be a bad man,—" a devil,"—but His omniscience, not the overt acts of Judas, taught Him thus, and so He received him into the church, leaving us an example that we should follow His steps.

16. Thus, too, we have a full refutation of the objection made to a connection with the visible church, because there are wicked men in her communion. The apostles certainly knew that among them was one bad man; but they did not therefore renounce their portion among Christ's professed friends. And Christ Himself held intercourse with Judas, just as if he were all he professed to be. So that, if one certainly knew another to be an enemy of God, and yet could not prove it to the satisfaction of impartial church authorities, this should not debar him from the Lord's table. And in all our dealings with men, it is better to be sometimes imposed on, than to be of a suspicious temper.

17. How difficult it is to bring home truth to the deceitful heart of man. Hypocrites are slow to improve close, discriminating preaching. They desire not to look into their real characters. It was not until all the rest had inquired whether Christ referred to them in foretelling His betrayal, that Judas said,—" Lord, is it I?"

18. Nor could one do a wiser thing than to inquire whether he has better evidence of piety than the great traitor had during his apostleship. Judas could heal the sick, raise the dead, and cast out devils. He was first a disciple, and then an apostle of our Lord. He often heard Christ preach. He held the only office of trust among the apostles. His reputation for piety stood as fair as any man's.

19. The case of Judas discloses the uselessness of that sorrow of the world which worketh death, hath no hope in it, and drives the soul to madness. It is not desperation, but penitence, that God requires. Regrets without hatred of sin are useless, both on earth and in hell.

20. In the case of Judas we have also a fearful example of

the terrible judgment of God against the wicked. How fearful must it be to fall into the hands of the living God, when on earth a drop of His wrath will make men choose hanging rather than life. And how dismal must be the prospects of all who die in their sins, when they shall have for their companions Judas and all evil-minded men, the devil and his angels. The society of the damned is good ground for earnestness in fleeing from the wrath to come.

21. The doctrine of universal salvation has no countenance in scripture. It is disproven by many express declarations, and by many fair and necessary inferences. It is disproven by the case of Judas. If, after many thousand years of suffering, he shall rise to everlasting happiness in the skies, it will be good for him that he was born. Eternal happiness far outweighs all temporal suffering, however protracted. Any existence which terminates in eternal glory will prove a blessing beyond all computation. All temporal suffering can be gauged. But who can fathom the sea of love,—the ocean of bliss,—made sure to all believers? And eternal misery is as dreadful as eternal glory is desirable. Oh! how fearful must be the doom of the incorrigibly wicked, when in their case existence itself ceases to be desirable, or even tolerable! It is true of every one who dies without repentance towards God, and faith in our Lord Jesus Christ, that IT HAD BEEN GOOD FOR THAT MAN IF HE HAD NOT BEEN BORN.

The Reign of the Saints.

By Rev. WALTER CLARKE, D.D., New York.

"And the kingdom and dominion, and the greatness of the kingdom under the whole heaven, shall be given to the people of the saints of the Most High."—DAN. vii. 27.

THIS is part of Daniel's prediction concerning the order of empire in the Christian ages. In a previous vision, the prophet had seen the world, with all its races, interests, institutions, and destinies, made over to Christ, the universal King. But, as this great empire, and every part of it, was then in alien hands, Daniel was permitted to complete the vision, and, by a second revelation, beheld the historic transfer of races, and governments, and trades, and destinies, to their appointed Owner—the King of kings and Lord of lords. These prophetic paragraphs, therefore, are a carefully prepared chart, revealing the course of empire, till it consummates and ends in the universal reign of our Lord Jesus Christ. This is the topic upon which I propose to discourse this evening : the empire of the world falling at length into the hands of the saints. Let me say, then,—

I. *That the doctrine of our text does not require us to believe that the Lord Jesus Christ is, at some future time, to return in person to our world, and set up a visible and theocratic empire upon all these continents.*

The kingdom of which we are to discourse is a spiritual kingdom. It asks and needs no visible manifestation of its Lord, no earthly metropolis, or sceptre, or throne. And though the reign of the saints is to be a wide-spread and universal rule, yet I shall need to say,—

II. *That the Scriptures do not require us to teach or to believe this doctrine even in any absolute, extreme, and unexceptionable sense.*

The meaning of the Scriptures, if I do not altogether mistake their sense, is, that the saints as persons, and their great Christian maxims as principles, shall ultimately win such an ascendency over all nations, interests, institutions, and affairs, that this whole world shall become an orderly and well governed Christian empire. If there shall be impenitent men, as there may be, they shall nevertheless, either of their own will, or by the constraint of others, submit to Christian usages, and acquiesce in just and salutary laws. We shall need to inquire, then, and with a discriminating and cautious care,

III. *As to the way in which this great conquest is to be achieved.*

Are the saints of the Most High, after a series of moral victories, wrought with peaceful weapons, and by the aid of the all-conquering Spirit of God, to change their tactics and go forth, in coming times, with their armies to dislodge the wicked, and settle as victors on all the continents ? The Scriptures everywhere discourage such conclusions. They that take the sword shall perish by the sword. The weapons of our warfare are mighty, but are not carnal,—are mighty because they are not carnal.

It is a great law of nature,—a law operating among all the orders of the animate creation,—that the superior race shall win ultimate ascendancy over the inferior. Put two children, two men, two tribes together, and let them associate, and interact, and adjust their relative forces and positions, and no matter what titles or what opportunities you bequeath to the inferior, or what stigmas and restraints you cast upon the stronger, as time advances, the weaker will submit to the mightier. The people of God have no need to assail the nations; they have no use for arms, and no license for invasion. They have only to keep their Christian virtues, and exercise them, and by this simple process they shall at length acquire a kingdom, and dominion, and the greatness of the kingdom under the whole heaven.

But there is another question touching the manner in which the saints are to get possession of this world, which we shall need to consider before we can fully comprehend the meaning of Scripture. Will the saints of the Most High, as they advance and take possession of the world, remove existing governments, offices, orders, and customs? And will they set up in their place the one great institution, the Church, making all offices spiritual? The Scriptures hold no such language. According to the pattern which they present, society, as she has many interests, must equip herself also with many executive institutions and organs. And, since civil order is as indispensable to social well-being as spiritual thrift, the State is an institution as truly divine as is the Church. The one is Christ's authoritative organization, for the control and government of things spiritual. The other is His twin organization, for the management and direction of things temporal. And the moment either of these bodies invades the other's territory, and undertakes to regulate affairs in which it has no jurisdiction,—the moment a Hildebrand ventures to dictate to states, or a Henry aspires to be head of the church, that moment the world is out of joint, and disorder and debasement must certainly ensue. Let me remark, in reference to this conquest of the nations for Christ,—

IV. *That according to all Scriptural intimations, it will be a very gradual conquest.*

We mistake when we imagine that the great revolutions which the Bible predicts, or any other great revolutions, are to be accomplished suddenly, so that either prophecy or history can determine the exact day on which they occur.

V. *That it is to be, and in a twofold sense, complete and universal.*

It will embrace all territory,—covering the continents, going forth to the islands, possessing the seas. It will include all races, it will embrace all arts, all sciences, all trades, all interests, all governments, all usages, all compacts, all relations. Taking possession of a country, a district, a race, on heathen or on Christian ground, merely taking possession is only the commencement of the great work which the saints have in hand. Having got possession of the territory, they are then to revolutionise and re-construct, revolutionise and re-construct till they shall build up upon the new site a Christian state, to be the habitation of righteousness, the city of the Lord, the new earth. That the people of God will one day possess and govern the world, might be conclusively argued,—

1. From the known nature of their religion. Take the religion of the New Testament, and give it to any race or people under heaven, and let it remain among them, and do its work in them, and that people, thus endowed, will ultimately possess and govern the world. The same conclusion might be argued,—

2. From the actual history of the church, since it has had a place among the nations. Impoverished and alone, the disciples of Christ began their work, and they and their successors have carried it forward through the centuries to the present time. Look forth, then, at this moment, and observe, for example, how much of the world's wealth has come into the hands of God's saints during these last eighteen centuries? How much of the world's wealth, and her sources of wealth, do the saints possess to-day? Or, take any other element of social power. Take intelligence, for instance: the mastery of all arts, the knowledge of all sciences, the ability to influence and affect the world, and what an accumulation of all forms of enduring and practical wisdom have the saints of these bygone centuries made? Who are the pioneers in all the sciences? Who lead the way in all the trades? Who explore the unknown seas? Who discover the unknown continents? Who pilot the ways of traffic? Who are the men that are thus the lights of the ages? For eighteen centuries, the saints have been gradually getting possession of the world,—of its intelligence, of its arts, of its property, of its positions of power and influence. The Church is wiser, stronger, richer to-day than she ever was before. Project this Church into the future now! Let the saints of God go on for the centuries to come, acquiring and accumulating as they have done in times gone by, and is not here an argument to attest what the prophet foresaw?

8. All the indications of providence point, as with a prophetic finger, to the same grand consummation, the delivery of the world into the hands of the saints. Within half a century, all the nations have been thrown open to the saints of God, and they may enter and ply their work diligently and mightily as they will. Within the same period, the mind of the world has awakened to universal consciousness and universal inquiry. Within half a century, all the powerful tongues on the globe have been impregnated and freighted with the truths of Christianity. The Bible has been translated into more than two hundred languages and dialects, and given to the nations. Meantime, all the old religions of the heathen have become confessedly effete and decrepit. Nor is this all. Mohammedanism, once so mighty, and Infidelity that had power in other ages to diffuse itself, and Roman Catholicism that once encircled the globe with its missions and its triumphs; all these systems, the last that time has power to breed, are to-day shorn of their power, and unable to extend to other races The saints of God are biding their time, and that time is not far distant. The world has, in its descent, thus far, followed exactly and step by step, the track of prophecy. Power and supremacy, in their way to the saints, lodged for a time with the Assyrian; went next to Rome, and perched for a period on the sceptre of the Cæsars; till descending once more, they were robed in scarlet, and went forth to change times and laws, and wear out the saints, and make the earth drunk with the blood of the martyrs. Thus far have rule and authority come along the line of prophecy. One step remains—for that the nations wait. When Antichrist falls, then comes the reign of the saints!

We may remark, then, in concluding our discourse, and by way of particular application of our subject,—

1. That in this great work of possessing and governing the world, the people of God must never allow themselves to confine their endeavours to any single achievement, but must preserve a breadth and amplitude of purpose, equal to their universal mission. Thus, in every field and in every place, there is something to be done to give strength, and success, and enlargement to the kingdom of Christ And what waits to be done; in one spot or another; afar in heathen land, or here in our own cities and churches: whatever work is yet unfinished, and yet on hand, that and all of it, is alike indispensable and alike important. So that we may not point to one field or another, and say, There is our one only work. Our work is everywhere, everywhere till the kingdom is set up. And this brings us to say,—

2. That neglect or debility in any one department of this great work of saintly conquest and control, enfeebles and endangers the whole enterprise. The cause, the kingdom, the church, are one; even as Christ, their Head and Owner, is one. Our religion, too, the animating principle of all our endeavours, at home and abroad, is one and the same. You cannot disable it for one of its appointed tasks, and have it strong and undamaged for the others. Take what care of hand and foot you will, if the heart be diseased,—if the lungs are unsound,—if there be weakness and decay at the fountain-head of life,—the extremities partake in the common decline; and no care of these far-off members can prevent the transmission of decay and impotence to them. The best thing the church of Christendom could do for the great work of missions to the heathen would be, to stir up their graces, and call into use their strength, and accomplish at once and to the full the work they have on hand at home. Here on the home field acquit yourselves with courage, fidelity, and unwearied zeal. Take up all these honest, inviting, and beneficent trades, holding and working them for Christ and His kingdom. Acquire what you may by every lawful means, of this precious, useful, and accessible property. Ascend, upon all legitimate paths, to posts of influence and seats of authority. Lay hold of government, possess the offices, compass all forms of knowledge, appropriate all liberal and honourable arts, wield the power of letters, put forth the energy of thought, get so much of the world as is within your reach into Christian hands; and then, make it your fixed purpose, as it is your high mission, your holy calling, your supreme and unalterable duty, to hold, use, and govern all that you possess, in a truly Christian way, making the field in which you dwell a miniature kingdom of Christ. Scatter instruction, suppress sin, overcome evil, diffuse good, build upon this waiting soil the empire of your ascended Lord. Show to the nations, and send to the nations, that true, that mighty, that transforming religion which can erect here among us, and there among them, the needed, the promised, the glorious kingdom of Christ.

The Deceitful Hope.
ANONYMOUS.

"And their hope shall be like the giving up of the ghost."—Job xi. 20.

WHEREVER the word of God is revealed, almost every person cherishes some kind of hope. Beside that one hope, which is as an anchor to the soul, sure and steadfast, there are a great variety which are all fatal. From the hardened infidel, up through all the grades of fundamental error, and through the influence of many deceptive impressions, multitudes gain and cherish a hope that all will be well. Until the very last moment, the self-deluded sinner will cling to this fatal hope, and then, when he must abandon it, it is like the giving up of the ghost.

I. *It is giving up that which is very dear.*

Like life itself, it has been ardently fostered. In order to maintain it, reflection has been shunned, Scripture perverted, the ministry derided, friendship grieved, and the Holy Spirit insulted. The delusions of error have been sought, and their preachers trusted. When conscience has warned him, he has refused to examine; when sickness assaulted, he has sometimes trembled, but still clave fast to his hope.

II. *Yet, dear as it is, it must be given up.*

The delusions of sophistry, the flattery of friends, the dread habit of self-deception, all are unavailing. We remember how Voltaire begged for the dread hour to be postponed; how Altamont raved in his irrepressible spasms. There was no escape; the hour and the man had met, and the false hope must die.

III. *Yes, it must be given up, and that suddenly.*

Death, even in lingering disease, is generally unexpected at the moment of its last effectual touch. So it is with the false hope.

IV. *Depend upon it, the giving up must be soon.*

Even at the longest, your end is near. Death standeth not far away. So is the hour when these delusive hopes must die.

V. *When given up, it will leave no substance but perfect despair.*

When life is resigned, death sits sole monarch of the mortal remains. All the bloom, and lustre, and indications of life forsake the corpse. So it is with the soul, when she is severed from her cherished hope. It is for her to sink in horrid despair. Then will she realize that the day of mercy has vanished, and that of retribution arrived,—that final despair no pen can describe, no heart on this side of eternity conceive.

Let us examine our hopes. Let us be sure to build only on the imperishable rock. By all that the soul is worth, resolve on thoroughness in turning to God.

The Anointing at Bethany.

By Rev. CHARLES W. BAIRD, Brooklyn, N. Y.

"Verily, I say unto you, Wheresoever this gospel shall be preached in the whole world, there shall also this, that this woman hath done, be told for a memorial of her."—Matt. xxvi. 13.

GREAT love can impose great obligations. It is when justified by a deep and strong affection, that the right of one man to act for others, engaging and covenanting in their behalf—as a king for his subjects, or a patriarch for his descendants—is most freely recognized and scrupulously respected. The unwritten wish, the implied request, will often obtain a fulfilment which no decree of chancery could secure. [Instance David and Jonathan's son—Rechabites.] Years after a parent's death, the son discovers, in some neglected corner, a manuscript which makes known the unsuspected destination of property left without bequest. It needs no signature or seal to prove the familiar characters. Whatever sacrifice the duty may involve, he cheerfully assumes, rejoicing that somewhat still remains, whereby to honour a memory so dear.

In the Testament or Will of our Lord and Saviour, my brethren, there are some legacies yet unpaid, to be discharged by you and by me. Let it be our congenial task to fulfil this Scripture on this day. We have here a pledge to redeem, a promise to make good, and that for Jesus' sake. To a poor woman who had done Him a valuable service, our Friend and Master gave this assurance in our name,—" Wheresoever this gospel shall be preached throughout the whole world, this also that she hath done, shall be spoken of for a memorial of her."—Mark xiv. 9.

I. *The deed.*
[Read the narrative fully as recorded by Matthew, Mark, and John.]

II. *The significance of the deed.*
One only of those present at this transaction was competent fully to declare its import. If Mary herself, by an instinct of that holy love prompting her to the performance, apprehended somewhat of its meaning, it could have been but a dim and shadowy conception at most. The disciples, from their more elevated stand-point, ought to have been able to form a just as well as generous opinion of this good deed wrought upon their Master, but they were not. Possessed for the time by the bad spirit of parsimony which their apostate companion diffused, their eyes were holden, that they could not see the fitness and the timeliness, the grace and the sweetness, and the glory of this loving, adoring prodigality. ONE saw it. But for His divine appreciation, the purest and most beautiful deed that ever woman wrought, had been forgotten out of mind, or had come down to us with the stain of a mean and sordid imputation. Yet the simple monument of Mary's love, disallowed indeed of men, but chosen of God and precious, rises at His command through the earth-born mists that strive to shut it in. Uncharitable judgments, my brethren, are not wholly precluded by our increase of light and liberality; and were it left us to make out the significance of this deed, perhaps we should go as wide of the mark as those who witnessed it first. But the monument bears its own record. Let us approach and read it there, traced by the same Hand that raised the memorial, in lines most legible and plain.

1. It was a useful work. Such is the first inscription,—" Let her alone; why trouble ye her ? She hath wrought a good work on me." The word thus translated means, primarily—fair, goodly, beautiful, as to external form and appearance. This it was, but the language implies more. It was moral excellence

that distinguished the miracles and teachings of the Saviour; and the quality pertaining to them, He ascribes to this humble performance. More precisely, however, the epithet refers to the effect and influence of the work possessing this quality. This is the ordinary sense of the word, where it is used to characterize the practices of piety among the followers of Christ.

2. Passing on to another side of this memorial pillar, we read its second inscription. It was a great work. Jesus said,—"She hath done what she could." The deed was co-extensive with her ability,—the ability of a rational and immortal creature to honour, extol, and glorify the Saviour who redeemed her with His most precious blood. To the eye which looked only upon the outward appearance, it seemed an act which nothing but its wasteful extravagance raised above insignificance; to the eye that searcheth hearts, it was grand, august, important. The value of a deed wrought upon Christ, or for the sake of Christ, though relative to us, is absolute to Him. If it be our best, though it were another's least, it is great and precious when its perfume ascends to heaven.

3. It informs us that this memorable deed was an act of faith in a crucified Saviour. Jesus said,—" Let her alone; against the day of my burying hath she kept this." The extraordinary commendation bestowed upon her in our text, was scarcely such as Christ would pronounce upon a blind instrument for the fulfilment of the divine will. There were others who unwittingly subserved that will, by procuring the Saviour's death, as Judas and Caiaphas. Of all the followers and friends of Jesus, we read of only one who pondered and treasured the sayings concerning Him with equal intentness; and she was that other Mary, the blessed mother of our Lord.—Luke ii. 19, 51. Even the less spiritual Martha had confessed her belief in Him as the Christ, the Son of God, which should come into the world. To Mary He was more than Messiah, the Anointed; more than Master, Teacher, Healer; yea, more than the Resurrection and the Life. By the clear illumination of that faith, which is always and in every case the gift of God, enabling us to discover and embrace the Redeemer in all His offices, as Prophet, Priest, and King, she now beheld Him also as the suffering Messiah, the atoning Lamb to be slain for the expiation of sins, and she anointed Him to the sacrifice of His body upon the cross.

III. *Such was the deed, and such, at least in part, its significance. Look now at its commemoration.*

"Wheresoever this gospel shall be preached in the whole world, there shall also this, that this woman hath done, be told for a memorial of her." For the most delicate service that mortal rendered Him on earth, our gracious Redeemer provides the most delicate reward. That it was unsought, we know; that it was unforeseen, we may be sure. We do not learn that our Saviour made to the twelve any promise of such distinction. It was for two lowly, loving, unaspiring women, that this honour was reserved,—for the one, that all generations should call her blessed (Luke i. 48); for the other, that wheresoever the gospel should be preached in the whole world, approving mention should be made of her good deed.

Upon the immediate disciples of our Lord the accomplishment of this declaration first devolved. Hence Matthew, John, and Peter (at whose dictation it is supposed that Mark wrote his gospel), the three who were present at the scene, all record it; the more fully perhaps, and the more ingenuously, too, because their own uncharitable temper furnished occasion for the reproof it implied. John indeed gives a pleasing instance of his own care to fulfil the command, for happening elsewhere to mention the name of Mary, he adds, with beautiful particularity,—" It was that Mary which anointed the Lord with ointment, and wiped His feet with her hair."—John xi. 2. And often, we may suppose, was the touching story of this woman's faith and devotion told by those living witnesses of the event, who preached this gospel to the multitudes of many lands. Once, however, inscribed on this imperishable page, they are "like words graven with an iron pen and lead in the rock for ever."—Job xix. 24. It has been true of the church of God, as of the dwelling of Simon, that the whole "house has been filled with the odour of that ointment."

What, after so many centuries, shall we do, worthily and honourably, to carry out our Master's purpose here made known? Two things are feasible: the one, which we have been endeavouring, by the story of her pious deed read and related from the gospel page, to keep in fresh remembrance one who was in Christ before us, and who ministered, as it were in our name and behalf, to His comfort. The other, which we shall now attempt, to appropriate this memorial to that one use and service which were all her desire, "the praise of His glory" for whom her deed was wrought.

1. Behold, then, dear friends, how exceedingly precious to Christ is the love of His people! Have you, like Mary, been called to part for a season with some cherished human friend! Has one or another channel of your affection been cut off! Then let the full tide flow out toward Him who was dead, and

behold, He liveth for evermore. Give Him, your Lord and Master, what you had thought to bury with a creature,—the precious ointment of your kindness, and service, and zeal!

2. See, too, how precious to Christ is the memory of His people! A signal proof we have in the declaration of our text. For I suppose the design with which it was made to have been rather the illustration of His regard for the memory of all His saints, than the elevation of one to a peculiar privilege.

3. Observe, again, how great the jealousy of Christ for the good fame of His people! "Let her alone; why trouble ye her?" "He that toucheth these, toucheth the apple of mine eye!"—Zech. ii. 8.

4. Mark also how generouly Christ estimates the offerings and services of His people! Mary was not so lavish of her ointment as Jesus of His praise. Be very sure that whatever others may do, He will put the best construction upon a work of faith and love wrought for His sake.

5. Learn how Christ would have us cherish the memory of His people. Records of good men's lives are among the means which God hath most emphatically approved and blessed for the sanctification of believers.

Longing for Sunset.

By the Rev. W. H. CORNING, New York.

"As a servant earnestly desireth the shadow, and as an hireling looketh for the reward of his work: so am I made to possess months of vanity, and wearisome nights are appointed unto me."—Job vii. 2, 3.

IN an illustrated edition of the book of Job, great vividness is given to this scripture by a picture of a slave, earnestly looking to the western sky, and longing for the evening shadow. The artist has succeeded in embodying the idea of the passage in a sketch for the eye, so that you see before you the over-worked and wearied labourer, looking anxiously for the expected signal of rest from his daily toil. By a happy stroke, condensing into a single phrase the entire passage, he has named his picture "Longing for Sunset." And when I looked upon it, I was most intensely impressed with a realization of that sad experience in the human soul which is imaged in the text. Tracing it, in the life-like lines of the graver, as it took visible shape before me, I felt that it had practical connections with human lives, of such importance as to make it a useful theme for thought before any congregation of world-worn, and world-wearied men. Not for himself alone, but for a great multitude, did Job speak these words.

I. *Let me set before you the different forms of that experience, in which the soul earnestly desireth the shadow, or the coming on of the night of death.*

The natural instinct of man is to desire to live. In all the ordinary moods of mind there is a shrinking back from the grim shadow of the grave. "Truly the light is sweet, and a pleasant thing it is to behold the sun." The work of life and its rewards have a charm even too attractive to the heart of man. As you pass around among your fellow-creatures, it is only here and there that you see written out upon the bowed head, and sad countenance, and wearied step, the words,—"I could wish to die." In naming the different forms of this experience, we may mention,—

1. That which arises out of painful and exhausting sickness. This was that which led Job to utter the words of the text, and long so earnestly for death. Months of bitterness and wearisome nights had worn away his instinct of life. The grave seemed to him a desirable refuge from his distresses. Many a poor, wasted, wearied sufferer, as he lay upon his bed of languishing, has felt with Job in his distress.

2. When the infirmities of old age creep on, and life continues after the loss of nearly all the friends in which it was passed, it is not uncommon that the soul turns with yearning towards the end of this earthly course. The future life appears much brighter from its contrast with the infirmities of the present.

3. I have seen those, under the shadow of a mighty sorrow from God, longing for sunset. Their earthly home was desolate, and they longed to pass into the heavenly. Earthly sorrow in its many forms makes the human instinct of life to yield before it, and even turns it into a prayer for death.

4. The baffled and disappointed hero of the church, after a long conflict with wickedness, often yearns for the end of his course. Thus the grand old prophet Elijah, upon Carmel,

would gladly have anticipated the chariot of fire with its horses of fire. Thus, with what a melancholy grandeur do we hear the great Martin Luther, at the close of his life, finding it impossible to mould everything to his will, sorely disappointed at results, passionately, and almost petulantly, praying to die.

5. Thus far we have mentioned forms of experience, all of which have their root in a loathing or weariness of life. We now mention one which differs from all these, and is perfectly harmonious with a deep love and joy in life. It is that high Christian experience, which, while it finds great delight in working for God upon earth, yearns also for a full communion with Him in heaven. It has no disgust of a life of Christian toil and duty, and yet it reaches after "the inheritance of the saints in life."

II. *Such, in its different forms, is the experience in which the human soul earnestly desireth the shadow. Is it healthy and desirable in any of its forms? We have seen that there are really but two kinds of this experience,—that which roots itself in a disgust of life, and that which is inspired by a clear realization of the celestial glories.*

This last is certainly both healthy and desirable. It shows great vigour of Christian character. It is both the flower and fruit of an earnest life with God. It brings a joy into the soul through communion with the upper world, which gives intensity to all Christian action. It is possible, indeed, that such an ecstasy of mind may arise in the soul, if too much time is given to contemplation and too little to action, as to unfit it for real duty. But this is not the danger of our age or time, or of our style of Christians. St. Bernards do not abound among us. The real Christian often needs this longing for God as the solace and hope of his work.

But every form of this experience which arises from disgust of life is both unhealthy and undesirable. It is not a normal condition of the soul of man to wish to die, simply as a relief from the cares and toils of the world. Men love activity. It is only the over-tasked and over-wearied, whose hearts have been long bowed and their spirits broken, who long for the shadow. Work is the natural element of man. It is therefore the sure sign of unhealth when the manly vigour of the soul succumbs to its sorrows, and longs for the rest of the grave. The physical system is itself broken down. The nervous wires, which thread so mysteriously the "harp of a thousand strings," and make such bounding music in a healthy frame, are out of tune, and make only discords now.

And as such a state of mind is unhealthy, so it is undesirable. It oppresses the soul with a heavy load, so that it can bear no burden of duty. It envelops the life in a cloud of darkness, so that it cannot see the light. Unless in those who are appointed unto speedy death, in which case it may lighten the passage to the tomb, it is to be regarded as an enemy to all that is good and noble. It is to be prayed against, laboured against, and lived against, with the utmost tenacity of will.

III. *There is still another question which the subject presses upon us. How far is it right or wrong to harbour this disgust of life, and "earnestly desire the shadow"?*

I answer,—God surely permits him in whom, by His Providence, He has destroyed the instinct of life, to long for the end. It surely cannot be wrong for one worn out by painful and protracted sickness,—to whom months of vanity and wearisome nights are appointed,—to yearn for the termination of his sorrows, even wishing to hide them in the grave.

But, while we cannot condemn this longing for death in the souls of those worn out by disease, we do not mean to be understood as sanctioning the very common notion that it is to any great extent the proof of grace in the heart. If there were not, indeed, a calm trust in Christ, with holy assurance, we could hardly expect that the soul would long to die. Still, a sinner with a callous conscience and a false hope, will just as earnestly often "desire the shadow."

But if it is right for him, whom God has visited with sickness, and so destroyed the instinct of life, to yearn for the close of his course, may not the aged man also be permitted to look joyfully towards the end? And if the aged man, why not the oppressed; the lone and wasted prisoners in the dungeons of despots, whose only crime has been their love of liberty, and from whom God's sunlight for years has been excluded?

But if those whom the providence of God has absolutely shut up to this prayer, may offer it, without offence to His infinite purity, it is equally certain they have no right to take it upon their lips whom the heavenly Father calls to the active life of duty. However great their sorrows or their disappointments,— though their dearest friends are in the dust, and their earthly all is swept away—they have no right, in moody melancholy, to sit listless down and wish to die. They have a higher, nobler work than to look into the shadows. They are to long for the sunshine, and not for the sunset. For them the clarion note of duty rings, summoning them onward. Elijah was out of place in the solitudes of Carmel. Luther should have spoken words more grand and inspiring to have formed the fitting conclusion of his glorious life. Every Christian is sinning against God, when he permits himself to loathe or neglect the actual work to which he is clearly called.

In the conclusion of this discourse, I shall not attempt to gather up all its practical suggestions, some of which have necessarily come into view, in the illustration of it. I will only call your attention,—

1. To the supreme dignity of a joyful, earnest, working life in God. This is better than a constant longing for sunset; nay, this is better than the most gorgeous sunset which has ever illumined a Christian's dying hour. To live like Payson would be better than to die like Payson, though one would love both to live and die as he did. In His holy word, God gives a higher importance to living than to dying—to our work in the broad daylight, than to our work amid the shadows. And yet, however much a working life is to be desired in itself, it is not true that a Christian is always best trained in the sunshine. Some of the most precious of the graces grow best in the darkness, and the choicest disciples very often pass their lives under a cloud. Perfect health and unbounded elasticity of life will not be a safe endowment except in heaven.

2. But while we all should love to live in the active performance of duty, we are never to forget the shadow, or to fail to prepare for death. There is such a thing as a Christian loving this life too well. The instinct by which he clings to it may not be properly subdued unto God; or the divine providence may have scattered so many blessings upon his home, that he is in danger of "laying up his treasures upon earth." There is much necessity for the children of God to seek, by positive effort, to break the cords which bind them too closely here, and to replace them with those golden chains, whose fastenings are in the throne of God and the Lamb. The apostle Paul occupied the right position upon this question. To depart was far better, and he greatly desired it; yet "to live was Christ," and if the Master still had work for him to do, he would choose, on the whole, for the sake of the dying world, to remain at his post.

3. The sunset will bring blessings to the weary saint. The shadow, which he so earnestly desires, lies just before the celestial city. Poor, sorrowing disciple! the Saviour keeps thy

crown in readiness for thee. Thy sun which, through all thy afflicted life, has seemed to be enveloped in thick darkness, shall go down without a cloud, even setting in a refulgent sea of glory. Oh! didst thou know it all, thou mightest well long and pray for sunset.

The Gentleness and the Energy of Christianity.

By the Rev. HENRY A. NELSON, D.D., St. Louis, Mo

"And James the son of Zebedee, and John the brother of James: and he surnamed them Boanerges, which is, The sons of thunder."—Mark iii. 17.

"Now there was leaning on Jesus' bosom one of his disciples, whom Jesus loved."—John xiii. 23.

WHEN we think of John as "the beloved disciple,"—when we figure him to us, leaning on Jesus' breast, at the Supper—we are apt to conceive of the meekest, and gentlest, and loveliest of the twelve. The artists who undertake to delineate the countenances of the apostles, and of their Lord, are wont to give to John a countenance of almost feminine mildness. There is somewhat in the writings of John, and in his history, which justifies the imputing to him of unusual gentleness. Yet we should greatly err if we were to conceive of him as of a soft and feeble character, or as deficient in the solid elements of manliness. He was one of the two brothers whom Jesus named "sons of thunder," a designation certainly indicative of the utmost force and energy of character.

That they were both naturally of a somewhat impulsive and fiery temper, may be inferred from the narration in Luke ix. 51-56. That they were naturally ambitious, seems evident from their desire to sit one on the right hand, and the other on the left, of the Lord, when He should be established on the seat of His kingly power.—Mark x. 35. In short, it is evident that they needed to have their fiery impulses curbed, and their aspiring dispositions repressed, by the example and instructions of their Lord.

Limiting our view to John, of whom the Scriptures give us the more full account, it seem to be evident that, under the training of Christ, he came to possess, in a very eminent degree, the meek gentleness and the resolute energy, which, being combined, constitute the best Christian character ; and I call your attention to the character of this individual for the purpose of presenting to your contemplation the *gentleness* which belongs to Christian character, in its proper combination with the *energy* which equally belongs to it.

I. *We will consider some things in Christianity that are adapted to give gentleness to the character.*

1. The view which it gives a person of himself. This, you know, is anything but flattering. The Christian estimate of human character is such, that when any person appropriates it to himself, he finds all the pride of his spirit abased and mortified. Christian humility certainly tends to promote gentleness.

2. I mention next the view which Christianity gives of God and of eternity. Not only is a person who has felt " the powers of the world to come " apt to feel that the paltry interests of time are not worth contending for, but habitual contemplation of eternal realities, and of Him who " inhabiteth eternity," will so awe and elevate the Spirit, that it will have the utmost disrelish for contention. Scarcely can such an one be induced to contend for anything except the sacred matters of truth and of conscience. Would it not be strange if two persons should quarrel while gazing together at the cataract of Niagara, listening to its solemn roar, and feeling its solemn tremor ? Is it possible to retain anger when you stand at a window, watching the coming up of a storm ; or at the foot of cliffs, that lift themselves ruggedly up to the sky ; or on the shore of the ocean, stretching away beyond the utmost reach of vision, endlessly rolling in its waves, and ceaselessly lifting up its voice ! Christianity, studied, believed, embraced, experienced, causes the soul to dwell habitually in the presence of sublimer objects than these, and under the influence of nobler contemplations.

3. The character of Christ, as it is delineated in the scriptures, and as the Christian contemplates it, is calculated to promote

gentleness. He is exhibited as "the Lamb of God,"—not only a *spotless* victim, fit for the sacrifice, but dumb and unresisting, when led to slaughter. The Christian not only trusts in the efficacy of Christ's sufferings, to atone for his sins, but he reads in his New Testament, that " Christ also suffered for us, leaving us an example, that we should follow His steps. The Christian, truly loving Christ, having his heart open to the influence which beams from all Christ's life and character, and by contemplation of Him, holding himself under that influence, is assimilated to Him more than himself perceives; and sometimes, in the higher degrees of this experience, he is like Moses, whose face shone with a light which he wist not of.

II. *Some things in Christianity that are adapted to give energy to the character.*

1. Look at the objects of effort which it presents,—all that is involved in one's own eternal salvation,—and all that tends to the well-being of mankind and the glory of God. One's own salvation, as Christianity proposes it, is not the gaining of a title to heavenly bliss hereafter, by submitting to some rite of priestly performance, or to some austerities of priestly imposition; nor by any bargained work, whereby such title is to be purchased. It is, after gratefully and believingly accepting as a free gift, that title, written in blood, to gird one's self for a race, and arm one's self for a warfare, the strenuous prosecution of which will engage all the highest powers of one's being, through the whole period of his earthly existence. Distinct from this, yet not separate, is the effort to which Christianity calls us, for the benefit of our fellow-men, and for promoting the glory of God. These are perfectly harmonious, and are best prosecuted together. We are then doing most for our own Christian improvement, when we are most faithfully serving God, and most benevolently labouring for the good of mankind. A dull and spiritless Christian,—with such fields of enterprise around him, and such enemies before him, and such a crown above him,—is such an anomaly possible?

2. Look at the motives to effort which Christianity supplies. These are indeed in great measure involved in the objects of effort already mentioned, but they are capable of distinct consideration. All the motives which appeal to one's regard for his own welfare—his desire for happiness, and for excellence of character—are furnished by Christianity in their highest and best forms. The highest motives of gratitude are also present—" for the love of Christ constraineth us." All the benevolence, too, which experienced Christianity awakens in the soul, practical

Christianity continually addresses with the most moving appeals. It must surely be a hard and cold heart that, in such a world as this, among such beings as people it, in such a condition, and with such prospects, is not moved to the most energetic endeavours to help, to benefit, to save them.

3. Consider the examples which Christianity exhibits. What other field, what other cause, can furnish nobler specimens of heroic energy? [Instance Paul, Peter, and the other apostles, and Jesus, the perfect Model.] Read the epistles of Peter and of John; read them attentively, and see if, while they are characterized by affectionate tenderness, they do not also burn with a steady and mighty energy. Familiarity with the life and writings of those New Testament men, while it chastens the spirit, is most effectual to rouse and to kindle it. The scriptures teach us to look unto Him,—to consider Him, " lest we be wearied and faint in our minds."

I hope you see that the energy which Christianity inspires does not mar the gentleness which is so beautiful an ornament of character; and that the gentleness which Christianity cultivates, does not soften and enervate the soul. The two elements do most harmoniously blend, balancing, and tempering,—not at all hindering each other. Doubtless, amid the many imperfections of exemplified Christian character, none is more common than the distortion which arises from the prominence of one of these elements, in the absence of the other. Our gentle and amiable Christians are apt to be too irresolute, and our heroes are apt to be too rough and coarse. We should be lenient toward the errors of all sincere and earnest souls.

In all our efforts at self-culture, let us seek for the attainment of both these elements in scriptural proportions and in scriptural combination. Let us cultivate that spirit which would befit us leaning on Jesus' breast, together with that which won the surname, " Sons of Thunder."

The Providence of God.

By Rev. LEWIS SABIN, D.D., TEMPLETON, MASS.

" Wherefore, if God so clothe the grass of the field, which to-day is, and to-morrow is cast into the oven, shall He not much more clothe you, O ye of little faith?"—MATT. vi. 30.

WHEN we think of the world in which we live, in comparison with the magnitude of creation, a sense of littleness comes over us, and a feeling of insignificance, which prompts us to say with the Psalmist,— "Lord, what is man, that Thou art mindful of him? and the son of man, that Thou visitest him?" This feeling has been appropriated to the use of irreligion and infidelity. It has been turned into a popular argument against Christianity. This objection of infidelity was answered by Dr. Chalmers, in his masterly "Astronomical Discourses," in such a manner that the work will never need to be done again. Still the feeling of our littleness, and a consequent apprehension of exposedness and insecurity is natural, and has power with many minds.

But there is another feeling, quite in contrast with this, to which calm reflection, in our evening walk, may reasonably lead us, not less deep and powerful than the crushing sense of our insignificance. We stretch out our hand to a flower, within whose fair bosom God has reared colonies and nations of animalculæ, in all the glow of their costume and in a perfection of beauty, after which art toils in vain. So the world of littleness stretches away beneath our feet. Over all this microscopic littleness, as well as all that greatness brought to view by the telescope, our heavenly Father presides, and has given man the princely faculties to be lord of this lower world which He has prepared for him. From this survey we may turn with reasonable loyal joy to Jesus, and listen to Him as He speaks in the words of the text.

I shall attempt, in this discourse, to exhibit some of the practical benefits of the doctrine of God's providence. In doing this, I must show what this doctrine is, and then we can discover how its application throws around the character of God an ineffable glory, and at the same time is of the highest practical utility to ourselves.

I. *When we speak of God's providence, we mean that God, by His invisible and almighty agency, guides and governs all His creatures and all their actions; or, in other words, that He takes care of every individual person, object, and event in the world.*

Many people have vague and erroneous ideas of God's great wonder-working processes, which we call providence. This is indicated by common modes of speech. Some speak of "luck," and "chance," and "accidental events." Many events are said to "happen." The scriptures teach us that not a hair falls from the head, and not a sparrow falls to the ground, contrary to His design, and without His agency. His wise and powerful direction controls all the good and all the evil that befalls mankind. Our life is full of changes. The wheel which God showed Ezekiel is a beautiful figure of divine providence. Life is a checkered scene, sometimes exalted, and sometimes depressed. But God's love to His people is unchanging. And He controls all things for their good. If you look back through the ages, by the aid of history, you see God working out His everlasting purposes. To His eye there are no chance events,—nothing out of place,—nothing out of time,—nothing really adverse to His great end.

Again, some people speak of the laws of nature in a way to exclude the wisdom of God from His providence. Old heathen philosophers held the doctrine of fate, with some differences of opinion among themselves. They supposed that "this universe is moving, as it were," in a groove of adamant. Nearly the same thing is meant by those who talk flippantly now about "natural laws," as governing the course of events. What law developed the muscles, with their power of contraction, for the purposes of motion, and pulling against each other, to keep the body even? By what innate tendency of matter was the heart developed,—that mighty forcing pump, beating a hundred thousand times a day, and never growing weary? Every tendency of matter would operate to prevent the formation of such organs as the heart, the lungs, or the eye. Whence came the exact adjustment which you observe between the eye and the light, or between the lungs and the air? The machinery of the eye had no tendency to give birth to the light, nor the light to form the eye. In both is seen the wisdom of God. It required the same hand to govern the world which first brought it into existence. The Creator has never given, and never could give it an independent existence. He upholds and governs it by a constant exertion of His power. The wisdom of God moves the wheels along, and if anything would go wrong, God puts it right. The doctrine of providence is not that "what is must be," but, "that what God in His wisdom ordains must be." This difference keeps us from being fatalists. It brings us into the presence of an infinitely wise, good, and powerful personal Deity, and brings God near to us as a Father, making all things work together for good to His children.

The doctrine of providence is one of amazing sublimity; and in this respect it comports with the true idea of the immunity of God. Like Himself, it is incomprehensible. It is so vast: God controlling all. It is so intricate,—"a wheel within a wheel." [Instance Joseph, Esther, the Christian church of the first century, &c.]

It is important to remember that the providence of God extends to the sins of men and the iniquities of nations. This it does in permitting them. Under this sovereign and universal providence of God we live and are free,—man does as he chooses, —and God does as He pleases. The facts are clear, and beyond these facts we cannot go.

II. *The practical benefits of the doctrine of God's providence have, to some extent, been brought to view in the progress of this exhibition of the doctrine itself. Let us consider some of them more particularly.*

1. The cordial reception of this doctrine leads the believer to honour God by trusting Him. We are sometimes in trouble and distress,—we are perplexed,—we cannot see the end. All is dark. Things around us seem to be entangled in a Gordian knot. We may be tempted to cut the knot by the hand of a heartless infidelity,—tempted, perhaps, to turn the cold, sharp edge of the scalpel of modern science against Christianity, and sever the world from its Maker. But this will not extricate us, nor in the least relieve our trouble. God can solve the difficulty. He sees it all,—His wisdom is in it all,—His love will shine in it all.

"God is His own interpreter,
And He will make it plain."

Thus the prophet Isaiah says,—"Who is among you that feareth the Lord, that obeyeth the voice of my servant, that walketh in darkness, and hath no light: let him trust in the name of the Lord, and stay himself upon his God." God means to have us trust Him.

2. This doctrine brings to the believer satisfying comfort. Earthly possessions are very uncertain and unsatisfactory in their nature. Man is born unto trouble. But he who has faith

in God's providence has comfort. He is not like the stoic. The stoic philosopher bore it, because he believed he must, and that it was manly to make the best of it. The Christian bears it because he believes that God will make it work for his good.

3. Another practical benefit of this doctrine is, that it represses violence and fretfulness of spirit, and produces a meek and gentle disposition. There are many important circumstances and events, the reason of which will probably remain to the end of time inscrutable; many that disappoint our hopes, and cross our wishes, and provoke our resentment. His providence is a shelter where meekness and gentleness may sit down and wait for the issue. Only do your duty, and leave the result calmly and cheerfully with Him.

4. Another practical benefit of the doctrine of providence is, that it shows the indispensable obligations of gratitude to God for every favour we enjoy. The Apostle says that "Every good gift, and every perfect gift, cometh down from the Father of lights, with whom is no variableness, nor shadow of turning." He has preserved you, watched over you, and provided for you every blessing that you have enjoyed. Give daily thanks to Him for the great and immeasurable blessings which have fallen to your lot.

5. The doctrine of divine providence lays the only true foundation of prayer, and is the great encouragement to Christian exertions.

The Sufferings of Christ.
ANONYMOUS.

"But rejoice, inasmuch as ye are partakers of Christ's sufferings."—1 Peter iv. 13.

"For as the sufferings of Christ abound in us, so our consolation also aboundeth by Christ."— 2 Cor. i. 5.

OUR fallen, ruined condition makes suffering an element of earthly life, and the plan of restoration makes suffering or sorrow an element of recovery. There is a conflict between sin and holiness,—between Satan and Christ,—for the possession of the human heart. And as the human subject is a moral being, the success of the struggle depends much on the decisions of the moral agent. Whatever may be the choice of man as a moral agent, there will be conflict and suffering, though the final results will be very different. Choosing Christ, and living in obedience to Him, conflict, and self-denial, and suffering, will be the law of life; but the result will be peace, joy, felicity. In this life, Christians are called to be partakers of His sufferings; because Christ also suffered for us, leaving us an example, that we should follow His steps. If the Captain of our salvation was made perfect through sufferings, His under-officers and soldiers cannot expect to overcome sin and Satan without partaking of His sufferings.

I. *Let us inquire how Christians are partakers of the sufferings of Christ?*

1. By sympathy with Him. There is an intimate connection between Christ and the renewed soul. His life is hid with Christ in God. There is a strong bond of sympathy uniting them. Christ is the Bridegroom; His disciples are the bride, the Lamb's wife. He is the Head; they are the members of His body. The sympathetic tie is strong,—what affects the one affects the other. Joy in one heart is transfused into the other. Sorrow filling the one oppresses the other. The sufferings of his Lord on earth oft excite deep feelings of commiseration in the bosom of the loving disciple. When these amazing sufferings are made real and vivid by the Spirit of God, then the disciple is a partaker of Christ's sufferings by sympathy.

2. The disciple of Christ is a partaker of suffering with Him in prayer. True prayer is a labour of the soul. It is the struggling of pent-up desires, which can hardly be expressed. It sometimes makes demands upon the heart, even to oppression of feeling, to deep sorrow. Dr. Payson once remarked, that he pitied the Christian who did not sometimes have such feelings that he could not express them in language. And the Holy Ghost is represented as making intercession for us with groanings which cannot be uttered. Now the Spirit dwells in the Christian's heart, and excites these overwhelming feelings in his bosom. Christians often possess this feeling in the midst of a revival. They wrestle for the salvation of souls. God honours their faith, and answers their prayer. They cannot rest while their fellows are plunging into hell.

3. The disciple of Christ is a partaker of sufferings with Him

by self-denial. The term self-denial conveys the idea of suffering. It denotes the renouncing of all those pleasures, profits, views, connections, or practices that are prejudicial to the true interests of the soul. It implies a crossing the natural desires, and pursuing a course opposite to them. It indicates diligence and zeal in the service of the great Master in heaven, even to self-sacrifice and self-immolation. Our Lord and Saviour denied Himself. His servant is called upon to deny himself, take up his cross, and follow Him. May I not safely affirm that the mass of the professed followers of Jesus do not know the meaning of the term self denial, as applied to sacrifices for Christ? They have never attained to it. They feel, and give, and do, rather what is convenient, than what is self-denying. But there is a self-denial which includes a partaking of Christ's suffering. It is that sacrifice of ease, or pleasure, or property, or life, which is implied in living, labouring, and dying for Christ. It is seen in the Apostle Paul. He counted all things but loss, that he might win Christ. His life is a history of self-denials. It is seen in the lives of such missionaries as Henry Martyn, who give up the brightest earthly prospects to preach Christ crucified to a perishing world. May God hasten the day when every disciple of Christ shall be a partaker of His sufferings, by self-denial, by prayer, by sympathy.

II. *They who suffer most for Christ will enjoy the greatest consolation from Him,*—"*For as the sufferings of Christ abound in us, so our consolation also aboundeth by Christ.*"

1. It is true in regard to this life. If we would enjoy the highest degree of happiness in this world, we must suffer much for Christ. We must sympathize with Him,—we must sacrifice for Him,—we must toil for Him. The more suffering, the more consolation. This seems a paradox, yet it is true. The source of suffering and the source of consolation are distinct. In the providence of God, where one is greatest, the other is given in largest measure. As the world embitters the cup of the humble, praying, self-sacrificing Christian, God fills it with joys from His own infinite fulness,—from the river of His pleasures. And although worn down with care and toil, disquieted with opposition and reproach, and oppressed with persecution for Christ's sake, yet he possesses a richness, a variety, a surpassing fulness of joy, that transports him to the very ante-chamber of heaven, and enables him, believing, to rejoice with joy unspeakable and full of glory. All his losses and sacrifices shall be compensated, even in this life, an hundred-fold; and though toil

may wear upon the mind, and self-denial may cross it, and persecution may overwhelm it, yet God will greatly enrich it with divine consolation. This led the Apostle Paul to exclaim,— "Most gladly, therefore, will I rather glory in my infirmities, that the power of Christ may rest upon me." This fact sustained the martyrs while on the rack,—while burning at the stake. It made them joyful; and their spirits were pluming their wings for their ascent to heaven, while their flesh was consuming upon their limbs. This abundant consolation enables the humble disciple cheerfully to leave country, family, home, with all their endearments, and to go forth to labour, to suffer, and to die, to recover lost men to God, and prepare them for heaven. Says an old writer,—"I feel a young heaven, and a little paradise of glorious comforts and soul-delighting in Christ, in suffering for Him and His truth. My prison is my palace—my sorrow is full of joy—my losses are rich losses—my pain easy pain—my heavy days are holy days and happy days. Oh! what do I not owe to the file, to the hammer, and to the furnace of my Lord Jesus! Grace tried is better than grace, and more than grace. It is glory in its infancy. Who knows the truth of grace without a trial; and how soon would grace freeze without a cross? Bear your cross, therefore, with joy."

2. But this is especially true in regard to the life to come. They who endure most for Christ shall shine brightest in glory. They that turn many to righteousness shall shine as the stars for ever and ever. They that do most for Christ, and suffer most for Him, shall have the highest seat, the brightest crown, the most seraphic harp, and the far more exceeding and eternal weight of glory. They shall be as constellations, ever marked as the most faithful and the most enduring of Christ's chosen ones. They shall drink deepest of the river of divine pleasures, and rejoice with joy unspeakable and full of glory.

My brethren, can we afford to lose the blessings of constant obedience and hearty sacrifice for our Lord and Saviour? Do we wish to enjoy the consolations? Then we must take pleasure in the sufferings for Christ. The call to us is not to endure persecution and death for His sake; but it is to endure suffering with Him in deep sympathy, in agonizing prayer, in active labour, in cheerful self-denial, and in the consecration of our property. The day of persecution may come; it is not now. But the day of activity is come, calling for personal effort and a large-hearted benevolence.

Are you willing, my Christian friends, in the private walks of life, to do only what is convenient for Christ? To engage in the labours of the Sabbath-school only when convenient? To maintain family prayer only when convenient? To attend the social meeting when convenient? To be in your place on the Sabbath only when convenient? To labour personally for the conversion of sinners when convenient? To contribute for the support of the gospel, and the deep necessities of a dying world, what is convenient? In a word, to pray, and labour, and sacrifice, and suffer, and give, for our Lord and Saviour, when and what is convenient? And shall we, my brethren, in our holy calling and sacred duties, do only for our Saviour what is convenient? Shall convenience be consulted? Had the Lord Jesus Christ consulted His convenience, when redeeming us from hell, what had become of us? Can we withhold anything from such a Saviour? Shall we not pray, and toil, and sacrifice, and suffer, and give, so as to feel it, for Him?

The Nature of Religious Sorrow.
ANONYMOUS.

"For godly sorrow worketh repentance to salvation, not to be repented of."—2 Cor. vii. 10.

THIS passage of Scripture contains a most important principle in the life of Christian experience. The mourning, or religious sorrow, which our Saviour pronounces "blessed," springs only from a correct state of moral feeling.

I. *It implies a disposition to serious thoughtfulness.*

II. *A promptness to recollect past sins with penitent regret, belongs also to genuine religious sorrow.*

III. *That sorrow which is unto life is likewise connected with a careful watchfulness over the temper and conduct.*

IV. *It includes a spirit of constant dependence upon God.*

The nature of religious sorrow has been thus briefly considered. And is there anything unlovely in a religion which is tinged with such a sorrow? Let them consider her serious, repentant, watchful, and self-denying spirit, until they feel its inspiration; and let them remember, that a rejection of offered mercy,—a refusal to yield to the influence of religion, because it implies sorrow for sin,—will deprive them of much present blessedness, and exclude them from all participation in those spiritual and undecaying consolations with which those who "now have sorrow" shall hereafter be comforted.

The True Estimate of Men.
By the Rev. S. D. PHELPS, D.D., New Haven, Ct.

"Honour all men."—1 Pet. ii. 17.

TWO grand objects, yet blending together, stimulate us in the missionary work. They are the glory of God, and the salvation of men. And from these come the influential motives to the efficient prosecution of that work. The Infinite Being we would glorify, in a faithful obedience to His commands, is ever before us. The great I AM sends us to our work, and hold us to it by obligations the most sacred; and because HE IS, and is what He is, we feel bound both submissively and affectionately to do His will.

But the text summons us to another duty, and suggests another motive that, if not equally high and commanding, is nevertheless of immeasurable importance and weight. This duty is as imperative as any other. We are enjoined in the same breath to "Fear God," and to "Honour all men." But as we gaze downward to the low level of our race, in its fatal apostasy and reeking corruption,—its consuming sins and appalling crimes,—ah! what do we find to honour? What to inspire and call forth the high sentiments involved in that term? It is easy, it is a pleasure to honour some men. Their endowments, their attainments, and especially their exalted Christian virtues, elicit for them the praise of all the good, and justify an "everlasting remembrance." But here is the divine command that bids us make no exceptions. The gospel breaks down every barrier, and makes every man our neighbour, claiming the respect due to a human being and accountable creature of God. Even the degraded, the vicious, the far heathen, powerfully appeal to us in this gospel duty. I invite your attention to some of the reasons of this duty enjoined in the text.

I. *The common parentage of all men urge it.*

All have the same high birth,—the same original royal ancestry. Amidst the national, social, and conventional differences among men, this essential truth should never be forgotten. However wide and marked these differences may appear—however unlike each other various nations and races seem to be,—they cannot obliterate the fact of man's common origin. We often see as great an unlikeness—as wide a dissimilarity in personal appearance, or mental and moral characteristics—in the members of a family. I know the truth of a common origin for the human race is humiliating to some, distasteful to a few, and repudiated by others, among whom are a small number of considerable eminence in physical science and ethnological studies. But they have not been able to establish their theories of a plurality of races springing from different and independent creations at the first. And still more absurd are the attempts to show that the origin of human beings is not from a single pair created by God, but from a process of development from inferior animals, or even vegetables.

Divine revelation interposes an insuperable barrier to all these wild and foolish speculations. At its commencement it states the question in a clear light, and near its close settles it, as the chief Apostle in his sublime discourse at Mars' Hill boldly declares, that God, who made the world and all things therein, also "made of one blood all nations of men, to dwell on the face of the earth." And as every man, the meanest as well as the grandest, has such a high original birth and parentage, he is entitled, on that account, to the regard required,—an honour due to a human being linked to us by the common ties of humanity.

II. *The fact that all are involved in common apostasy is another reason for the duty enjoined in the text.*

Not one of our race has escaped the effects of the fall. All of human born—the child that knows not good from evil, that dies before it commits a sin, and is saved, yet in its sufferings and death experiences the effect of sin,—the aged, beginning to sink under the infirmities attending the decay of vitality,—the most amiable and lovely in the circle of home and its affections, as well as those of the very opposite cast and character, feel alike the stupendous shock. "The trail of the serpent is over them all." You could not despise even a degraded and wretched human being in the solemn reality and severe agony of death, because such an experience will some time be yours. Neither should you look with unfeeling contempt upon a living victim of vice and suffering. Is he going direct to perdition—to utter shipwreck and eternal ruin? So are you, unless you have taken refuge in the cross of Christ; and though you may not walk in the gutter and filth of the broad way to destruction as he does, yet, if unconverted, you are somewhere in that way, and will reach the same destination with him, unless you repent.

III. *The fact that all men are immortal, entitles them to the honour that Divine Revelation declares to be their due.*

This mysterious, wonderful, sublime, and awful element— IMMORTALITY—this astonishing gift, this amazing endowment, is the grand heritage, the priceless possession, the unspeakable destiny of every human being! Not merely the great and good —the mighty names embalmed in the pages of inspiration— the heroes and philosophers of the past—the eminent scholars and statesmen of the present—but the dense masses of men, the vast crowds that throng the thoroughfares of the world, and dot its whole surface with life and activity, and the miserable multitudes that jostle along the avenues of ignorance and degradation, or that fester and rot in the way-stations and by-places of vice and crime. Man's soul shall survive, shall live on, eternally. It might, it may, it was fitted to live in glory with its God.

> "O grandest gift of the Creator! O largess worthy of a God!
> Who shall grasp that thrilling thought, life and joy for ever?
> Yea, where God hath given, none shall take away."

Can we regard human nature thus mysteriously, grandly, and surpassingly endowed, even in its humblest and lowest forms, with other than emotions of reverence and awe? That ignorant and unsightly being that you chance to meet, is the possessor of a soul that cannot cease to exist. That wicked wretch who hates you and your religion, is immortal. As in mining districts the unpolished fragmentary rock, the useless sand, and the besmearing lump of earth have within them the precious ore, the silver, the gold, the diamond, and are therefore of great value; so in every depraved, polluted, shattered, and perishing human form, whose very presence, it may be, is loathsome and pestilent, there dwells imprisoned, and though defaced, marred, stained, and crimsoned with guilt, an unspeakably precious, living, susceptible, imperishable, immortal thing !

IV. *In the discharge of the duty enjoined, we do but imitate our heavenly Father, who has honoured man in what He has done for his happiness, his recovery, and salvation.*

Look upon God's unspeakable gift, bestowed in virtue of his great love, and honouring—how much !—the recepient race. That divine gift—God Himself manifest among men, infinite to pity and mighty to save—how did it appear?—in what form was it revealed? Bad as our nature is in its fall and ruin, Jesus did not scorn to assume it, and wear it from infancy to manhood, and do in it His works of mercy and power, and bow with it in the garden, and die in it on the cross, and go with it into the darkness of the tomb, and thence rise with it in triumph, and ascend to heaven with it, while He still wears it on the throne of intercession and dominion, all glorious in the imperishable splendours of the source and substance of immortality. And in all this He has opened the gate of life and of heaven for the recovery and salvation of man, the humblest as well as the loftiest—the bruised and scarred by sin, if they will receive His mercy, and follow Him to those celestial heights and joys. O brethren ! does it not become us to honour those whom God has honoured ?

V. *And our duty in this regard may be urged in view of the capability of all men for angelic excellence and dignity.*

Not that all will attain to this high and glorious state ; for many there are with all the means necessary to reach it, and under the most favouring influences to make those means effectual, who nevertheless fail ; but their failure is the result of their own wicked neglect and choice. The gospel, wherever preached or known, offers its rich provisions to all—its invitations, its promises, its inducements, are presented to all alike ; and every one who believes the gospel, trusts in the Saviour it reveals, and lives according to its precepts, shall share in its redeeming grace, its immortal honours. High or low, learned or ignorant, king or subject, master or servant, Christian or heathen, every one who accepts of salvation in God's method of grace, shall rise to angelic excellence, and dignity, and glory—he " shall be equal to the angels." Such is the high destiny of our ransomed humanity. "If any man serve me," said Jesus, "him will my Father honour." How different from anything like contempt should be our emotions in looking upon a human being, however degraded, who is capable of rising to such a height of glory, and honour, and immortality!

Such I conceive to be some of the reasons for the duty enjoined in the text, and required by the very spirit of the gospel, which commands us, as we have opportunity, to do good to all men. If this duty and obligation were fulfilled, what blessed practical results would follow. This true estimate of men would be a powerful motive for their evangelization.

1. How would crimes against humanity cease?

2. Carry out this Christian requirement, and how would injustices and dishonesty cease among men, and in what important respects would society be remodelled?

3. On this principle, how would all humane institutions be sustained and multiplied? What sympathy for the unfortunate!—what help for the needy!—what relief for the distressed! Who would be neglected?

4. If we fully understood and endeavoured to act on this great principle, what a higher, nobler estimate we should place upon a human soul, wherever it is found? Its value, how great! Its interests, how overwhelming! In a just regard for the souls of others, we should have a better idea of the unspeakable preciousness and high destiny, the perils or hopes of our own.

5. And, lastly, in bringing our duty up to the obligation of the text, how would efforts be multiplied for the diffusion of the gospel—for the evangelization of the nations! The number of missionaries would increase. Funds for their support would be vastly augmented. We should catch the spirit of Jesus, who, knowing what was in man—what an immortal nature—what capabilities of joy and sorrow, came "from the highest throne of glory to the cross of deepest woe," to seek and to save the lost. In the midst of all other theories and appliances of human progress, we find the old sins and sorrows, the degeneracies and passions ever returning and asserting their sway, and endeavouring to maintain it in crime, and blood, and woe. The only remedy is in the cross—in the empire of Christ in human hearts and lives. Catch anew the inspiration of the great commission, and under it bear the message of life to dying men, realizing the honour of such a service in the light of that day when the Judge shall declare,—"Inasmuch as ye did it unto one of the least of these, ye did it unto me."

"Lo! another age is rising—in the coming years I see
Hopes and promises of blessing, light, and love, and liberty;
All the good the past hath garnered, all the present yet hath won,
Fade before the glorious future, like the stars before the sun!

"Truth for every eye is shining, in the fulness of that day,
Joy and Hope, descended angels, rest, no more to pass away;
Freedom comes, and lifts the captive from the dungeon of his woe,
And all streams of mortal being deeper, purer, sweeter flow.

"There,'the thunder of the captains,' and their shoutings die away,
Melting into love's sweet music, like the darkness into day;
And the chorus of the nations, as the rolling years increase,
Rises in harmonious numbers, peaceful, to the Prince of Peace."

Confounding Right and Wrong.

By Rev. SAMUEL G. BUCKINGHAM, Springfield, Mass.

"Woe unto them that call evil good, and good evil."—Isaiah v. 20.

WHAT is there in a name? Is it anything more than a word?—a word, perhaps, hastily uttered, and when another might have been used just as easily. And then, is it not a mere sound?—an articulate and intelligible sound, to be sure; but one that is uttered, then heard no more, and usually forgotten. And what difference can it make what anything is called? Is it not the same thing, whatever name it bears, and can a word—a mere breath—change it at all, and make it either better or worse than it was before? As Shakspeare says,—

"What's in a name?
A rose by any other name would smell as sweet."

And yet the Bible pronounces its woe upon those who merely call certain things by wrong names. It curses such as call good evil, and evil good, as if it were a grievous crime, and deserving of the heaviest punishment. Wherein, therefore, consists this sin?—and what makes it such a crime?

The sin, we must suppose, relates to moral good and evil, or to moral distinctions, as we call them, to right and wrong. It is with duty that the Bible especially deals. It is pre-eminently of what is good for man as a creature of God's, and subject to His law, and of what would bring evil to him in that most important of all relations, that the scriptures treat. These are distinctions that must not be confounded. Their names must not be interchanged. Right must not be called wrong, nor wrong right. This is to unsettle all the foundations of moral obligation. It is to sweep away all the landmarks of duty; or, rather, it is shifting all the buoys and beacons by which we navigate the sea of life, so that, instead of warning us of danger, they shall rather draw upon shoals and rocks. No wonder, therefore, that the Bible says,—" Woe unto them that call evil good, and good evil."

Let us, therefore, treat of this subject : THE GUILT OF CONFOUNDING RIGHT AND WRONG, BY CHANGING THEIR NAMES.

Names are not mere words. They have a meaning, and a force of meaning which make them the most efficient instruments we know of. How much meaning and force single words have in them ! The name of a place suggests to us all that we know, or have conceived of, about that place.

Words are the representatives of ideas. The word upright represents the ideas which we attach to such a character. The name of Paul stands for the man himself, for his character, and labours, and usefulness. The statement of a fact in language is the expression of our ideas of what exists, or has taken place. The statement of a truth expresses what we conceive to be, and if it is really truth, what is a correct account of the matter. An abstract proposition expresed in language is something which, if true, corresponds with the reality of things. This is the nature of language. True, it is all words—syllables—breath ; still, as the representative of ideas, thoughts, conceptions upon every subject, it is just as valuable as thoughts and ideas are. And if these ideas are just and true, it is worth just as much as truth is. Or, if they are false, it becomes just as injurious as error and falsehood are. And it is just as necessary that language should be used aright as it is that it should teach truth rather than falsehood and error. And when it is wrongly used and misapplied, it is just as great a calamity as it is to have falsehood and error taught. And he who misapplies language thus, disseminates falsehood and error, and is guilty of the crime, and deserves the curse of such.

Here, then, we begin to see what the sin of changing the names of right and wrong, and calling good evil, and evil good, consists in.

I. *It confounds moral distinctions, and perplexes one in regard to his duty.*

It makes that seem right which is wrong, and that seem wrong which is right. They are made to change names. It is as if Judas was introduced to you under the name of Paul, and Paul by the name of Judas. Take the word "religion" as it is misapplied in Catholic countries. With us it means piety, the fear and love of God, heartfelt reverence for His character, and sincere devotion to His Son. It has special reference to the heart, and he who has not a truly pious heart, we do not regard as having any religion. But religion with a Catholic is very much a matter of forms, and ceremonies, and ritual observances. A "religious house," is not a Christian family, where husband and wife are "walking in all the commandments and ordinances of the Lord blameless," like Zacharias and Elizabeth, and "training up their children in the nurture and admonition of the Lord;" but a family of monks or nuns, who are under vows of celibacy, and subject to the rules of St. Benedict or St. Theresa. It is religion when seen aright that is appreciated and admired, if at all; and not when so misrepresented and reduced to outward forms and mechanical observances.

II. *But it not only perplexes men—it deceives and misleads them.*

To have right and wrong confounded, and called by wrong

names,—to call formality piety, when there is no piety except of the heart, and they who worship God at all, must "worship Him in spirit and in truth," is to mislead one. To call that Christianity, and teach for "the doctrines of God, the commandments of men," is to deceive men. We easily deceive ourselves with names. If we wish to believe anything, we call it truth, whether it is so or not. If we wish to think well of anything, we call it good, however bad it may be. We never could receive an unmitigated villain into our confidence and friendship in his true character; but how easy it is to overlook his corrupt principles and palliate his vices, and admit that he possesses all the excellences to which he lays claim, and, under this assumed name of a man of worth, grant him admission to our hearts and homes.

And in this, too, consists the art of deceiving others. Call bad things by good names, if you wish them to find favour. Call religious error the true doctrine and orthodoxy, if you wish to have it pass current. Call vices justifiable practices, or innocent indulgences, if you want them to be allowed. In this consists the skill of every successful errorist. He can dress up error in the garb of truth: he gives it the name of truth, and arrays it in the garments of truth, and so arranges that drapery about it, and gathers it in here, and lets it flow loosely there, as to hide this deformity, and make it seem to have that grace, until it passes under the name it bears. In this, too, consists the skill of every corrupter of public morals. He calls vice by some innocent name, and makes her talk of love and harmless enjoyment, and wreathes her face in roses and smiles, until she passes for the lovely maiden whose name she bears. It is doing mischief on a grand scale, and doing it most effectually, to confound right and wrong, and give them false names. It is calling irreligion piety, and having it revered and practised as if it were such. Well might the prophet pronounce a curse upon such,— "Woe unto them that call evil good, and good evil."

And now we are prepared to see how right and wrong are confounded by changing their names, and this "woe" incurred.

1. We slander one another by giving false names to each other's acts. We call that pride which is only dignity; we deem that parsimony which is nothing but economy; we say one is sceptical and perhaps infidel, because he is fond of investigation and discussion, and not willing to receive anything as the teaching of the Bible, except as it is plainly taught there; we charge another with being a bigot, when he only loves the truth of God, and dares not surrender it; we charge men perhaps with being hypocrites, when God knows that they are sin-

cere and for the most part conscientious and exemplary Christians, though they have certain striking faults. In such cases we give others a false name.

2. In like manner we deceive ourselves in respect to our own character and conduct. We call ourselves firm, when we are obstinate. We think we are conscientious, when we are only wilful. We call that a sense of justice in our hearts, which is the bitterest revenge.

3. Men relieve their consciences by giving to their actions false names. Their forgetfulness of God, and guilty indifference to all His claims and all His commands, they style only thoughtlessness. Their wickedness, and even gross vice, they call only gaiety. Their cheatings and their fraud they laugh over as only keenness and shrewdness. Their deceptions, and lies, and mean trickery to carry their point, they speak of as nothing but good management, and as justified by the object that was contemplated by them.

4. The standard of public morals is lowered, and the community is corrupted, by giving decent names to gross sins. There is no better way of reforming a corrupt public sentiment than by giving vices and crimes their true names. Call stealing, "stealing," and oppression, "oppression," as the Bible does, if you would bring men back to the Bible standard of duty.

Be not deceived, then, by names. Receive not that as right which calls itself such, unless it is really such; nor believe that to be truth which goes by that name, unless it is such in reality. Names are worth nothing if what they represent is worthless or injurious. All is not Christianity which goes under the name of it. All are not prophets who come in the name of the Lord. "If any man speak, let him speak as the oracles of God." Do not deceive yourself by giving things wrong names. Do not deem yourself a Christian because you bear the Christian name.

Do not attempt to practise such impositions upon others. It is bad enough to deceive yourself, but worse, if anything, to deceive another. To teach some humble and confiding soul that falsehood is truth, and that wrong is right; to take that feeble one by the hand, and offer to lead him to heaven and salvation, and set him in the broad road to destruction, when he thinks it is the narrow way to life, and send him forward to stumble on over rocks and pitfalls, and through darkness and danger, until he plunges at last into the bottomless abyss—there is no crime like this, and none deserves such a curse. If those denunciations of the Hebrew law were just, "Cursed be he that removeth his neighbour's landmarks; and all the people shall say, Amen!" and, "Cursed be he that maketh the blind to wander out of the way;

and all the people shall say, Amen!" a still heavier curse must light on that man who deceives his brother, to lead him into sin and on to ruin.

Learn, then, to call things by their right names—not that you should publicly, and in all places, and all times, speak of every thing and every body just as they are; not that you are to be publishing to the world every villain that you know of, or telling every body of all the misdeeds that you have discovered. This might be as needless and as cruel as it would be mischievous. Where duty does not call you to make such disclosures, Christian compassion would forbid it; but where duty requires it—duty to the community, duty to those who are ruining themselves by their self-deceptions, duty to truth and righteousness, and to the God of both—then set things in their right light, and hold them there, till all shall see them as they are, call them just what God calls them in His word.

Christ Wounded in the house of His Friends.
By Rev. E. H. GILLETT, New York City.

"And one shall say unto him, What are these wounds in thine hands? Then he shall answer, Those with which I was wounded in the house of my friends."—Zech. xiii. 6.

WHATEVER may have been the prophetic reference of these words, they are strikingly illustrative of the treatment of Christ.

It is not merely a beautiful but an affecting thought, that Christ identifies Himself with His people. He is with them to the end of the world. He is in them, and they in Him. The Church is the body of Christ. "Inasmuch," He says, "as ye have done it to one of least of these, ye have done it unto me."

In like manner Christ identifies Himself with His own cause on the earth. Whoever touches it, touches the apple of His eye. Its interests are His interests; its triumphs are His triumphs. He is glorified by its purity, He is dishonoured by its shame.

We see, then, how it is that He can be wounded still on earth. He is no longer present, indeed, in His bodily form. The nails are no more driven through those hands of flesh; the Roman spear is no longer thrust into that bleeding side; the agony of the wooden cross can never again be repeated: and yet Christ's spiritual body—His Church, His cause—can be exposed to suffer.

Need I say that this is the case? Who does not know it? Who does not see the deed done? Sometimes in heedlessness, sometimes in the haste of passion, sometimes by deliberate purpose, Christ's spiritual body is doomed to suffer, not only from the blows of open enemies, but of professed friends. I do not believe that a true friend could deliberately do it. A foe might, a Judas might, a hypocrite—a wolf in sheep's clothing—might; but the deliberation of the act would preclude friendship. How much of it there is in the world, God only knows. We wait for the judgment day to unmask hypocrites. Human insufficiency must pass them over to the hands of God.

But, wittingly or unwittingly, through a culpable negligence or haste, Christ is wounded in His cause, or in His spiritual body, in the house of His friends.

I. *He is wounded when Christians grow cold in zeal, slack in duty, or forgetful of their solemn vows.*

They show indifference, and indifference strikes like a dagger into the loving heart. They show ingratitude; and among men, no wounds sting, and bleed, and rankle like those of ingratitude. They betray selfishness, and selfishness is anti-Christ, and smites at that self-denying love which led Christ to die.

II. *Christ is wounded in the house of His friends when His cause is injured by the unbecoming conduct of His followers.*

Scandal in the church is scandal heaped upon His name. They are not to live as others do. The world expects, and rightly expects, more of them, and, although often unwarrantably, it judges the cause by the men. Religion is stabbed by the vanity, pride, ostentation, envy, luxury, selfishness, dishonesty, meanness, uncharitableness, deception, trickery of those that wear its garb. The world does not distinguish between the man and his uniform; and so, by the fault of one, that glorious cause, which aims to regenerate a world, or bring from its sad wreck many sons and daughters home to glory, is darkened and defaced.

III. *Christ is wounded in the house of His friends when indifference is shown by them to the success of the instrumentalities by which His cause is promoted.*

These instrumentalities are vital with Christ, as though His blood flowed through them, and His voice spake by them, and His heart beat in them. He is in the word, the sermon, the prayer, the praise. They are His eye, piercing the souls of backsliding Peters; His breath, withering the "vipers" of the temple—lawyers, scribes, and Pharisees; His fingers, touching the sick of the palsy or the blinded eye of the soul; His hands, stretched out in blessing to the little children whom He calls around Him. Yes! Christ so identifies Himself with His own ordinances and means of grace, that He suffers when they suffer, is slighted when they are slighted, wounded when they are wounded. Your influence, by your presence or absence, your sympathy or alienation, tells on Christ's cause; cheers or disheartens your brethren, speaks to sinners for weal or woe; and if that influence or example helps to thin the sanctuary or the praying circle, then do you stifle, as it were, the breath of intercession; you wound or contribute to strike down the hand that, in the name of Jesus, breaks the bread of life to dying souls. Are you guilty? If Christ should turn and look on you with an eye like that which smote through Peter's soul, and should hold up before you His pierced hands, and show you the print of the nails driven perhaps by your cold-hearted neglect, would not the very falsehood of the plea your heart may be suggesting now carry out to its conclusion a darker parallel?

IV. *Christ is wounded in the house of His friends by inattention to the gospel, with its messages of duty, its invitations and exhortations.*

True, they are presented in what the Apostle calls "the foolishness of preaching;" the treasure is committed to earthen vessels; but it is treasure still. Christ Himself speaks, although through lips of clay. Yet some listen just as though it were but a man talking,—just as though they were hearing a political speech; and so they yawn, or doze, or sleep, or turn away the head!

V. *Christ is wounded in the house of His friends by their lack of sympathy and co-operation, within their sphere, with the institutions of charitable beneficence for the spread of the gospel.*

It is for us to sustain them—to pour through them the full tide of our sympathies, till they beat strong and healthy with the life-blood of a true devotion.

VI. *Christ is wounded in the house of His friends, when Christians, instead of keeping the unity of the Spirit in the bond of peace, treat one another with superciliousness or bitterness; when their intercourse is not marked by that gentleness and forbearance which the gospel requires.*

Here looks may be daggers, and words blows. The laceration of Christian feeling by the wantonness of passion, is, between members of the same body, a self-mutilation, a wounding of the body of Christ. So the lack of Christian sociability, an indulgence of an exclusive spirit, is a wounding of Christ's members, and thus of Christ Himself. He is stabbed through His members. He is lacerated by the blows that fall upon His disciples. "Inasmuch," he says, "as ye have done it to one of the least of these, ye have done it unto me."

Now, I appeal unto you whether Christ be not, in view of these considerations, wounded in the house of His friends? Are there not those who, by inconsistent conduct, by neglect of the ordinances of the sanctuary, by worldliness, by passion, by unbrotherly feeling and act, dishonour their profession, disregard their solemn vows, and do injury to the cause of Christ? Is He not wounded, then, in the very house of His friends? Is it not a fact, that all the assaults of infidelity, all the rage of profanity, all the recklessness of vice and crime, do far less to check the power of the gospel than the scandals or offences of professed disciples? He that creeps into Christ's bosom can strike a blow such as no one else can; and He feels it, for His cause feels it, His members feel it, the Church feels it in palsied energy and enfeebled devotion.

But is it not something sadly aggravated? When the child lifts his hand to strike her that bore him and nursed him at her breast; when the son requites a father's counsels by mockery or vice that breaks his heart, and brings his gray hairs down with sorrow to the grave, even the world cries out,—"For shame!"

And when a pardoned rebel abuses the forbearance of a ruler, and steals into his confidence to smite him down, the execration of ages is heaped upon the culprit's head. But where is princely forbearance, or fatherly anxiety, or mother's love, to be compared with the tenderness and affection of Him by whose blood we are redeemed? And how shall that love be requited? By wounds? By wounds in the house of His friends! Forbid it heaven! Oh! for one more prayer like that which once fell from dying lips,—"Father, forgive them, for they know not what they do!"

Solemn Responsibility.

By the Rev. HEMAN HUMPHREY, D.D., Mass.

"Abstain from all appearance of evil."—1 Thess. v. 22.

THIS, like our Saviour's golden rule, is an injunction which every person ought to carry in his memory, wherever he goes. Our example, whether good or bad, will have an influence upon many, and may either save or destroy some.

The text includes two ideas. First, it requires every person most scrupulously to avoid whatever appears to him sinful, or even of doubtful character. And, secondly, as far as he can, to shun whatever may carry the appearance of sin to others, even where the motive is right, and the action, in itself considered, would be entirely unexceptionable.

It is obvious, at a glance, that the apostolic injunction, "Abstain from the appearance of evil," is much broader, and strikes much deeper, than the most perfect human legislation. The duty of avoiding whatever is positively sinful, and is known to be so by all parties, is seen instantly; but the reasons of our being required to abstain from all appearance of sin, are not so obvious. Many a tender conscience has been perplexed here. Many a sincere Christian has thus communed doubtingly with his own heart,—"Why this more than legal strictness?" In reference to such inquiries, let the following considerations be seriously weighed.

I. *We are bound to abstain from all appearance of transgression, because actions indifferent in themselves, or safe for us, may become positively criminal, by leading other men into sin.*

Of this we have a striking illustration in the eighth chapter of Paul's first Epistle to the Corinthians. Perhaps Paul never appeared greater than here. Rather than mislead the weakest and humblest believer, he would go to the extreme point of self-denial. He would wholly abstain from any, otherwise innocent, indulgence, not for a month, or a year, but to the end of time. This goes fully to establish a very important general principle, which it becomes every professor of religion to regard with a trembling conscientiousness. It binds you to submit to the greatest self-denial, rather than, by asserting your liberty, to bring in jeopardy the soul of your weakest brother. This great principle admits of innumerable applications.

II. *Professing Christians of enlarged views, are bound to give great heed to the scruples and remonstrances of their weaker brethren, in regard to many unessential points of Christian practice.*

I am aware that we here stand upon very delicate, not to say difficult ground. A brother may entertain extremely contracted and even erroneous views of Christian liberty. He may choose to find something wrong in the most innocent or indifferent action, and to be hurt every day where no harm is intended, and where no offence ought to be taken. Now, to admit that an individual of such a temperament may bring a whole church into bondage, would doubtless be carrying the matter quite too far. For no man has a right thus to "lord it over God's heritage,"— thus to fence the church about with unscriptural jealousies and restrictions. On the other hand, we are required to regard the feelings, and even the prejudices and extreme scrupulousness of the weaker brethren with great tenderness and indulgence. It is in this way that the strong should "bear the infirmities of the weak, and not seek to please themselves."

III. *It is only by abstaining from all appearance of evil that an unblemished Christian character can be maintained in the sight of the world.*

My meaning may be illustrated by Christ paying tribute money. In the same spirit are the following exhortations of the Apostle Paul,—" Provide for honest things, not only in the sight of the Lord, but also in the sight of men." According to this rule, in all our intercourse with the world, we are to consider not only what is honest and right in the sight of God, but what is so in the sight of men. As we must never transgress any law, or come short in any duty, so likewise we must not, if we can help it, seem to transgress, or to come short.

IV. *We, as professing Christians, are bound to maintain the most scrupulous circumspection in our deportment, to keep back others from presumptuous sins.*

With whatever indifference or scorn the wicked may affect to look down upon evangelical religion, and whatever sneers they may cast upon serious professors, they have a conscience, and they cannot always keep it under the power of opiates. It will sometimes whisper in their ears, when they are alone, or on a sickbed, or at the grave of a friend, and tell them that religion is true, that the Bible is God's book, and that they can never be safe without an interest in His promises. At such times they narrowly watch the example of professing Christians, and are influenced to a much greater degree by what they observe, than they are willing to admit, or than they are aware of themselves. It will never be known till the day of judgment how many souls are ruined by evil examples, nor how many are saved by a contrary influence.

V. *Another cogent reason for the injunction in my text is this : The limits between right and wrong actions, between lawful and unlawful indulgences, are often extremely indefinite.*

I am persuaded God never meant to say to us, "all is lawful till you reach that hair line, and all beyond it is sinful." There is often a doubtful space of very considerable extent, between what we may certainly know to be right, and certainly know to be wrong, and we tread upon this doubtful ground at our peril. The very fact of its being doubtful warns us to keep off; and this is the only safe course. It is the course which every consistent Christian will take. And how much better it is, never to venture within the limits of uncertainty, even though we should not actually transgress in a given case, than to run the hazard of it by our temerity. That there is such a doubtful region as I have alluded to, might be illustrated by a great variety of examples, such as appetite, relaxation, amusements, dress, expenditure, &c.

VI. *There is no safeguard against the power of temptation, but in abstaining from all appearance of evil.*

The firmest resolution cannot be trusted. The most settled convictions of duty are liable to be subverted. No man is safe who relies upon the strength of his religious principles, and in this vain confidence goes as far as he can, without actually violating God's holy law. Whoever stops to parley with temptation is already more than half overcome. The man who would be secure from danger, must keep so far away that he cannot hear the song of the syrens; and should he ever find that he is approaching any of their enchanted retreats, he must fly and deliver himself, "as a roe from the hand of the hunter, and as a bird from the hand of the fowler."

And now, dear brethren, in view of this subject, "what manner of persons ought ye to be, in all holy conversation and godliness?" Let me earnestly exhort you to abstain from all appearance of evil. For in no other way can you be safe from the power of temptation. In no other way can you keep yourselves unspotted from the world,—in no other way can you show your ardent love to all the brethren,—in no other way can you uniformly honour the Saviour,—in no other way can you "present your bodies a living sacrifice, holy and acceptable unto God, which is your reasonable service."

Encouragement only to the Devoted and Obedient.

By Rev. W. C. WALTON, A.M., Alexandria.

"Who is among you that feareth the Lord, that obeyeth the voice of His servant, that walketh in darkness, and hath no light? Let him trust in the name of the Lord, and stay upon his God."—Isaiah l. 10.

THE *fear of the Lord* is a phrase often used in the Bible to express true religion. Accordingly, the Divine blessing is pronounced upon *every one who fears the Lord*. It is, therefore, to be distinguished from that *fear which hath torment*. It is a *filial* fear; such as a good child has towards a good father, whom he loves, whose favour he highly prizes, and whose displeasure he dreads to incur.

It is here supposed that the person who thus fears the Lord, and obeys the voice of His servant, may, in some sense, walk in darkness and have no light. My object is to explain this figurative language, and to show how it was intended to be applied.

Light is emblematic of joy, *e. g.*, "Light is sown for the righteous, and gladness for the upright in heart." It is also an emblem of knowledge,—"Whatsoever doth make manifest, is light." Knowledge is to the soul what light is to the eye. When I have light, I see where to walk; so, when I have knowledge in regard to my duty, I see what course I ought to pursue. Or, if I have knowledge in regard to the manner in which Providence will deliver me from evils under which I suffer, I have light,—I do not walk in darkness, with respect to such deliverance. If, on the contrary, I cannot see, nor even conjecture, *how* I am to be delivered from existing or impending evils, I may be said to walk in darkness: and in that case, if I *fear the Lord, and obey the voice of His servant*, I am encouraged *to trust in His name*, and to *stay myself upon Him*. This is manifested by His word and by His Spirit.

If such be the meaning of the phrase in question, it would involve a palpable contradiction to apply the text to those from whom, according to their own acknowledgement, the light of God's countenance is withheld, and who are consequently walking in darkness, as to any evidence of the Divine favour. We must, therefore find another meaning.

In the preceding chapters, the prophet speaks of the Babylonian captivity, and of the oppressions of the Israelites during that dark period of their history. He also predicts their deliverance and restoration to their own land, and the subversion of the Chaldean empire. There was a pious remnant of the nation answering to this description. They feared the Lord and obeyed

His voice under the darkest and most discouraging circumstances. God had said, I will sift them as wheat is sifted in a sieve, yet shall not one grain be lost. He tells them, in effect, that although they had no light as to the manner in which He would accomplish their deliverance and restoration, yet they might confidently trust His power and faithfulness, for *it should be done.*

Such is the obvious meaning of the text. I would now improve the subject by stating a few similar cases, to which it might properly be applied.

I. *It might be applied to a case like that of Joseph, while lying under the reproach of a crime which he never committed, and which he abhorred.*

This was a great trial to his pure mind. From a situation of high respect and unbounded confidence, he was suddenly reduced to that of the basest criminal, stripped of all his honours, covered with infamy, immured in a prison, and without any earthly prospect of relief, because the circumstances of the case was such as to render it impossible for him to prove his innocence. But, as he feared the Lord, and obeyed His voice, he was authorized to trust in Him, and to stay himself upon the Divine faithfulness.

II. *The situation of David, during the life-time of Saul, was such as would have justified the application of the text.*

God had promised that he should be king over His people; and yet he was obliged to fly for his life, and to wander among the mountains, and to hide himself in dens and caves of the earth. Thus he was walking in darkness as to any prospect of relief, except from a Divine interposition.

III. *The last case that I shall state as justifying the application of the text, is that of the Church at the present day, when looking at the moral condition of the world in connection with the prophecies.*

The conversion of the world is predicted in the Bible with as much certainty as was the restoration of the Jews from the Babylonian captivity; and the obstacles which opposed the accomplishment of this prediction are far greater than those which darkened the prospects of the captive Jews. In the view of all who disbelieve the promises of God, then, the attempts of a company of children to level the Alleghany or the Andes, with such little instruments as they are able to wield, would not appear more hopeless than those which the Christian church is now making to convert the world. Therefore, the church may be said to be walking in darkness with respect to this event. She does not see how the immense obstacles are to be removed. She knows that the means she employs are in themselves perfectly inadequate to accomplish the work, and that it cannot be accomplished without a Divine interposition greater than any ever yet witnessed. She is, therefore, as entirely thrown upon faith, in relation to this matter, as the Jews were with regard to their restoration. It was written, that after seventy years, when the Lord had accomplished His purposes in their affliction, they should be released from their captivity and restored to their own land; and they were encouraged in the meantime to trust in the Lord, and stay themselves upon His promises, confidently believing that he could and would remove every obstacle. So it is written that "the earth shall be full of the knowledge of the Lord, as the waters cover the sea;" that the time will come when it shall be proclaimed in heaven, that "the kingdoms of this world have become the kingdoms of our Lord and of His Christ."

The only additional remark which I shall make, by way of improvement, is that it is a principle which runs through the whole economy of grace, to connect comfort with the active and faithful performance of duty.

This principle, it is believed, has not been generally recognized. Hence the perversion of the text; and hence the low state of religious enjoyment in the church. If the practical error which prevails on this subject could be rectified, the effect would soon be seen in the improved aspect of all the churches, and it would soon be felt to the ends of the earth.

Necessary Preparation for the Millenium.

By Rev. W. C. WALTON, A.M., Alexandria, D. C.

"Ye that make mention of the Lord, keep not silence, and give Him no rest, till He establish, and till He make Jerusalem a praise in the earth."—Isaiah lxii. 6, 7.

A RIGHT understanding of the purposes of God in relation to His Church is highly important. It will not only heighten our religious enjoyment, but furnish a powerful stimulus to exertion. Without such understanding, we have no certain ground of hope that the cause of Christ will finally triumph : and hope is in all cases essential to vigorous action. Let all Christians know and feel that it is God's purpose to establish and to make Jerusalem a praise in the earth ; that His omnipotence is pledged for the accomplishment of this purpose ; and let them be fully convinced that He designs to accomplish it through the instrumentality of His people, and the effect must be a great increase of their zeal and activity. The victory will be more than half won. The church will immediately assume that character and attitude which will ensure her speedy triumph. In the discussion of this subject, then, I shall first attempt to show,—

I. *What is implied in establishing Jerusalem, and making her a praise in the earth.*

Jerusalem is a figurative name of the church. It is, therefore, the church that is to be established and made a praise in the earth. This church is also frequently called a kingdom ; being composed of those who professedly submit to the Lord Jesus Christ. Let us, then, consider the church as the kingdom of Christ, and apply the language of the text accordingly. If His kingdom were of this world, it is plain that it could not be universally established, but upon the ruins of all human governments. But Christ has declared that His kingdom is not of this character ; and, therefore, its establishment will not require the subversion of other kingdoms. On the contrary, it will add strength and stability to every government whose principles are consistent with the liberty and happiness of man.

The *establishment* of Christ's kingdom implies its pervading influence among all ranks of men, in all lands : it implies the destruction of idolatry and of infidelity, the extermination of heresy, the conversion of the heathen, of the Mahomedans, of the Jews, and of the multitudes of merely nominal Christians ; in a word, it implies the universal knowledge and reception of the truth, and a universal submission to the authority of Christ. And when the whole church, thus enlarged, shall cease vain wrangling, and love as brethren, then may Jerusalem be said to be established, and then, too, will she be a praise in all the earth. There will be nothing like her for beauty, and grandeur, and glory under the whole heavens.

II. *I now proceed to show, that it is the purpose of God to accomplish all this for His church.*

He has said that Christ must reign until He has put all enemies under His feet; that He shall have dominion from sea to sea, and from the river to the ends of the earth. Yea, all kings shall bow down before Him, and all nations shall serve Him. "From the rising of the sun unto the going down of the same, my name shall be great among the Gentiles, and in every place incense shall be offered unto my name and a pure offering." The same is predicted by the prophet Daniel. After speaking of the rise and fall of other kingdoms in succession, until he came to the Roman Empire, he says, "In the days of these kings shall the God of heaven set up a kingdom which shall stand for ever." "And the Lord shall be King over all the earth. In that day there shall be one Lord and His Name one." This can mean nothing less than the universal prevalence of one religion, or the universal establishment of the kingdom of Christ. HE is to be KING over all the earth, for all kings shall bow down before Him, and all nations shall serve Him. If this is not predicted, then nothing can be certainly gathered from the language of prophecy. It is, therefore, the purpose of God to establish Jerusalem, and to make her a praise in the earth

III. *In accomplishing this work, God will employ human agency.*

The command to evangelize the nations was given, not to angels, but to men. Go ye, and preach the gospel to every creature. Go ye, and teach all nations. Again, the Saviour says to His disciples, Ye are the light of the world. Ye are the salt of the earth: *i. e.*, you are to be the instruments of enlightening, and purifying, and saving the world. But, in order to answer this description, and to execute this high commission, Christians must be a *peculiar people;* they must have a distinct character, —a character as distinct from that of the world, as light is from darkness. If a lighted candle did not produce an effect essentially different from darkness, it would not answer the purpose for which it is intended. Darkness would never enlighten itself. And God has revealed it as His purpose, to fit His church for the great work which He intends to accomplish by her instrumentality. Then shall the sanctuary be cleansed (Dan. viii. 13, 14). THE CHURCH THEN IS TO BE PURIFIED, BEFORE SHE WILL BE THUS

EXALTED. This conclusion from the prophecy of Daniel accords with the still clearer prediction of Isaiah. The sixtieth chapter of his prophecy contains the most striking representation of that state of the church to which the text refers, that is to be found in the Bible. Every advance, therefore, which the church makes in holiness, or in conformity to the image of Christ, is an approximation towards that character which she must attain, to be fitted for the great work to which she is called; or, in other words, it is an approximation towards that state of things which must precede and prepare the way for the millennium. The work of converting the world must, according to the revealed purpose of God, be done by her; and yet it will not be done until she be fitted for the work. This fitness, then, is the first grand object to be attained. Let all Christians and ministers consider this, and let them pray, and preach, and labour, with this object distinctly in view.

The language of the text is addressed to Christians. Ye that make mention of the Lord,—or ye who are His "remembrancers,"—who, to speak after the manner of men, are allowed to remind Him of His promises,—ye are to give Him no rest, till He establish, and till He make Jerusalem a praise in the earth. No intelligent and consistent Christian will say, that because this is the work of God, He does not need our co-operation; and because the event is here certainly predicted, and will assuredly take place, therefore, we need not urge the matter in prayer, or be very solicitous about it. No; this is the language of infidelity. But happy, thrice happy shall we be, if, instead of hindering, we now come to the help of the Lord, and do His work faithfully, in the true spirit of the text. When the Lord shall establish Jerusalem, and make her a praise in the earth, her triumphs will be our triumphs, her glory will be our glory; while those who act a different part will sink, condemned of God and of all holy beings; and at the day of final retribution, will rise only to shame and everlasting contempt.

The Heavenly Mind.

By Rev. EDWARD D. GRIFFIN, D.D.

"To be spiritually minded is life and peace."—Rom. viii. 6.

THE Apostle is contrasting a carnal with a spiritual mind. By a carnal or fleshly mind, he means that which is natural to man, according to those words of our Saviour, "That which is born of the flesh is *flesh*." By a spiritual mind, he means that new and holy temper which is produced by the Spirit of God, according to the words of Christ subjoined to the former, "That which is born of the Spirit is *spirit*." The whole movement of that which is called a spiritual mind is contrary to fallen nature. It is an up-hill motion, and requires great effort. Every step of its course is self-denial. A man who would live easy and go where nature leads him, will never attain to a spiritual mind. He must enter in earnest on a conflict with nature, and wage a war, if not of extermination, at least of absolute conquest. There is no life, no peace, further than he does this.

But that part of the spiritual mind to which I wish to draw your attention is what is called a heavenly mind. It consists of the following ingredients:—

1. A deadness to the world.
2. An eye habitually fixed on heaven, like Abraham, who "looked for a city which hath foundations, whose Builder and Maker is God."
3. Such a walk with God as Enoch maintained, consisting in an intimate communion with Him (involving a clear view of Him, and a consciousness of living in His presence), and consisting also in a will moving in the same line with His will.

The heavenly mind, thus constituted, is supported by that faith which is "the substance of things hoped for, the evidence of things not seen," and is accompanied with a sense of acceptance, and, in its higher actings, with "the full assurance of hope," which brings with it that "peace of God which passeth all understanding."

This is the heavenly mind. To attain this is the greatest happiness on this side of heaven. How, then, shall it be obtained? This is a question of the greatest personal importance to us.

I. *I remark that it must be received from God, and of course must be sought with a deep sense of dependence on Him.*

II. *We must ask Him for it in a course of habitual and earnest prayer.*

III. *We must be much employed in heavenly meditation.*

IV. *The man who would attain to a heavenly mind must be conscientious and punctual in his attendance on all the means of grace.*

V. *He must watch.*

VI. *The man who would attain to the exalted dignity and serenity of a heavenly mind, must pursue a course of habitual and universal obedience.*

VII. *It is necessary to the attainment of a heavenly mind, that a man possess a single eye; that he be not divided between the world and God, and keep a double object in his view.*

VIII. *A man cannot expect to ascend to this holy and happy elevation without setting his mind npon it as the personal good, to which all others must submit, and decreeing in his heart (with a proper dependence on God), that he will attain to this though everything else be lost.*

He must say, and continue to say, "God helping me, I must and will have this. Let everything else go; this is my point,—this is my all." The man who thus resolves and perseveres, in the manner already described, *will* obtain this most desirable good. It is an old maxim, that if a man says, I will be rich, he will be rich. The meaning is, that if he resolves to be rich at all hazards, and makes everything else bend to his purpose, and has no other object day or night, and sticks at no hardships or self-denials, the probability is that he will succeed. The same may be said of a resolute pursuit of learning, and indeed of almost every other object. But there is a certainty in the present case which does not attend any other, for God has promised success. "Seek and ye shall find,"—" The soul of the diligent shall be made fat,"—" Delight thyself in the Lord, and He shall give thee the desires of thy heart,"—" How much more shall your heavenly Father give the Holy Spirit to them that ask Him."

Here then is a good within the reach of every man who will feel right and do his duty. And it is worth more in the present life than thrones and kingdoms. And now the question is, will you drop every other concern and rise up to this pursuit? Not one of you is excluded from spending your life high under the arch of heaven, far above the world, in full view of the heavenly city, knowing that to be your eternal home, and sheltered there from all the cares and troubles of life. The means by which you can make the ascent have been pointed out. And now the question is, will you come up to this high and holy life, or will you grovel still in the dust, sighing, suffering, dying? There is but one mind that can decide for you, and that mind is your own. What say you now, my brethren?

God Entitled to our Obedience.

By the Rev. CHARLES COFFIN, D.D., East Tennessee.

"Who is the Lord that I should obey His voice?"—Exod. v. 2.

THE interrogation is equivalent to the boldest assertion that the Lord is not a Being of such greatness and excellency as to deserve the obedience of man. At least the king of Egypt wished to excuse himself, and he spoke the heart of every sinner. In thus confidently addressing Moses, he doubtless expected to awe him into silence, and so to escape any decisive reply. But that Omnipotent Being, whose authority was disputed, came forth in terrible majesty, and took the answer upon Himself.

Although comparatively few are so bold as to repeat the question, which God answered in so awful a manner, yet the sentiment which it avows is continually echoed by the conduct of sinners. Indeed, all sin proclaims the principle, that there is no God worthy to be obeyed. Else why is He ever disobeyed? In almost all nations now called Christian, there are those who not only refuse to obey the commands of God, but make sport of His perfections and deny His being. But professed atheists only display the tendency of that sinful nature which is common to us all. "Who is the Lord, that I should obey His voice?" is the practical question of *all* who do not live, by evangelical faith, that life which God requires, and which is the only acceptable acknowledgement of His being and perfections. This question I shall attempt to answer by a general exhibition of the Divine claims to our obedience.

I. *We ought to obey God, because He is the benevolent Creator of the universe.*

II. *We are bound to obey God, because He is the constant Preserver of the creatures of His power.*

III. *We are under yet greater obligations to obey God, because He is the perfect Governor of the universe.*

IV. *We are obligated in the highest degree to obey God, because He is the merciful Redeemer of sinners.*

From this general view of the character and works of God, we infer, in the first place, the greatness of our obligations to love and obey Him with all the heart.

It may be inferred, in the second place, from the infinite excellency of the Divine character, that to be destitute of the love of God is to possess a heart entirely depraved.

Let me then exhort the impenitent, "Be ye reconciled to God." He has graciously set on foot a plan of reconciliation through the mediation of His Son, Jesus Christ, offering pardon and blessedness to all who will renounce their opposition and become His friends. There is every possible motive to immediate compliance with this overture. We must either comply, or, by obstinately rejecting it, widen the distance between God and ourselves, and render it eternal.

Fatal Hindrance to Prayer.

By Rev. LEONARD WOODS, D.D., Andover.

"If I regard iniquity in my heart, the Lord will not hear me."—Psalm lxvi. 18.

THERE is no subject on which the Prophets and Apostles speak with more earnestness and decision, than on *the necessity of holiness.* They teach that although God will save *sinners*, He will give no encouragement to *sin ;* that the whole work of redemption is intended to promote moral purity,—to establish a kingdom of holiness. The sentiment that God is holy, and cannot look upon sin, was deeply impressed upon the mind of David. It was a truth familiar to his thoughts that, although God was so much inclined to hear prayer, and to grant the desires of all who call upon Him, He would have no favourable intercourse with those who lived in sin. That God will not hear the prayer of those who regard iniquity in their hearts, is made very evident from the infallible instructions of holy writ. The same truth may be deduced from a consideration of the known attributes of God, such as benevolence, wisdom, justice, and truth. The doctrine which I have thus briefly established, is essential to the Christian religion, and has a direct bearing upon various subjects of high practical importance.

I. *It exposes, in clear daylight, the falsity of every scheme of religion which stands in opposition to the Divine law, or in any way detracts from its authority and influence.*

If there is any one who encourages himself in disobedience to God, because he hopes for pardon,—any one who is less impressed with the authority of the divine law, because Christ died to redeem us from its curse,—any one who can live quietly in the neglect of duty, because he thinks he has believed in Christ,—finally, if there is any one whose confidence in divine grace renders him less grieved and distressed with the evils of his own heart and life, and less desirous of becoming holy,—let such a one know that, however highly he may think of himself, God looks upon him with an awful frown, and will not hear his prayers.

II. *Our doctrine is important in relation to Christians, and may assist them in accounting for the fact that their prayers are so seldom heard and answered.*

The prayers, brethren, which we have offered to God cannot

be enumerated. We have often prayed that He would enlighten our minds, that He would make us holy, harmless, and undefiled, cause all the fruits of the Spirit to abound in us. We have prayed, too, for the growing holiness and usefulness of Christians, for the conversion of sinners, for the effusion of the Holy Spirit upon our churches, and our literary and religious institutions, and for the universal spread of the gospel. Such prayers for ourselves and for others we have offered up hundreds, and perhaps thousands of times, and have offered them up to that God who heareth prayer. And yet, where is the answer to our prayers? Is not here something very strange! God has promised to hear prayer,—the prayers of Christians constantly ascend to Him for spiritual blessings,—and yet few of these blessings are bestowed? Has God ceased to be gracious? Has He forgotten His promises? Is His ear heavy that He cannot hear? No, brethren, the reason is not to be found in God, but in ourselves. We are chargeable with regarding iniquity in our hearts, we are deficient in our obedience to the divine law. This is the reason, and the only reason, why God does not hear our prayers. And, my brethren, is not this a sufficient reason?

Christian brethren, this is a serious subject. Let us not pass over it lightly. Let each one for himself faithfully inquire,— What is the particular sin, which causes the divine displeasure against me, and hinders my prayers from being heard?

Our attention to this subject may be rendered more profitable if we will examine ourselves in regard to a class of duties and sins which are considered less frequently, and are more likely to pass unnoticed. I speak now of the hidden motives which govern us in those actions which are externally right. I speak of those thoughts and feelings which are seen only to the eye of God. As what I have now hinted at is specially important, I shall turn your thoughts to a few examples.

1. It is the requisition of the sacred scriptures, that we should be governed in our conduct by love to God and love to man. Suppose, now, that in all our actions, even when we show the greatest respect for God, and the greatest benevolence to man, we still have in our hearts an ultimate reference to ourselves; and instead of seeking the welfare of our fellow-creatures, and the honour of God, do in reality make our own interest the grand object of pursuit. Is not this regarding iniquity in our hearts?

2. If we receive an injury from others, God requires us from the heart to forgive them, to wish them well, and to overcome evil with good. In doubtful cases, He requires us to avoid evil thoughts and suspicions, and to possess that love which hopeth

all things. Suppose, now, when we receive any injury, we put the worst construction possible upon it. Is not this iniquity?

3. If we have injured or offended others, our Lord requires us to make ample confession and reparation. If any of our fellow-Christians have aught against us, it is our first duty to go and be reconciled to them. The neglect of this is a sin, which will deprive us of the happiness of communion with God.

4. We are required not to think of ourselves above what we ought to think; not to seek great things for ourselves, but to be meek and lowly in heart, and to be content that our names should be unknown, if the name of our blessed Lord may be honoured. Suppose that we seek the gratification of ourselves, instead of the welfare of others; and care for our own things, not for the things of Christ. Is not such a state of mind highly offensive to God?

Let us then, brethren, examine ourselves with incessant care. For sin is a deceitful, subtle thing.

III. *Impenitent sinners may learn from this subject why God does not hear their prayers.*

On this point those who are disposed to give some attention to religion, especially those who are solicitous for their eternal happiness, often feel distressing difficulties. They are unable to account for it, that, after they have offered so many prayers, they are not relieved from trouble, and comforted with the tokens of divine forgiveness. That the prayers of such persons are unavailing, and their souls destitute of peace, is not owing to the want of stronger excitement of feeling, nor to the want of greater frequency or length in their prayers, nor to the enormity of past sins, and least of all to any want of compassion in God. The dreadful fact, that God does not hear their prayers, is owing to this one cause,—that they regard iniquity in their hearts,—that their affections cleave to sin,—that they dislike the service of God, and will not be bound by His holy law. It is this which bars them from the presence of God, and closes His ear to their prayers. Let them give up their sins, and let their hearts give up the love of sin, and God's ear will be open to their cry. There will be no need of any tumultuous excitement of feeling, and no need of great frequency, or length, or loudness in their prayers. God will hear the gentlest whisper. Yea, God is so merciful, that he will hear *the desire* of the humble, though never uttered in words. When any are disposed to confess and forsake their sins, God graciously attends to their requests. And sometimes He anticipates their wishes, and bestows the blessings they need, before they ask for them. Thus it was with the prodigal son.

Let, then, all impenitent sinners ponder well the reason why God does not hear their prayers. Their hearts are still wedded to sin. They still cherish in their bosoms that abominable thing which God's soul hateth. A holy God can be brought into no alliance with a heart that loves what He hates. You must sacrifice the pleasures of sin, or the friendship of your Maker. You must part with sin, or part with heaven.

Wealth a fearful Snare to the Soul.
By Rev. GARDINER SPRING, D.D., New York.

"How hardly shall they that have riches enter into the kingdom of God!"
MARK x. 23.

THIS extraordinary remark was made by our Lord to His disciples on observing the conduct of the rich young man whom He had required to "sell whatever he had, and give to the poor." What a snare riches are to the soul! Wealth does not, indeed, form an insurmountable obstacle to the possession of piety. If there were nothing to obstruct the salvation of the rich except their affluence,—if there were no opposing heart to be overcome,—the rich might be saved as easily as others. There are not wanting examples of piety among the affluent. Abraham and Job were rich, and David, Solomon, and Joseph of Arimathea were men of princely fortune, and yet were men of great devotedness to God. The scriptures represent wealth, when used aright, as a distinguished blessing. It may, and ought to lead men nearer to God, instead of driving them far from Him. But, while these facts show that it is not impossible for rich men to be pious, they do not invalidate the sentiment that there are serious difficulties in the way of their salvation. Among the obstacles which oppose themselves to the salvation of the rich, we may refer,—

I. *To the pride of life.*

The scriptures speak of this as one of the most operative causes of human destruction. An inordinate and unreasonable self-esteem excludes God from the heart. It is a spirit diametrically opposite to all which the gospel requires, and therefore rejects the gospel salvation. There is everything in the condition of an affluent man to foster and cherish his pride. The ease with which his desires are gratified, the obsequiousness which attends the fulfilment of his wishes, the decoration and show, the ostentation and splendour which he imagines becomes his station, and which distinguish his person, his family, his dwelling, his business, and his enjoyments; in a word, that "pride of life" which "is not of the Father but of the world," inflates his inconsiderate mind, insensibly puffs it up with notions of self-importance, and has a powerful, if not a fatal tendency to close every avenue of his soul, and banish from his mind every thought of God and eternity.

II. *A strong impression of their personal independence.*

Though men are absolutely dependent on God, and to a great extent on one another, there is in all a natural feeling of independence. There is nothing in which poor dependent man glories more than exemption from control. Nor will it be denied that wealth is very apt to foster this unseemly self-reliance, and this haughty contempt of God. When, therefore, you see a man who reluctantly admits the thought, that in God he lives, and moves, and has his being,—who revolts at the idea that he himself is God's property, and rigidly accountable to Him as his Great Superior, you can feel how hard it is for such a man to enter the kingdom of God. It was from the high elevation of his affluence and grandeur, that Pharoah demanded, "Who is the Lord, that I should obey His voice?"

III. *Their attachment to this world.*

How many, like the rich man in the gospel, have the most pungent and solemn reflections; have made the most anxious inquiries relative to their salvation; have formed most salutary resolutions, and have become "almost Christians;" who, when they have learned that the indispensable condition of discipleship is a hearty renunciation of this world, have come to the affecting conclusion to choose this world as their portion, and have gone away from Christ, "because they had great possessions." "Covetousness is idolatry." There is no room in the heart for God, where it is pre-occupied by the world. The love, and worship, and service of God are excluded by the love, and worship, and service of another. The loyalty which belongs to God is forcibly transferred to another sovereign. "No man can serve two masters: for either he will hate the one and love the other, or else he will hold to the one and despise the other. Ye cannot serve God and mammon."

IV. *Their cares and perplexities.*

Wherever you find the greatest amount of secular care and solicitude, there, rest assured, is the greatest danger of losing the soul. The thoughts are busied about other concerns, the time is occupied in other pursuits, the attention is wearied, the vigour of both body and mind is exhausted in business, and the whole soul so immersed in harrowing avocations, that there is little opportunity to think, or read, or converse, or hear about spiritual and eternal things. And thus, in the midst of these conflicting claims, no place is found for the claims of religion. Eternity is forgotten, and the soul is lost! Now, the pressure of this perplexity falls upon two classes of men,—the rich and the poor,—but especially the rich. Rich men, with few exceptions, are men of calculation, business, and enterprise, and, from the force of habit, are almost always pre-occupied in concerns remote from God and heaven.

V. *The best means of grace are rarely used with the rich and affluent.*

God has formed no purpose to save any man irrespective of the appointed means. If there is any class of mankind who, from their condition in society, are separated from the means of salvation, their doom is written in the fearful sentence, "Where no vision is, the people perish." But rich men, as a class, are very apt to put themselves at a distance from the means of grace. You do not find the rich generally so well acquainted with the Bible as persons in more humble circumstances. If a poor man, or a poor family, or a neighbourhood is destitute of the scriptures, Christian benevolence will seek them out and supply their wants. But who distributes Bibles to the rich? Who gives tracts to the rich? It will not be denied that those individuals and families who are born and brought up in the more fashionable ranks of life are greatly prone to neglect the duties of religion. I have often observed, too, that men who have been prospered in business, and raised from poverty to affluence, more generally evince an increasing disregard of religious institutions with the increase of their wealth.

Nor do the rich usually attend upon the most faithful ministrations of the gospel. A fashionable church is too apt to be but another name for a very smooth gospel. For myself I must say that, in the course of my ministry, with few exceptions, I have not found the rich frequenting the weekly lecture and prayer meeting. And when ministers are roused with anxiety for the souls of their people, and testify the grace of God, not only publicly, but from house to house, whose door are they likely to pass? The door of poverty? No. But it is that sumptuous dwelling, that pile of marble, so splendid without and so decorated within, that he passes without reluctance, from the chilling apprehension that no such errand of mercy as that which guides his steps would be welcome there.

There is another aspect, too, in which the rich are sufferers. Ministers are not faithful with them in those few personal interviews on which they venture. They heal the rich where they would probe the poor,—they comfort and build up the rich where they would distress and pull down the poor,—they administer premature consolation, and cherish false hopes, and make hypocrites of the rich where they would make converts of the poor.

Nor are ministers alone unfaithful to the rich. Private Christians have no bowels of compassion for them. Who thinks of instructing them, and praying for them, and teaching them to pray? You may see a collection of humble individuals engaged in religious conversation, and if a family servant should happen to enter the room, no one feels embarrassed, no one is alarmed; the conversation proceeds, and the poor servant is profited by it, and it issues in her salvation. But if some rich and distinguished personage should perchance obtrude upon their sacred familiarity, mark how every tongue is silent! None now can speak a word for Christ. The rich may not share in this spiritual repast. No; there is no mercy for the rich. Bibles there are, and ministers there are, and tracts, and pastoral faithfulness and prayers, and tender and solemn instructions there are, in a thousand forms for the poor; but the "poor rich" must remain unadmonished, and go down unpitied into hell.

Thus we see that scarcely any class of men are destitute of so many of the best means of salvation as the great and the affluent. There is pity for all others, and from all other classes the kingdom of God suffers violence, and the violent take it by force; but, O! how hardly shall they that have riches enter into that kingdom? And now from these views several reflections may naturally arise.

1. What melancholy evidence does this subject furnish of the strange depravity of the human heart. Why is it that the rich are so much more in danger of perdition than other men? Sim-

ply because they enjoy so much of Divine goodness! "I spake unto thee," says God, "in thy prosperity, and thou saidest, I will not hear. This has been thy manner from thy youth." "Let favour be shown to the wicked: yet will he not learn righteousness; in the land of uprightness will he deal unjustly, and not behold the majesty of the Lord."

2. Let me say, do not envy the rich. You recollect the sentiment of David, when he gave way to his sinful spirit,—"I was envious of the foolish, when I saw the prosperity of the wicked." And you recollect how he was cured of this envy, when he considered the influence of wealth on their spiritual character, and their final condition. Will you envy a man that which ensnares his soul?—which presents obstacles to his eternal salvation?—which throws mountains in his way to heaven? Wealth is a privilege when enjoyed and used as it should be. But I should be afraid to pray for wealth, either for myself or my children. If I knew I should devote it to God, I should be glad to possess it. But I do not know; and observation shows that large possessions are much more likely to injure and destroy us, than we ourselves are likely to devote them to God.

3. Our subject then admonishes us to take care how we heap up riches. What mean all this anxiety, and watchfulness, and effort, and bustle to lay up to yourselves treasures on earth? What doth it profit? It will give you the means of an independent subsistence—it will give you influence with your fellow-men—it may render thousands obsequious to your desires; but this is not all. It will inflate you with the pride of life—it will beguile you into a proud contempt of God—it will rivet your heart to earth—it will multiply the cares and embarrassments which detach your thoughts from eternity—it will put you at a distance from some of the best means of salvation—it will be an obstacle to your entrance into life eternal, which thousands have in vain attempted to surmount. O let me say, "Seek ye first the kingdom of God and His righteousness, and all these things shall be added unto you." Do not defer this momentous concern till you are rich. For the probability of your becoming the humble followers of Christ is less and less, as your wealth increases. I remark,

4. Our subject affectionately addresses itself to the rich. Of all those who have hope towards God, the rich are most in danger of losing the savour and usefulness of piety, and of being scarcely saved. And that your riches may prove a blessing, and not a curse, "set not your hearts upon them,"—"be not conformed to this world,"—"use this world as not abusing it, for the fashion of this world passeth away." You are God's stewards, and must

give an account of your stewardship. How suitable, then, the injunction,—" Charge them that are rich in this world, that they be not high-minded, nor trust in uncertain riches, but in the living God, who giveth us richly all things to enjoy; that they do good, that they be rich in good works, ready to distribute, willing to communicate; laying up in store for themselves a good foundation against the time to come, that they may lay hold on eternal life." And to the rich who are not pious let me say, Respected friends, is there not fearful reason to apprehend that you will never enter the kingdom of God? Everything is leagued against you. O this pride of life—this forgetfulness of God—this confidence in riches—this incessant care and vexation —these golden treasures—how are they like a millstone about your neck, sinking you down to perdition! But if you perish in the midst of mercies, is not the fault your own? O tell me, will you perish because God is kind?—because He gives the means of great usefulness, as well as happiness? It may be He is now saying, "Sell that thou hast, and give to the poor, and thou shalt have treasure in heaven." Obey God's voice. For "what is a man profited if he gain the whole world and lose his own soul; or what shall a man give in exchange for his soul?"

5. Let me say to all, while you envy not the affluent, study to do them good. An appropriate tract, a faithful sermon, a religious periodical, a word fitly spoken, may be to them the message of eternal love, and may give a new and heavenly direction to all their wealth and all their efforts. How exceedingly great, then, the guilt of neglecting those whose souls are at least as precious as those of the poor, and whose influence may be a thousand fold more important.

The facility with which Sinners go to Destruction.

BY REV. WM. MITCHELL, A.M., NEWTOWN, CONN.

"Enter ye in at the strait gate; for wide is the gate, and broad is the way that leadeth to destruction, and many there be which go in thereat."
—MATT. vii. 13.

HE who made the human soul, and laid down His life for its redemption, knows perfectly well what is necessary to salvation, and knows our liability to be ruined by a delusive hope. In the greatness of His compassion, with His omniscient eye upon the deceitfulness of the heart, and the many temptations of the world, He has clearly described the Christian character, and the character of every traveller in the broad way. He has exhibited the features of the carnal man, and the spiritual man in the nicest shades of distinction; presenting to the vision of the one unclouded immortality, and to the vision of the other the horrors of everlasting death. The path of life is so plain that "the wayfaring men, though fools, need not err therein." But notwithstanding all the light shed from heaven on the ways of wisdom, there are "few that be saved." Such is the blindness and desperate wickedness of men, that the multitude throng the broad way, bent on their own destruction, in despite of the entreaties and the mercies of the Lord. The passage leads us to consider the facility with which sinners go to destruction. This will appear,—

I. *From the fact that it is agreeable to the nature of man to pursue a sinful course.*

The natural character of all men as delineated in the scriptures is this,—They roll sin as a sweet morsel under the tongue. They love darkness rather than light. Their hearts are fully set in them to do evil. They possess the carnal mind, which is enmity against God. They are dead in trespasses and sins. The heart is deceitful above all things, and desperately wicked. The natural man is fully persuaded that the pleasures of sin will make him happy, while godliness would rob him of his present enjoyments. He is thus persuaded, because sinful pleasures are agreeable to his depraved nature, and the pleasures of holiness are contrary to his nature. And now, if "the wages of sin is death," and "to be carnally minded is death," and if sin is altogether agreeable to the natural heart,—and if it is very difficult, impossible, indeed, without grace, to persuade the transgressor to exchange the things he dearly loves, for things which he cordially hates, then it is easy for him to continue in sin, and go to destruction.

II. *The facility with which men go to destruction is apparent from the spiritual sloth of the transgressor.*

This dreadful insensibility to eternal things, natural to all men, is represented in scripture by the words *sleep* and *death*. They are significant epithets when applied to the moral condition of man. A man sleeping on the brink of destruction is in a dreadful state. A man spiritually dead to his everlasting welfare—dead while the day of grace is gliding away—is in an awful condition. And such is the state, such the condition of the sinner. Means, various and abundant, are employed to awaken him, but still he sleeps. How awfully sure that he will sleep, and sleep, and perish everlastingly, unless God quicken him by the energies of His Spirit, and call him from death to life ! Look at all the facts in the case, and you will see how deep is the slumber of the natural man, and how easy it is for him to continue in his slumbers, till he awakes amid the realities of eternity to sleep no more.

III. *The truth of the text is illustrated by the blindness of the carnal mind.*

"The natural man receiveth not the things of the Spirit of God, because they are foolishness unto him; neither can he know them, because they are spiritually discerned." There is no passage of scripture better illustrated by matters of fact. The gospel is foolishness to the sinner. How erroneous all his conceptions of God and the heavenly kingdom! He thinks that what men call morality will save him; and therefore he needs no repentance, faith, regeneration. You will find him benighted in all his views of God, of duty, of Christ, of holiness, of the great salvation. How easy it is for him to remain in this spiritual darkness, and be illuminated too late only by the light of eternity.

IV. *The strength of unbelief, the many allurements of the world, and the devices of Satan show with what facility sinners may go to destruction.*

If they would believe the eternal and tremendous truths which God has revealed, they could not remain destitute of the good hope through grace. But they will not believe. And "this is their condemnation." Their whole guilt is summed up in the single word "unbelief." And the difference between the righteous and the wicked all along, in the scriptures, consists in the fact, that the one is a believer, the other not. The allurements of the world, too, which tend directly to confirm the sinner in his unbelief, are in number almost like the stars of heaven. There is the legion of enticements which feed the lust of the eye, the lust of the flesh, and the pride of life. There is the combined influence of ungodly companions, and the persecution and derision of a wicked world. Add to this the devices of Satan. He commenced his wily labours in Paradise, and will pursue his prey, till he shall be finally bound with the great chain of the angel, who has the key of the bottomless pit.—(Rev. xx. 2.)

V. *The effect of things present, compared with the influence of things distant, still further illustrates the truth of the text.*

Present good exerts a strong influence against the importance of distant good. The child will prefer a small gift to-day to a greater one to-morrow. And this is one of the traits of natural character. The sinner seizes on the present good, and regards salvation as a distant thing. Sinful pleasures may be enjoyed now, but heaven seems to be afar off, and this exerts no small influence in determining his present choice. Under the influence of these erroneous views he chooses the present good, and how easily may he drop into the "everlasting burnings," from this dying world, while relying for safety on future amendment!

VI. *The imperfections and sins of professing Christians make the broad way still broader.*

"Ye are the light of the world. Ye are the salt of the earth," said the Saviour. These are very significant comparisons. If the church is the only light of the world; and if this light become dim, the transgressor will discern the narrow way very obscurely. If the church universal felt the full import of this language, and lived in accordance with these precepts, the broad way would be much narrower, and trodden by a smaller throng of travellers. But the imperfections and sins of the best Christians are many, and ruinous are the consequences. The sinner is kept quiet on his way, and confirmed in his unbelief. Merciful God! keep the skirts of thy people's garments from being stained with the blood of souls!

VII. *The example of the multitude demonstrates the facility with which men go to destruction.*

The simple fact that so great a multitude are crowding along through the wide gate, furnishes a reason why they continue in their ruinous course. They imagine their safety to be in proportion to their numbers. As if a host could contend with the Almighty, and wrest from Him the sceptre of dominion, or prevail on Him to change His unalterable purpose "by no means to clear the guilty." Thus they go hand in hand, strengthening each other's hands, till "the destruction of the transgressors, and of the sinners, shall be together, and they that forsake the Lord shall be consumed."

Another reason why the multitude encourage each other in the broad way, is found in the stillness which broods over the grave and the world of departed spirits. It is natural for us all to feel and desire to believe that the grave is a place where all the weary are at rest, and all troubles find their end. But the scriptures assure us that the conscious spirit enters, at its departure from this world, into happiness or misery, according to the works done in the body, and that the body itself lies in its resting place till it awakes to the resurrection of life, or the resurrection of damnation. The departed Lazarus, in the parable, is said to be "in Abraham's bosom,"—"the rich man in hell, being in torment." The grave, then, is for all the suspension of bodily, but not of spiritual suffering. But the multitude will not believe these revealed truths. They say, None have returned from the unknown world to inform us of their state. We do not know but all are happy there, and we will hope in the mercy of God, without disquieting ourselves with things beyond our knowledge.

We now close the subject with one reflection,—It is a very difficult thing to be saved.

The many obstacles we have enumerated must be overcome, or we inevitably perish. And we may well ask, with the disciples, "Who then can be saved?" Have you considered that while you neglect salvation, time is hurrying you to that world where no ray of hope can penetrate the everlasting darkness— where Despair, surveying the walls of her prison-house, shall, age after age, lift up her broken voice, and ask,—How long?— and on the anxious ear shall fall back no answer, but—Forever! Awake, awake now, lest you knock at heaven's gate when none shall open. To-day, harden not your heart. Behold, now is the accepted time, now the day of salvation. Escape for thy life; tarry not in all the plain, lest thou be consumed!

The Gospel Harvest and Christian's Duty.
By Rev. THOMAS DE WITT, D.D., New York.

"Then saith He unto His disciples, The harvest truly is great, but the labourers are few. Pray ye therefore the Lord of the harvest that He will send forth labourers into His harvest."—MATT. ix. 37, 38.

THE words of our text were spoken by Jesus to His disciples as He contemplated the multitudes destitute of the means of religious instruction. "He was moved with compassion on them because they fainted, and were as sheep without a shepherd." The compassion that dwelt in the heart of Jesus is not foreign to the hearts of His people, for they are of one spirit with Him. The text,—

I. *Presents an argument for missionary effort,*—"*The harvest truly is plenteous, but the labourers are few.*"

1. It is great in view of the field which it will cover. "The field is the world."

2. The harvest is great in view of its many blessings. The religion of Christ blesses the life which now is, and prepares for happiness in the life to come.

3. The harvest must appear great, in view of the instrumentality it requires. The great result is to be accomplished by the faithful use of those means which God has in His wisdom and goodness appointed.

4. The harvest is great in view of the means and prospects furnished by Providence. God, in advancing His kingdom on earth, prepares the way, in arranging the events of His providence.

II. *The text urges our duty in relation to missionary effort,*—"*Pray ye the Lord of the harvest, that He will send forth labourers into His harvest.*"

The spirit of the Christian is that of love to Christ and to Zion: his life is in sincere and unreserved devotion to his Saviour's glory and Zion's prosperity. Prayer is his vital breath. In proportion as his own soul prospers will intercession constitute a leading part in his addresses to the throne of grace. It should never escape our remembrance, that of the six petitions in the summary of prayer furnished us by our Saviour, three respect the display of His glory and the extension of His kingdom on earth. "Pray for the peace of Jerusalem: they shall prosper that love thee." The discharge of this duty enjoined by our Saviour supposes,—

1. That we cherish a deep and constant sense of our dependence upon divine grace.

2. This duty requires habitual and fervent remembrance in our private devotions. Love to the Redeemer's cause is not a transient emotion in the Christian's heart; but it is a fixed principle and growing habit of soul. He prefers Jerusalem above

his chief joy. He should then be frequent, fervent, importunate, and persevering in his intercession.

3. This duty requires union in Christians. Addressing His assembled disciples, Jesus said, *Pray ye.* The true disciples of Jesus are united in spirit and service.

4. This duty requires the use of all proper means for suitably training labourers for the missionary field.

5. This duty requires that all the churches of Christ should systematically and efficiently aid in the promotion of the cause of missions. Christians should learn to give, not from the impulse of momentary excitement, but from the deliberate conviction of duty, in the discharge of which the heart seeks its highest joy. Where the churches are blessed with the Spirit's influence, cherishing the graces of the pious, and converting sinners to Christ, there will be found free-will offerings brought liberally, cheerfully, and continually, in behalf of this cause. Look, on the other hand, to the churches indifferent to this cause, and neglectful of duty. There mildew and blasting spread, and spiritual barrenness reigns.

Influence of the Atonement on the Believer's Conscience.

BY REV. GEORGE C. BECKWITH, A.M., CINCINNATI, OHIO.

"If the blood of bulls and of goats, and the ashes of an heifer sprinkling the unclean, sanctifieth to the purifying of the flesh; how much more shall the blood of Christ, who through the eternal Spirit offered Himself without spot to God, purge your conscience from dead works to serve the living God."—HEB. ix. 13, 14.

THE Law of Moses was but a shadow of good things to come. It could do little more than watch over the infancy of true religion, and keep alive the hope of a new and far better dispensation. It consulted the infirmities of man,—it wore a drapery adapted to his senses,—its rites belonged to the twilight of an early age, and all its types were designed only to prefigure the realities of a brighter and more glorious era. It was but a pioneer of Christianity,—a schoolmaster to teach a few of its elementary principles, and thus prepare mankind for a prompt and cordial reception of the gospel.

But, aside from this prospective connection with Christianity, had the ritual of Moses any power to sanctify and save? It did, indeed, prescribe rites to cleanse the body from ceremonial impurities; but could it purify the soul, and provide an antidote, or anodyne, for the anguish of a wounded spirit? It taught that without the shedding of blood there could be no remission of sin; but was it possible for the blood of bulls and of goats to take away the sting of guilt? Could all the gifts and sacrifices, prescribed in the law of Moses, make the comers thereunto perfect, and disarm a guilty and exasperated conscience of its power to disturb the sinner's peace? No.—[See text.]

But how is this done? Is it *by dethroning or destroying his conscience?*

Is the Christian relieved from remorse *by forgetting his sins?*

Or *by becoming conscious of ill-desert?*

In none of these ways can the burden of conscious guilt be removed. Still, the gospel does remove it from the conscience of every penitent believer, and permits him to rejoice in the favour of a reconciled God. But how does the blood of Christ thus purify and relieve his conscience?

1. *By preparing the way for his repentance, and his ultimate deliverance from all sin.*

This purification is absolutely essential. Sin produces misery as its natural, inevitable result; and the sinner must therefore become holy, before he can be happy. Repentance is the beginning of holiness; and so far as it makes the sinner holy, it tends to promote his happiness. It cannot, indeed, alter the fact of his having been a sinner; nor can it ever destroy the remembrance, or conscious guilt of his transgressions; but it will check the progress of sin, and thus prevent the future increase of its miseries.

Mere law, however, makes no provision for repentance, nor could it consistently permit the pardon even of a penitent transgressor. It is a system of pure, unmingled, uncompromising justice. It acknowledges no principle but that of righteous retribution; it denounces death to the man who offends in a single point, and the soul that sinneth but once can never live again under a system of mere law.

But the gospel so far modifies the government of mere law, as to prepare a way for the consistent reformation and forgiveness of sinners. It renders repentance possible, encourages it by the promise of pardon, and provides means, motives, and divine influences sufficient to restore the sinner to the lost image of his Maker. I am fully aware, however, that repentance alone can never restore the sinner to the favour of his Maker; because it cannot repair the evils he has done to God, to himself, and the universe.

II. *Here the atonement of Christ comes to relieve the believer's conscience by counteracting the evils of sin.*

We may not see all, but we can easily see some of the ways, in which this great expiatory sacrifice for the sins of mankind may prevent or repair the evils of transgression. Sin tends to tarnish the character of God, to shake the stability of His throne, and destroy the influence of His moral government over His intelligent creatures. Thus do the general interests of His kingdom absolutely require that God should preserve the moral influence of His law, either by inflicting its penalty on the transgressor, or by devising some other expedient of equal power to maintain His authority, secure the obedience of His subjects, and accomplish all the other purposes of His moral government.

Such an expedient is the death of Christ. It counteracts the evils which sin had done or threatened, and thus becomes a sufficient and satisfactory substitute for the penalty of the law. It upholds the authority of Jehovah, confirms the moral influence of His government, and accomplishes even more important results than could have been secured by inflicting all the penalties of the law on transgressors. It expresses, in the strongest manner, God's deep and unchanging abhorrence of sin, His steady regard for His law, and His inflexible determination to preserve its influence unimpaired, by enforcing all its claims and all its sanctions. If He spared not His only Son, but from His own bosom gave Him up even to the death of the cross, rather than relax one iota of that law on which are suspended the dearest interests of the universe, can any of His subjects now hope for impunity in transgression? If God spared not His own Son, will He spare the impenitent rebel against His throne?

Thus doth the death of Christ counteract the evils of sin. It restores to the violated law all its moral energies, repairs the injury done by sin to the character and government of God, and prepares the way for Him, consistently with all His attributes, with the honour of His throne, and the interests of His kingdom, to pardon every one that believeth in Jesus.

III. *But the atonement does even more than repair the evils of sin.*

By this I cannot surely mean that it will restore to the favour of God more than all, or even all that have sinned: but that it will eventually bring more glory to God, and a greater amount of happiness to the universe, than would have resulted from the punishment of every transgressor, or even the prevention of sin itself.

I know very well how difficult it is for us to conceive of such a result being accomplished, without restoring every sinner to the image and favour of God. We are so engrossed with the interests of our own little world, as to overlook other parts of the universe, whose welfare, equally with our own, depends on the character and government of Him who doeth His pleasure in the armies of heaven and among the inhabitants of earth. Is He not bound, as an impartial Sovereign, to consult alike the interest of all worlds? Shall He, for the gratification of a few hell-deserving rebels, sacrifice or endanger the happiness of all the unfallen beings scattered through His boundless empire?

Consider, then, the vast extent to which the atonement of Christ may diffuse more or less of its benign influence. Its redeeming efficacy is probably confined to our world, but the story of its wonders will be known through the universe; and so far as it displays the glory of God, and strengthens the moral influence of His government, just so far will it tend to promote the holiness and felicity of all His faithful subjects.

And is not this the actual effect of the atonement? Yes; it makes a new and most glorious display of that character which forms the confidence, hope, and joy of the whole universe. It develops traits which must otherwise have been for ever concealed from the view of God's creatures. If the morning stars sang together, and all the sons of God shouted for joy at the birth of creation, with what emotions of wonder, and love, and bliss must the bosoms of all His faithful subjects glow on beholding the operations and results of redeeming grace! May not the gospel thus promote, to an extent altogether inconceivable, the holiness and felicity of the universe? May not its blessed results far outweigh all the evils that sin will ever inflict on the comparatively small number of its unreclaimed victims?

Thus may we imperfectly see how the death of Christ prepares the way for the restoration of mankind to the image and favour of God. It modifies His moral government over our world, and adapts it to our ruined condition. It provides a power to renew men to His image, an anodyne for the anguish of remorse, and a sovereign remedy for all the maladies of sin; it renders our repentance possible; it furnishes means sufficient for our entire purification; it not only counteracts and repairs the evils of sin, but accomplishes additional purposes of great importance to the general interests of the universe; and thus does it render our salvation not only consistent with the justice of God, but subservient to His glory, and the happiness of His whole moral kingdom. Our forgiveness now infringes on no principle of His administration. Our salvation, so far from tarnishing the lustre of His character, shaking the stability of His throne, or putting in jeopardy the great interests of His kingdom, tends to display His perfections, to enhance His glory, to increase the moral influence of His law, and promote the holiness and happiness of all His obedient subjects. Reflections,—

1. Let the Christian, then, dwell with devout admiration on the cross of Christ.

2. Make the cross of Christ, also, a source of consolation.

3. Use this precious truth, also, as a means of promoting your spiritual improvement.

4. Let me also assure the awakened sinner that his burden of guilt can be removed only by applying to that blood which will purge his conscience from dead works to serve the living God.

5. But a cordial acceptance of these invitations is indispensable to the sinner's salvation.

The Living Epistle.

By Rev. JOSHUA LEAVITT, New York.

"Ye are our epistle, written in our hearts, known and read of all men."
—2 Cor. iii. 2.

PREACHING the gospel is the main instrument of salvation. But notwithstanding this, the concurring weight of a Christian example is necessary to the proper effect of a preached gospel. It is not merely needful that Christians should avoid counteracting the influence of the gospel by unholy lives; they must help it forward by a living exemplification of its appropriate efficacy. A Christian life is a living epistle. The importance of this living epistle to the advancement of religion is the subject of discourse.

I. *The necessity of the living epistle appears from the nature of language.*

Preaching is an attempt to produce an impression by means of language, and words have their influence according as they are understood, *i. e.*, by their received meaning. Words have no inherent meaning. They mean precisely what those who use them agree to mean. Religion has its peculiar dialect—it speaks a language of its own. Religious people speak of a change of heart, of being born again, and of being reconciled to God; of pardon and peace; of finding peace of conscience through the blood of Jesus Christ; of having the spirit of adoption, enjoying the presence of God, and the light of His countenance; of holding communion with God, and having the witness of His Spirit: of living to the glory of God, and seeking first the kingdom of God and His righteousness; of having the terror of death taken away, and of triumphing over the grave; of receiving the earnest of the Spirit, and a foretaste of the joys to come. Now, what are people to understand by all this phraseology? According to the principles laid down for understanding language, people will understand by it just what those who use this dialect *agree* to understand by it. It is to be expected that those who hear it will be impressed by it, just according to the common consent of those whose language it is. The great body of mankind will not receive any further ideas from it than the lives of Christians exhibit.

These things are indeed spoken of in the Bible as being literal realities; and the descriptions given of them are very bright and magnificent; and preachers often attempt to paint them with something of the colours of reality and glory which they bear in the scriptures. But no great impression is made, any further than these things are exhibited in the lives of Christians. Written descriptions have no force without the living epistle. The great portion of mankind undoubtedly get their actual ideas of religion in this very way. They can understand the living epistle.

And all the art and eloquence of man do not convey anything more to careless minds than they see in Christians.

II. *A second reason for the importance of the living epistle to the success of the gospel is found in the nature of religion itself.*

True religion consists in holy affections. Its essential ingredients are, the hatred of sin, and the love of God, and a hope of salvation only through the death and resurrection of Jesus Christ. Nothing but the living epistle can make religion appear desirable for its own sake. Under other influences men may wish to have religion. They may desire it as a refuge from the compunctions of conscience and the apprehensions of coming wrath. But they can hardly be expected to be smitten with the love of holiness, or to desire religion for its own sake, until they see its divine lineaments drawn out and exhibited in the living epistle. The eloquence of a holy life is never wasted; it arrests the attention, and carries conviction to the heart, of the reality and value of religion.

III. *The influence of the living epistle removes many difficulties which prevent men from embracing religion.*

The grand object of Christianity is to convert men to God. The labourer in the gospel must proclaim distinctly that Christians alone are right, and all the rest of the world wrong. He has, moreover, nothing to offer, but a salvation consisting in the first instance only of a free pardon to an humbled rebel. He must enforce acceptance also, by the evangelical alternative,— "He that believeth shall be saved, and he that believeth not shall be damned."

In this encounter with passion, and pride, and sin, the advocate of religion finds all his arguments and persuasions rebutted. The mind, by all these prejudices, is barred and fortified against the gospel. There can be no hope of success till this prejudice is removed. And nothing will open the door like the mild influence of a life of simplicity and godly sincerity. The best reply which ministers can make to the calumny about priestcraft is a life of usefulness. Let it be evident that the church and the minister have no other than a common interest and a common end, and that end a benevolent one—the salvation of souls. Let it be so that he can boldly appeal to his brethren, and say, "Ye are my epistle, written in my heart;" and can point the world to them and say, "These are my letters of commendation, known and read of all men." In such a state of things, truth will make its way to men's hearts like a two-edged sword.

IV. *The value of the living epistle, in promoting the cause of religion, is abundantly confirmed by facts.*

How important an auxiliary it was to the ministry of the apostles! They could appeal to their own lives, and say to the people, "Ye are witnesses how holily and unblamably we had our conversation among you." Why was the blood of the martyrs the seed of the church? It was because that when "they counted not their lives dear unto them," the surrounding world read the evidences of true religion in the pages of the living epistle. In modern times, nothing awakens the sensual Hindoo, or opens the mind of the ignorant savage, or the stupid Greenlander, to the benign influences of the gospel, like the evidence which he sees of sincerity and benevolence in the devoted missionary.

The same remark holds true in places where the church has long been planted. Facts crowd upon the mind of every one who is acquainted with the history of revivals. There is probably not an instance of any considerable work of grace, while the body of the church are asleep, or in a state of conformity to the world; nor an instance in which a church, however small, have continued for any considerable time to hold up to men's view the testimony of the living epistle, without effect.

1. The subject shows the grand obstacle to the progress of religion, where the gospel is preached. It is the indistinctness of the living epistle. It is because ministers and other Christians do not live better. Unaccompanied by the living epistle, the boldness of Peter, the earnestness of the sons of thunder, the reasoning of Paul, and the eloquence of Apollos, are insufficient to give the gospel its proper influence. Poor preaching is bad enough in its influence, but poor-living is much worse.

2. The subject shows the vast responsibility which rests upon professing Christians, for the lives they lead before the world. They are God's witnesses; and the bulk of mankind take the gospel just as it is set out before them in the lives of Christians. They are the lights of the world. God has scattered them through the wilderness. And if the light that is in them be darkness, how great is that darkness? How great his guilt, who bears false witness for God, by misrepresenting Christianity in his life!

Brethren, we must be more holy. We must live down the suspicions of jealousy. We must live down the reproaches of calumny. We must live down the cavils of infidelity. We must live down the indifference of stupidity. Talking, and preaching, and wondering never will do it. We must "study by well-doing, to put to silence the ignorance of foolish men." If we wish to see religion making progress, we must live a life of religion, and it will not fail to prosper. For God has said, "Then shall the heathen know that I am the Lord, when I shall be sanctified in you before their eyes."

Call to Professing Christians on Temperance.
By Rev. AUSTIN DICKINSON, New York.

"To him that knoweth to do good, and doeth it not, to him it is sin."— JAMES iv. 17; also ACTS xvii. 30; LUKE xxii. 32; MALACHI iii. 11.

IN professing the religion of the Bible, we covenant with God to make His word our rule of life. This requires us to "present our bodies a living sacrifice, holy and acceptable unto God;" to "purify ourselves, even as he is pure;" to "give none occasion of stumbling to any brother;" to "give none offence to the church of God;" to "love our neighbour as ourselves;" to "do good to all as we have opportunity;" to "abstain from all appearance of evil;" to "use the world as not abusing it;" and, "whether we eat or drink, or whatsoever we do, to do all to the glory of God."

Any indulgence, therefore, not consistent with these divine precepts, is actually sinful, is inconsistent with a holy profession, and must disqualify us for "standing in the judgment." Such a sin, very obviously, is the habit, which some professing Christians still indulge, of drinking and tempting others to drink distilled liquor, in this day of meridian light. To those who admit the binding authority of God's precepts, and whose minds are not clouded by "sipping a little," this sin must, on examination, be perfectly manifest.

I. *The use of such liquor, instead of enabling us to "present our bodies a living sacrifice, holy and acceptable," actually degrades, impairs, and prematurely destroys both body and mind.*

II. *This habit of drinking is incompatible with that desire of eminent holiness and growth in grace, which a consistent profession implies.*

III. *The use of this liquor is inconsistent with anything like pure and high spiritual enjoyment, clear spiritual views, and true devotion.*

IV. *The use of ardent spirit by professing Christians is inconsistent with the good order and discipline of the church.*

V. *The use of distilled liquor by professors of religion is inconsistent with the hope of reforming and saving the intemperate.*

VI. *The use of distilled liquor by professing Christians is inconsistent with the hope of ever freeing the nation from intemperance.*

VII. *The use of this liquor by professing Christians is utterly inconsistent with the proper influence of their example.*

VIII. *The use of ardent spirit by a part of the church is inconsistent with that harmony and brotherly love which Christ requires in His professed followers.*

IX. *The use of distilled liquor by members of the church, in this day of light, is incompatible with their receiving any general effusion of the Holy Spirit.*

X. *The waste of property in the use of distilled liquor is inconsistent with the character of faithful " stewards for Christ."*

XI. *For Christians to indulge in the use of ardent spirit is inconsistent with all attempts to recommend the gospel to the heathen.*

XII. *The use of ardent spirit by the church is inconsistent with any reasonable hope that the flood of intemperance would not return upon the land, even should it for a season be dried up.*

XIII. *The use of distilled liquor as a common article of luxury or living is inconsistent with the plain spirit and precepts of God's word.*

XIV. *To manufacture or use ardent spirit is inconsistent with a grateful reception of the bounties of Providence.*

XV. *For a professor of religion to persevere in making, selling, or using ardent spirit, as a common article of luxury or living, while fully knowing its effects, and possessing the light Providenceh as recently poured on this subject, is inconsistent with any satisfactory evidence of piety.*

The duty of professing Christians, then, in regard to distilled liquor is very plain. If their vision be not clouded by reason of the poison, they cannot but see that it would be pleasing to God, happy for themselves, beneficial to the world, and conducive to the highest interests of Christ's kingdom, for them to adopt with one consent the principle of TOTAL ABSTINENCE, and make generous efforts for disseminating this principle.

Conviction by the Law.

BY REV. SHEPARD K. KOLLOCK, NORFOLK, VIRGINIA.

"I was alive without the law once, but when the commandment came, sin revived, and I died."—ROM. vii. 19.

THERE have been but two ways ever revealed, in which man may obtain eternal life—the law and the gospel—the covenant of works and the covenant of grace. By the first mode, Adam, had he remained innocent, might have secured everlasting felicity. But, on his apostacy, this way to heaven was barred for ever; and to show the impossibility of being thus saved, cherubim and a fiery flaming sword guarded all access to the tree of life. To fallen man there is no hope, except through the sovereign grace of God, by the Redeemer revealed in the gospel; there is no hope till, sensible of his deep guilt, and trembling at the curse of the broken law, he penitently betakes himself to that Saviour who is "the end of the law for righteousness to every one that believeth."

Yet many who acknowledge these fundamental truths are careless and unconcerned, while they have no interest in the Redeemer; are hoping for heaven, though they have never fled to the Saviour, and accepted His righteousness for justification.

Let all such listen to the text, in which the Apostle gives not only his own experience, but that of all true believers,—"I was alive without the law once, but when the commandment came, sin revived, and I died."

These words will lead us to consider,—

I. *The character and sentiments of the unregenerate,—* "*I was alive without the law.*"

Three inquiries here arise,—What is the law of which the Apostle speaks? How was he without it? And what is implied in his having been alive?

1. The law to which St. Paul refers is evidently the MORAL law; that law which was impressed upon the heart of man at his creation, and which was published with such solemnity from Sinai. It consists of a system of precepts, and of a sanction for their enforcement. The sum of its precepts is perfect obedience to the Divine Lawgiver. Its sanction is an assurance of eternal life to the obedient, and of death to those who "continue not in all things written in the book of the law to do them."

2. How was the Apostle "without the law"? Not that he was under no obligation to it. From its very nature it must always be in force. It was binding upon Paul; it is obligatory upon every child of Adam; since it is founded in the perfections of God and the relations He sustains to us. While these perfections and relations continue, the law cannot be abrogated; Jehovah can no more free us from its obligation than He can renounce His Godhead.

When the Apostle is said to be "without the law," it does not imply that he was unacquainted with its letter. A clear, speculative knowledge of it he no doubt possessed, for he was brought up at the feet of the celebrated Gamaliel,—there studied it,— there made in it the greatest proficiency.

Neither does it imply that he paid no regard to it in his external life. He himself tells us that he outwardly complied with its precepts: that "as touching the law," that is, the formal and external observance of it, he was "blameless."

But to be "without the law" implies an ignorance of its extent, spirituality, and purity,—implies that the Apostle had no proper sense of its commanding authority, or of its condemning power.

3. In what sense was Paul, before his conversion, "alive"? Not in the estimation of God and angels; they beheld him "dead in trespasses and sins." But he was alive in his own estimation,—he thought himself upright, and holy, and entitled, by virtue of these qualifications, to life eternal. He entertained the strongest confidence of his high standing in the favour of God. He "verily thought he was doing God service," and advancing towards heaven. This case is common with the unregenerate. They are "without the law,"—without any knowledge of its strictness and purity,—without any sense of its dignity and perfection: While thus ignorant, as the Apostle once was, like him they are "alive,"—alive in their feelings, unapprehensive of danger, unconcerned about the terrors of the Almighty.

Some of the grounds of this security in sin are natural ignorance, abuse of the Saviour's grace, false evidence of the love of God, incorrect views of the privileges of the church, and the hope of a long and protracted life. These are so many springs to feed and maintain this life of delusion in the unregenerate.

We proceed,—

II. *To consider the nature of true conviction.* "*Sin revived,*" adds the Apostle, "*and I died.*"

A clear and lively sense of sin impressed his soul. He saw himself chargeable with aggravated guilt, in consequence of which his vain conceit fled, and his presumptuous hopes expired. This is the experience of all who have had true conviction of sin. They see the depth of their guilt, they behold themselves lost, they acknowledge that they are justly liable to eternal death.

But we must distinguish between the occasional fears and those genuine convictions which end in conversion. The former generally arise from the apprehension of God's power and justice; the latter from a sense of His goodness, love, and infinite hatred to sin. The former endured but for a season, the latter are permanent. In the former there is a view only of the penalty of the law, in the latter of the propriety of this penalty. The sinner who is truly convinced, perceives the odious nature as well as the awful consequences of sin. Now his great inquiry is, "How shall I escape the wrath to come? How shall I be reconciled to God? How shall I save my poor, neglected, perishing soul?" Ah! he knows what Paul meant when he exclaimed, "sin revived!"

III. *In the next place, consider the cause of this conviction,—"The commandment came," shining in its purity, and operating with power.*

In this manner only can the sinner be effectually convinced; by the law sent home to his heart, not in the "deadness of the letter," but in all the energy of the Spirit. The moral law insists upon an obedience that is perfect—perfect in its principle, perfect in its parts, perfect in every degree—and pronounces condemnation upon the least violation. When it is thus revealed to the sinner in its wide extent, in its high demands, in its rigorous sanctions, it must convict and humble him before God.

There is another intention of the law equally useful; it "reveals the wrath of God against all ungodliness and unrighteousness of men." Having set before the sinner his innumerable offences and enormous guilt, it denounces the doom which he deserves; it unsheaths the sword of justice, and threatens him with "everlasting destruction from the presence of the Lord."

But let us remember that this power which the law has is not inherent, but is derived solely from the Spirit of God. Without His influence it never did, and never can savingly convince the soul. It is the sword that pierces the heart, but the Holy Spirit wields it. Thus "the commandment comes," to accuse, to convict, and to condemn; to prepare him for the reception of the Mediator's righteousness; to drive him to the atonement of the Lord Jesus Christ.

In applying this subject to practical purposes, I remark,—

1. It teaches us that we may live in this world without apprehensions and fears, and yet perish for ever. Is not this the case with the generality of men? Their conduct evinces that they have no sense of God upon their souls, no preparation for death and eternity, and yet they are careless and gay; they indulge in pleasure and mirth; they confidently expect everlasting felicity. Do you ask, "Why is this?" "The commandment" has never come to them in all its purity, in all its spirit, in all its power, as a solemn reality.

2. This subject addresses those who are under conviction of sin. By the Holy Spirit, the law has, in some degree, come home to you, shining in its purity, and operating on your conscience.

You have seen its demands to be reasonable. In view of the desperate wickedness of your hearts, your contempt of God's authority, and your rejection of a Saviour's love, I hear you exclaiming, "For these things I deserve to die,—I deserve to be forever damned." Remember there is no necessary connection between conviction and conversion.

3. The subject before us should excite the gratitude of those whose conviction of sin has issued in true conversion. Bless God that you are experimentally acquainted with the language of the text. Though the law has "no condemnation" for you, if you be "in Christ Jesus," yet as a rule it is still binding, and has lost none of its authority. Having driven you to the Saviour for salvation, it serves as a rule for your conduct, and shows you how to order your conversation and to adorn your profession —how to glorify God, and express your gratitude to Christ.

4. This subject addresses those who are insensible of their guilt. Remember, sinners, it is the law of God you are contemning,—that immutable law which is the transcript of the Divine perfections,—that holy law which has broken the hearts of thousands, and driven them to the only citadel of safety, the Lord Jesus Christ. I tell you, upon the authority of Him who "cannot lie," that you are under the curse of this law; daily, hourly exposed to the infinite wrath of Almighty God. From your childhood you have been in this awful state. The cloud of Divine vengeance, big with awful thunder, has long been hovering over you, and nothing but the restraining hand of God's sovereignty has prevented it from suddenly bursting upon you. But this wonderful forbearance cannot always continue; the sentence denounced may soon be executed. There is but one way of escape—the Lord Jesus Christ, who is "a hiding-place from the wind, and a covert from the tempest." Guilty as you are, you are invited to this refuge. An opportunity is now offered for securing pardon and salvation; the uplifted arm of vengeance is suspended; the collected wrath yet waits for a moment. Oh, then, flee to that Redeemer who can "save to the uttermost."

The Duty, the Benefits, and the Proper Method of Religious Fasting.

By Rev. SAMUEL MILLER, D.D., Princeton, N. J.

"And I set my face unto the Lord God, to seek by prayer and supplication with fasting."—Dan. ix. 3.

THIS is the language of the Prophet Daniel. He is speaking of that which occurred in Babylon, where he and his brethren were in captivity. It was a dark and distressing day. Religion was at a low ebb among the professing people of God. Even their deep adversity had not led them to repentance and reformation. And idolatry, attended with the most deplorable moral corruption, reigned among the heathen around them. Everything, to the eye of sense, appeared in the highest degree discouraging, not to say desperate. But this holy man trusted in God, and in the exercise of faith saw, beyond the clouds which encircled him and his people, a ray of light which promised at once deliverance and glory. Instead of desponding, he "encourages himself in the Lord his God." Instead of allowing himself to indulge in a spirit of presumption and indolence, on account of the certainty of the approaching deliverance, he considers himself as called to special humiliation, fasting, and prayer; to humble himself before God under a sense of the deep unworthiness of himself and his companions in captivity; and to pray with importunity that their unmerited emancipation might be at once hastened and sanctified. Such is the spirit of genuine piety. It was with him a season of special, earnest, elevated devotion.

I shall take occasion, from the example of Daniel, to consider,—

I. *The duty of religious fasting.*

The Christian, as such, refrains from choice, denying his appetite from religious principle, and with a view to spiritual benefit. Now, when it is affirmed that occasional fasting, in this sense, and with this view, is a Christian duty, it is not intended to be maintained that it is one of those stated duties which all are bound to attend upon at certain fixed periods, whatever may be their situation, or the aspect of Providence towards them. It is to be considered as an occasional, or, perhaps, more properly speaking, a special duty, which, like seasons of special prayer, ought to be regulated, as to its frequency and manner of observance, by the circumstances in which we are placed. But although the times and seasons of religious fasting be left, as they obviously must be, to the judgment and the conscience of each individual, it may be confidently affirmed that it is a Divine institution; that it is a duty on which all Christians are bound, at proper seasons to attend. This, it is believed, may be firmly established by the following considerations.

1. The light of nature seems to recognize this duty. Abstinence from food, either as an aid or as an expression of piety, has been common in all ages, and among all nations. Was it a dictate of nature? Was it the result of tradition, handing down to all generations the practice of the first parents of our race? From one or other of these sources, the practice must have been derived; and either of them will go far towards furnishing the warrant in question.

2. The examples of religious fasting recorded in the word of God, are multiplied and very decisive in their character. Out of many which might be selected, the following are worthy of special notice.—Joshua, Nehemiah, men of Nineveh, Ezra, David, Daniel, Paul.

3. Again, we may infer that religious fasting is a Divine institution from a variety of precepts and direct intimations found in various parts of Scripture, especially in the New Testament.

II. *The benefits which may be expected to result from the proper performance of this duty.*

In reference to this point, it behoves us to be ever upon our guard against the dictates of a vain superstition. For, as the practice of fasting for religious purposes has probably been in the world ever since the fall of man, and we have every reason to suppose was thus early received from the Author of our being, so this practice began very early, like every other Divine appointment, to be perverted and abused. The heathen evidently considered it as highly meritorious, and as purchasing for them the favour of the deities whom they vainly worshipped.

Christians began very early to be corrupted by Gnostic dreams and Pagan habits. As early as the close of the second century, they seem to have commenced the practice of observing Wednesday and Friday of every week as days of fasting. Not long after, we find them observing one great annual fast, to commemorate the death of the blessed Saviour. Of this annual fast, as well as of all the Fridays in the year, the Romish church has long been in the habit of making a most superstitious use.

Now, all this is weakly and criminally superstitious. For "meat," as the inspired Apostle expressly tells us, "commendeth us not to God; for neither if we eat are we the better; neither if we eat not are we the worse." And, therefore, in estimating the benefits of religious fasting, we ascribe to it no mystical charm—no sanctifying power. But we consider religious fasting, when properly conducted, as attended with the following benefits:—

1. It is a natural and significant expression of our penitence for sin.

2. Another very important benefit of religious fasting is that, by denying the animal appetite, we "keep under the body, and bring it into subjection."

3. A third benefit to be derived from fasting, when properly conducted, is, that it renders the mind more active, clear, and vigorous.

4. A further advantage accruing from well conducted religious fasting is, that it ministers essentially to the bodily health.

5. There is one more advantage of frequent religious fasting by no means to be despised. I mean making it systematically subservient to the purposes of charity.

III. *Consider that method of observing a religious fast which will render it truly profitable.*

The great end of the duty is to be regarded. God "will have mercy and not sacrifice." Fasting, like the Sabbath, was made for man, and not man for fasting. No one, therefore, ought to carry abstinence to such an extreme as to impair or endanger his bodily health, of which there have been, undoubtedly, some mournful examples, both in ancient and modern times. We have no more right to injure our bodies than we have to enfeeble or derange our minds. Yet this, it must be acknowledged, is by no means the extreme to which the mass of professing Christians, at the present day, are inclined. On the contrary, it is manifest that the tendency, in general, is to deficiency rather than excess in this important duty. For one who injures himself by the excessive frequency or protraction of his seasons of abstinence, thousands, it is probable, either wholly neglect this self-denying duty, or perform it in a most superficial and inadequate manner.

The duty of fasting may be considered as devolving on men in all the circumstances and relations in which they are placed. Seasons of devout fasting ought, undoubtedly, to be observed by individuals, in private, with a special reference to their own personal sins, wants, and trials; by families, who have often much reason, as such, for special humiliation and prayer; by particular churches, whose circumstances are frequently such as to call for seasons of peculiar mourning, penitence, and supplication; by whole denominations of Christians, who have very often occasion to humble themselves before God on account of the absence of His Spirit, and the prevalence of some great evils in the midst of them; and finally, by nations, when suffering under the righteous displeasure of God, or when sensible that, for their sins, they are exposed to His heavy judgments. Of all these we have examples in the word of God; and if the spirit of the gospel were reigning in the midst of us, we should often see examples of them all at the present day.

But to pursue the inquiry. In delineating the method in which a religious fast ought to be kept, let it be observed,—

1. That it will be outwardly kept in vain, unless the heart be sincerely engaged in the service.

2. While the state of the heart is everything here, a real abstinence from aliment is also essential to the proper and acceptable performance of this duty.

3. It is important to the proper observance of a religious fast, that we retire, during its continuance, as much as possible from the world, shut out its illusions, and endeavour to break its hold of our hearts.

4. Days of religious fasting are to be devoted to a deep and heartfelt recollection of our sins, and unfeigned repentance for them.

5. As days of religious fasting ought ever to be marked by a special recognition, and a deep sense of our sins; so this recognition, if it be the right stamp, will ever be followed by genuine reformation.

6. In keeping a religious fast, everything like ostentation, or self-righteousness, should be put far from us.

7. Christian fasting ought ever to be accompanied with more or less of sympathy and benevolence to the destitute.

The foregoing discussion suggests a number of practical reflections, to several of which your serious attention is requested.

1. From what has been said, it is evident that the great duty of religious fasting is by far too much neglected.

2. We are led to reflect, by what has been said, on the reason why fast-days, even when appointed, and decently observed, are productive of so little beneficial effect.

3. Another reflection suggested by what has been said is, that every part of the service enjoined upon us as Christians is a reasonable service.

4. From the foregoing [view of the subject, the reflection is obvious, that we have no less reason for fasting and humiliation than our fathers of former ages. Human nature is the same, religion is the same, and the causes of Christian mourning are the same now as they were when Joshua, Nehemiah, and Paul fasted and lay in the dust before the mercy-seat. How many millions of our fellow-men around us still remain in hardened rebellion! How many churches in our land, notwithstanding all the precious revivals with which it has pleased God to favour us, are to this hour as cold, as desolate, and almost as lifeless, in a spiritual sense, as the tombs which surround their places of worship! How many personal, domestic, ecclesiastical, and national sins press heavily upon us, as a people, and cry aloud for the judgments of a righteous God! Think, also, in how small a degree multitudes even of the professing people of God seem to be awake to the great responsibilities and duties of their high vocation, and then say, whether we have not reason for special humiliation and prayer?

Conviction of Sinners at the Judgment.
By Rev. JOEL PARKER, New York.

"Behold, the Lord cometh with ten thousand of His saints, to execute judgment upon all, and to convince all that are ungodly among them of all their ungodly deeds which they have ungodly committed, and of all their hard speeches which ungodly sinners have spoken against Him."—Jude 14, 15.

THIS passage, we are informed, is a prophecy of Enoch. It obviously refers to the day of judgment. It places before us, in one view, the solemn majesty in which God, the Judge, will appear, the universal personal interest with which men will attend, and the conviction of all the incorrigibly wicked. I invite your attention to but one of these thoughts—"The ungodly will be convicted of sin in the day of judgment."

The text asserts that it is one of the ends of that great trial "to convince all that are ungodly of their ungodly deeds."

I. *It will exhibit scenes of such an interest as will arrest the sinner's attention, and fix it upon his character.*

A principal difficulty in convicting sinners in this world arises from their being so much engrossed with other subjects, as to prevent a serious contemplation of themselves. This difficulty will be entirely removed. Before the bar of God, that wealth which was once looked upon as the treasure of the soul will have lost its value. Those fashions which once occupied the mind with their ever-changing varieties will be all forgotten, or only remembered as having been the occasion of ceaseless levity and folly. Ties of earthly attachment will have been sundered. To a mind thus divested of all earthly interests, the scenes of judgment must possess the most affecting character, when its destiny is about to be settled for ever,—how certainly will every wayward passion be hushed, and the whole soul be fixed with keenest intensity upon its guilt.

II. *To increase this conviction of guilt, the perfect law of God will there be held up to the sinner's mind.*

One difficulty in convicting sinners here arises from the fact that they set aside God's law, and adopt other rules of conduct. When the great God is enthroned, and worlds are assembled, these standards, mere morality and worldly honour, will appear very small. It will no more be inquired before that tribunal whether a man has been honourable, or whether he has been moral, than it will be asked whether he has been respectable, or whether he has been fashionable. The great question there will be, Has he followed "holiness, without which no man shall see the Lord"? To decide this question, the infinitely holy law will be produced; that law which says, "thou shalt love the Lord thy God with all thy heart, and with all thy soul, and with all thy mind, and with all thy strength, and thy neighbour as thyself." This will wake up thought in the sinner's bosom. He will at once compare with it his life, his heart. His felt conviction will then be, By this holy law I am damned for ever.

III. *Another source of conviction in the day of judgment is the manifest preparation for the immediate execution of justice.*

When a judicial process is going on, if the criminal supposes that he may possibly escape punishment, or that a temporary respite at least will be granted, he feels a slight relief. The least hope of impunity enfeebles the convictions of a guilty mind, and the delay of punishment exerts, in some degree, a similar influence. But suppose his trial is to take place this hour, and his execution the next. Suppose, that while the criminal faces the court, and the testimony is condemning him, he sees before him the fatal block, and a grim executioner sitting upon it with his axe in his hand, waiting to do his office; do you not see that this prospect of the immediate execution of justice must tend strongly to fix his mind upon his guilt, and to give him a lively sense of ill-desert?

Precisely like this is the condition of the sinner before the bar of God. Mercy has been spurned before the judgment arrives. All hope of pardon is extinguished. Not the least respite is expected. The execution and conviction are simultaneous. "The Lord cometh with ten thousand of His saints, to execute judgment upon all, and to convince all that are ungodly."

We have only to suppose the principles of the human mind to remain unchanged, and it is easy to see that the judgment will place the sinner in such circumstances, and exhibit such scenes, and hold forth such prospects as must produce a full conviction of sin. We learn from our subject,—

1. That conviction of sin is no evidence of conversion. The wicked will experience a more full and perfect conviction at the day of judgment than any ever feel in this world, yet they will not be converted to God, but will remain His enemies for ever. Convictions which do not lead to a life of humble piety, are but premonitions of the judgment and foretastes of damnation.

2. The most pungent conviction does not necessarily lead to conversion. If the ungodly will be convicted at the judgment, certainly there can be nothing morally good in conviction. Facts teach us abundantly that conviction of sin may be deep, distressing, and long-continued, and yet the soul may remain in the gall of bitterness, and in the bond of iniquity. Look, then, convicted sinner, to your real condition. All your tears are unavailing—all your distress arises from sin which you will not forsake—all your trouble of mind arises from your unwillingness to go with an humble heart to your Saviour, and accept His freely offered grace. If, then, you would make your salvation sure, put no trust in your convictions. Repent and "believe on the Lord Jesus Christ, and thou shalt be saved."

3. Sinners may become convicted of sin if they desire it. Though conviction does not necessarily lead to conversion, it is nevertheless of great importance to the impenitent sinner. With

it he may indeed be lost, but without it he can never be saved. He may be the subject of deep conviction for years, and neglect to repent, but without it repentance is impossible. But to show that this conviction may be attained, let us call your attention again to the condition of a condemned criminal. His circumstances compel him to reflect. Things with which he was formerly engrossed are taken from him. The solemn trial, the violated law, and the prospect of the execution of justice awaken his attention, and fix it upon his character, and deprive him of every motive to estimate that character falsely. As his sentence is pronounced, he sinks under the sense of conscious guilt. Yet that same criminal, before he was arrested, perhaps felt no more conviction than the most thoughtless sinner does for his sins against God. But *could* not he have felt the pangs of conviction? Might he not have brought *voluntarily* all those considerations to bear upon his mind which the court of justice has compelled him to think upon? Every one must see that he *might*, and that he *ought* to have felt a sense of his guilt. Just so may sinners, before they are arrested for the judgment, bring the very truths to bear upon their minds which that day will compel them to dwell upon. Indeed they may do this at any period. It is the greatest folly imaginable for men to pretend that they want conviction, but cannot obtain it. The truth is precisely the reverse. The gospel presses upon their minds considerations which would overwhelm them, if they would only reflect.

4. We learn from this subject, that the character of God will appear glorious in the final condemnation of the wicked. God has introduced a system which secures the detection and punishment of every unreclaimed offender. The principles of this system commend it at once to all holy beings; its operation produces a full conviction in the minds of sinners. While heaven breaks forth in a song of admiration on discovering the perfect vindication of the Divine character in the execution of justice; while ten thousand times ten thousand, and thousands of thousands of voices swell the anthem of "salvation, and glory, and honour, and power unto the Lord our God, for true and righteous are His judgments," hell responds by its deep, eternal wail, and its loud laments, "The law is holy, and the commandments holy, and just, and good." While all heaven shouts "Alleluia," hell responds "Amen." All the holy *see* the justice of God, and all the wicked *feel* it. As often as the one look down, and see the justice of God, and shout "Alleluias," the groans of the other, as a responsive "Amen," are borne upwards upon the smoke of their torment. Oh, what an unspeakable lustre will

be thrown over the Divine character when the whole universe,—righteous and wicked, friends and enemies,—shall consent together in bearing testimony to the wisdom and goodness of God in the vindication of His law.

O sinner, would you now turn, your fainting soul might look up to Christ and live. Though covered with shame, you might accept a pardon, and be adopted into the family of God. Think *now*. Take a full view of yourself as a sinner against God, a transgressor of His law, and a despiser of His mercy. Come, come to the refuge provided for the guilty.

The probability of Perdition inferred from present Impenitence.

BY REV. WM. B. SPRAGUE, D.D., ALBANY, N. Y.

"He that is unjust, let him be unjust still; and he that is filthy, let him be filthy still."—REV. xx. 11.

THERE is a depth of meaning in the descriptions which the Bible has given of the final condition of the ungodly, which the boldest human mind is utterly inadequate to fathom. There is the most fearful imagery employed on this subject which lies within the compass of human language. There is weeping, and wailing, and gnashing of teeth. There is the smoke of the torment that ascendeth up for ever and ever. There is the worm that always gnaws and never dies. There is the pit over which hangs the blackness of darkness. There is the resurrection of damnation, and the lifting up the eyes in torment, and the being trampled under foot by Jehovah in His righteous indignation. No one can know all that is implied in the loss of the soul, until he learns it by experience. Why, then, this entire unconcern which prevails in so many minds in respect to the salvation of the soul? If there be a fearful hell before the ungodly, wherefore is it that the ungodly do not fear it? I will tell you the solution of this: it is that they do not after all expect to perish. They have some loose calculation in their own minds, that at some period or another they shall become religious. But it is my business, in this discourse, to attempt to show you that this will probably prove to be a delusion; in other words, that the fact that an individual is at this moment putting off religion furnishes ground for a strong probability that that individual will perish. Listen, and see if it is not so.

I. *You can never expect that any better adapted means will be used for your salvation than have been used already.*

Look back upon your life, and see how God has been dealing with you. When do you expect that any other or better means will be used for your salvation than have been already used? When can you expect that the invitations of the gospel will be urged upon you with more persuasive tenderness than they have been in years that are past? All these are the means of God's own appointment for bringing sinners to repentance: these means you have hitherto enjoyed, and by your own confession they have not accomplished their object. Suppose you should enjoy them to your dying day, where is the ground for concluding that they will hereafter be more effectual.

II. *Another consideration to prove the truth of our doctrine is, that probably, in respect of most of you, the greater part of life is already past.*

It will be acknowledged, on all hands, that life is the only period of probation; that whatever is done to secure the salvation of the soul must be done on this side the grave. You who have lived to the age of twenty, strangers to religion, will probably go to the grave strangers to it; because you have lived out more than half the common period of probation, and that part of it, too, in which, judging from all analogy, the chances for your conversion were most numerous. Far be it from me to say you never will be converted. But if we form our conclusions on this subject as we do on other subjects, in relation to which we can reason from facts, I see not how you will avoid the conclusion that the probability is much against you. And if this be true of those who have lived only to the age of twenty years, and even less, what shall be said of the condition of those who have already passed the ordinary limit of life—who have attained to forty, fifty, or even threescore years? Does not the fact of your being unreconciled to God at this moment have a fearful bearing upon your probable destiny throughout eternity?

III. *The probability that those of you who are unconverted will always remain so, is to be inferred from the nature and power of habit.*

You well know that it is the tendency of every habit to grow strong by indulgence. It is true of sin, even in the most general and least startling forms—such as inconsideration, the love of pleasure, practical unbelief—the longer they are indulged, the harder it is to forsake them. But sin, in any form, habitually indulged—even the principle of sin in the heart, where its operations are entirely concealed from the world—I hardly need say will destroy the soul. Now tell me, you especially who have lived a considerable time in a course of sin, whether you see nothing appalling in this consideration?

IV. *It is probable that those of you who are unreconciled to God will always remain so, from the fact that the idea of your being converted supposes a change of which there is not at present the least indication.*

Now I ask you to look, and judge for yourself, and say whether you can discern, in your present condition, a single symptom of conversion; whether, in all this carelessness, and giddiness, and worldliness, there be anything which even seems to indicate the prospect of a change? Do you not perceive that, in taking for granted a future conversion, you take for granted that you will be willing hereafter to submit to that which revolts your feelings now? But can you give any reason why you should submit to it with more alacrity hereafter than at present? But suppose that you are in some degree awakened, and are even oppressed, not only with a sense of danger, but guilt, I dare not say that the probability is very much in your favour, even then. That it is a more hopeful case than the one which we just contemplated, admits not of question. But how many times have you been awakened before? Perhaps once, perhaps twice, perhaps thrice, perhaps even more. And, notwithstanding these repeated scenes of conviction, you have never been converted. But suppose that instead of looking at your own experience, you look at the experience of others, and see if you will be brought to any different result. I appeal, then, to the testimony of Christian ministers, who have been most conversant with cases of conviction of sin,—I appeal especially to records of revivals of religion,—I appeal to your own personal observation, for the truth of the fact, that the greater number of persons who are awakened do not become the subjects of even a hopeful conversion.

V. *The truth which I am endeavouring to establish is evident from the consideration, that, at any given period, by far the greater number of individuals in a Christian land are, to all human appearance, unconverted.*

It is true we are always liable to mistakes in the estimate which we form of men, as we know nothing of the heart except by the external conduct. But though there are cases in which the application of the scriptural rule may be attended with great difficulty, yet this difficulty does not exist in respect to persons who are immoral, or who are manifestly thoughtless of religion, and seeking their whole enjoyment from the world. We say unhesitating, and even with their own consent, that *they* are unconverted. How few are there, comparatively, who even profess to be the followers of Christ; and may I not add, with fearful emphasis, how much fewer who give evidence of being His followers? Take out of the church all the lovers of pleasure, all who make religion a mere matter of form, all, in short, whose Christian character is in any way equivocal, and how large a number do you honestly believe would be left? If the proportion of the whole number be very small, and if, so far as we can judge, it has always been so, I ask again, whether there is nothing here that looks ominous in respect to your own destiny? You are now among the unconverted; and the unconverted are the majority, and always have been the majority: by far the greater part who have come down to the bed of death have given the most melancholy evidence that they were unprepared to die. Do you not perceive, then, that the analogy against your being converted is just so much stronger than it is in favour of it, as the proportion of those who are not converted is greater than of those who are? Is not the conclusion equally irresistible and overwhelming?

I here close my argument. And I now appeal to you whether I have not dealt fairly and honestly with your understandings; whether the doctrine which I propose to establish, startling as it might at first have seemed, or as it may still seem to you, is not sustained by considerations which it is impossible to gainsay? Rely on it, when you have been calculating on a future conversion, your depraved feelings have got the better of your understanding; sober reason, as I trust you are now satisfied, conducts to a directly opposite conclusion. I ask you again, will you not hold this conclusion to your minds? Will you not let it mingle itself with your thoughts after you have retired from this house, and in coming days and weeks? Will you not suffer it to have its legitimate influence on your conduct?

But methinks I hear some one say, "That would be a discouraging influence. If the fact be really so, that there is a probability that I shall perish, then it were useless to attempt any exertion; I will fold my arms, and sit down, and submit to my fate as quietly as I can." But, my friend, you are taking counsel here of the depravity of your heart, and not of reason or common sense. You do not act thus in your worldly concerns, and you would say of the man who should act thus that he was at least on the verge of insanity. Let it be remembered, also, that notwithstanding the truth of our doctrine, yet the reason why it is true is not that men are doomed to perdition, by an arbitrary decree that has no respect to their own character *(that were a perversion of the true doctrine of Providence)*; but because they choose death, or the course which leads to death, rather than life, when life and death are both set before them. The probability, then, that you will perish, results not from the fact that you cannot be saved, but that you will not be saved,—that you will continue till you die, to reject the offers of eternal life.

And now, beloved hearers, if I do not mistake, the subject on which we have been meditating has, as it respects some of you, raised a conflict between your judgment and conscience on the one hand, and your inclinations on the other. On the one hand you cannot resist the conviction that these things are so; that the probability is decidedly in favour of your being doomed to an eternal communion with the wailings of the lost; and reason tells you that this is an appalling consideration. On the other hand, you shrink from the effort necessary to escape from this tremendous doom; and there is the plea of business, and the plea of pleasure, and the plea of carnal apathy, all united in favour of some future, more convenient season. In this conflict, shall reason or feeling be triumphant?

I have said, you may refuse to look at this subject now, but the day is coming when it will urge itself upon you, and you will not be able to turn away from it. When sickness shall have taken you out of the ranks of pleasure and business,—when death, with its clustering horrors shall look you in the face, and show you his mandate, and point you to the pit; and one step farther onward,—when the everlasting abyss opens beneath the eye, and the sound of wailing ascends from it, and the storm and the lightning of God's wrath are blazing and raging over it,—oh, tell me, how will the subject of this discourse appear to you then!

The Wicked surprised by their own Destruction.

BY REV. WM. B. SPRAGUE, D.D., ALBANY, N. Y.

"She remembereth not her last end: therefore she came down wonderfully."—LAM. i. 9.

THE tremendous calamities that now came upon the Jewish nation, seem to have been an occasion not only of great distress, but of great surprise. Jerusalem came down wonderfully, inasmuch as she came down at a time when she did not expect it, in a manner which she did not expect, and to a doom which she did not expect. From having been the joy of the whole earth, she became a field of utter desolation.

There are certain great principles in the Divine administration, the operation of which gives a degree of uniformity to the Divine proceedings. For instance, it is the manner of our God to visit with signal destruction those who have proudly set at naught His authority in a course of prosperous wickedness. Such was His treatment of Jerusalem. So it has been with individuals. Witness the case of Nebuchadnezzar, and of Herod, and a multitude of others. Destruction came upon them, not only in a terrible form, but at an hour when they did not expect it; and it was the more awful because it came as a surprise. And, let me say, the same thing will hold true, in a greater or less degree, of all sinners, as it respects their final doom; while it will be especially true of those who have sinned against great light, and with a high hand.

The precise point, then, which I propose to illustrate

in this discourse is, that the destruction which will overtake sinners at last will be to them a matter of awful surprise. It will be at once unexpectedly dreadful, and dreadfully unexpected.

I. *This will appear, in the first place, from the fact that God's wrath against the wicked is constantly accumulating.*

If the first sin you ever committed provoked God, do you think that the second provoked Him less; and that as He saw you become accustomed to sin, He came to think as little of it as yourself, and has not even charged your sin against you? Do you not remember that the Bible speaks of the sinner treasuring up wrath against the day of wrath? And can you reflect a moment without perceiving that reason and conscience both decide that it *must* be so? To suppose that it were otherwise, would be to annihilate God's moral government, and to trample the Divine character in the dust.

II. *The destruction which will come upon sinners will be to them a matter of fearful surprise, inasmuch as in the present life God's wrath, for the most part, seems to slumber; at least they perceive no direct expression of it.*

It is true, indeed, that God is giving them warnings enough, both in His word and providence; and if they did not close their ears against them, they could not fail to be alarmed; and they will never be able, in the day of their calamity, to charge God with having concealed from them their danger. Nevertheless, He treats them here as probationers for eternity; He sets life and death before them, but He does not unsheath His sword, and point it at the sinner's heart. The sinner reads, perhaps, of the awful terrors of God's wrath, but he does not now experience them. He does not find that the elements are armed for his destruction. The thundercloud rises, and rolls, and looks terrific, as if it were borne along by an avenging hand, but the lightning that blazes from it passes him by unhurt. Pestilence comes, and if he sees it cut down the sinner, he sees it cut down the saint also; or perhaps the saint dies, and the sinner lives. He sleeps quietly upon his bed; no invisible being whispers in his ear anything in respect to the wrath to come, and he dreams perhaps of beauty, and of pleasure, and of mirth, without the intrusion of a solitary image of gloom. In short, not one of the vials of God's wrath can be said to be open upon him. There is nothing which he interprets as an indication of anything dreadful in the future. Now, must not all this be a preparation for a fearful surprise at last?

III. *Not only have the wicked, during the present life, received no signal expressions of Divine vengeance, but they have been constantly receiving expressions of the Divine goodness; and this is another circumstance which will serve to increase the surprise that will be occasioned by their destruction.*

They have food, and raiment, and houses, and friends; they have the means of intellectual improvement—of regaling the taste and imagination among the beauties of nature; they have the comforts of social intercourse, and the endearments connected with domestic relations; and, little as they profit by them, they have the means of grace—the Bible, the Sabbath, a preached gospel, and even the influences of God's Spirit—everything that is necessary to fit them for heaven. They secretly flatter themselves that it is impossible that a God who does them so much good here, should inflict any great evil upon them hereafter; or, if they are too thoughtless of the whole subject even to make this inference in form, still their long experience of God's mercies must prepare them for a tremendous disappointment when the change actually comes. What a fearful transition will it be from this world, in which there are so many blessings, to a world in which existence itself becomes a curse! Oh, will not the sinner feel that he has "come down wonderfully"?

IV. *God sometimes not only gives to the wicked a common share of temporal blessings, but distinguishes them by worldly prosperity; hence another reason of the surprise which they will experience at last.*

Sometimes they become rich by inheritance, without any exertion of their own; and sometimes their own ingenuity and enterprise in acquiring property are crowned with signal success, and they rise from absolute poverty to the possession of millions. Sometimes they acquire an extensive influence, are elevated to stations of high worldly honour, and are even permitted to rule over a state or an empire. Sometimes they are gifted with distinguished intellects, and rise high in the scale of mental improvement, and their productions are sought for with avidity even beyond the limits of a continent. All this is a sad preparation for the approaching change.

Do you not readily perceive that these worldly distinctions, of which the wicked are often the subjects in this life, are fitted to heighten their surprise when they come to experience God's wrath in another? Think of the rich, and the great, and the noble of this world, who have been accustomed to receive a homage which has sometimes fallen little short of idolatry, finding themselves in the prison of despair, with no sound but the sound of their own wailing—with no society but the society of the reprobate—with no light but the light of everlasting burnings! Have not these persons come down wonderfully!

V. *I observe, once more, that the destruction which will finally overtake the wicked will be to them a matter of great surprise, inasmuch as they will, in some way or other, have made confident calculation for escaping it.*

It will be found, no doubt, that many of them had flattered themselves with the hope that the doctrine of future punishment might turn out to be false; and some will have been left through their own perverseness to believe the lie that the good and the bad will at last be equally happy. There will be others who will have wrought themselves into a conviction that destruction might be averted by some easier means than those which the gospel prescribes, and may have chosen to trust to the orthodoxy of their creed, or the kindness of their temper, or the morality of their life. There will be others who will have intended ultimately to escape destruction by becoming true Christians, but who were looking out for some more convenient season. One thing will be certain in respect to all,—they will have intended to come out well at last. Not an individual among all the sufferers in hell but will have expected finally to be saved.

There are probably those in this house who will hereafter be examples of the awful cases to which I have now referred, but I venture to say there is not one here who really expects it, and has made up his mind to encounter this dreadful doom. The gayest youth before me does not intend to perish—the greatest worldling before me does not intend to perish—the oldest sinner before me does not intend to perish; and you never will intend to perish; but notwithstanding all your intentions, there is great reason to believe that such will be your doom; and oh, what a surprise would it be to you, if you should really find yourself in the arms of the second death!

1. In the review of our subject, we may see, in the first place, how blinding is the influence of depravity. The secret of it lies in the fact that in respect to their spiritual interests they are blinded by sin. The devil whispers falsehood in their ears, and they believe it; the great God, who cannot lie, thunders truth in their ears, and they doubt it.

2. Our subject teaches us that it is a most awful calamity to relapse into a habit of carelessness after being awakened. For the sinner to awake out of sleep is to take the first step towards escaping from the wrath to come. The fact, therefore, of his being awakened is a fact of deep interest to him; and if he should relapse, he would go back into a state, continuing in which there is no hope for him: he would, in all probability sink into a deeper slumber than ever.

3. We learn from this subject that there is no class of men so much to be pitied as those who are perhaps most frequently the objects of envy, and none whose condition is so much to be envied as those whose circumstances are often looked upon as the most undesirable. I have no doubt that there are many who regard the proud, opulent worldling with envy, while the humble, pious child of want is perhaps only thought of for his supposed degradation and wretchedness. Wait a few years and see how these two characters will change places; or rather how inconceivably degraded and miserable will be the former, how inconceivably happy and blessed the latter.

4. Who of you will turn a deaf ear to the warning which this subject suggests, to flee from the wrath to come? I am anxious to know whether this warning is to be lost upon you or not. Do you sleep still? Is there no sign of waking? Are you resolved that you will go away and be just as you have been before? Go, then; but remember there will ere long be a change; and remember, that as God's word is true, you will at last "come down wonderfully."

Duty of Praying for Rulers.

By Rev. EBENEZER PORTER, D.D., ANDOVER.

"I exhort, therefore, that, first of all, supplications, prayers, intercessions, and giving of thanks, be made for all men: for kings, and for all that are in authority, that we may lead a quiet and peaceable life in all godliness and honesty."—1 TIM. ii. 1, 2.

MORE emphatically than any other duty towards rulers, that of *praying for them*, is one of universal obligation. That Paul meant to be so understood, is evident from the language used in the text. After enjoining prayer for all men, he does not specify, in reference to rulers, the emperor and the several officers of the Roman court, but says, "for kings," and because this was too restricted, he adds, "and for all that are in authority,"—a designation broad enough to indicate every form of government in any age or country. The precept is enforced, too, by a reason that is general, viz., "That we may lead a quiet and peaceable life in all godliness and honesty."

In conformity with the plain import of the text, the subject to which I shall now invite your attention is the duty of praying for rulers. We proceed, then, to consider the grounds of our obligation to pray for rulers.

I. *It is only a becoming acknowledgment of that superintending Providence which overrules the affairs of nations.*

Prayer is in all cases a direct acknowledgment of God and His government. Prayer for national blessings, is an acknowledgment that His government extends to the concerns of nations.

II. *This obligation is enforced by considering the ends of civil government, and the agency of rulers in accomplishing or frustrating these ends.*

III. *We are bound to pray for rulers, because their duties are often difficult as well as important.*

IV. *The habit of praying for rulers is important to the welfare of our country, by its tendency to make good citizens.*

V. *The duty enjoined in the text is important, from its salutary influence on rulers.*

VI. *Prayers for rulers tend to prevent the prevalence, or diminish the mischief of party spirit.*

Permit me now to call your attention to some practical results growing out of this subject.

1. We may see why it is important that national habits should

be formed under the influence of religious principle. No permanent basis for enlightened social order can exist in a community, unless public sentiment recognises the government of God as extending over all the affairs of men; and unless this sentiment has the force of national habit, in commending to the blessing of God the public interests of a country. It is not single events or qualities, but habits, that constitute national character. Britain has never been accounted an infidel nation, because she had one Hume; nor Spain an enterprizing nation, because she had one Columbus. The character that continues and pervades a community, and becomes habitual, is national character. Whatever causes contribute to the formation of this, more than to all other things, is to be ascribed the religion of a country.

2. We see what is the true connexion between religion and government. It is a practical result from the subject that good government is dependent for its success on true religion, while religion is not, in any proper sense, dependent on government. When each man is left to choose his own mode of faith and worship, voluntary civil contracts to support religion doubtless ought to be enforced by law. But without any aid, and even against opposition from government, experience has proved that religion can prosper. As the world is constituted, state patronage of the church will be the death of religion, and of civil liberty too. But leave the church untrammelled with secular alliances, and she will diffuse a vital energy around her. Religion, like the air and the light, is an element not subject to the regulation of government. Subjects have as good a right to see and breathe as rulers; both are absolutely and equally dependent on God for this privilege. Just so as to rights of opinion and of conscience. Human governments do not confer these rights, and have no concern with them, except to protect individuals from violence in their enjoyment, and to prohibit any extravagant abuse of these rights to the public injury. Religion stands in its own strength, or rather stands by leaning on Omnipotence. Government stands, if at all, by leaning on religion. Take away from a free community belief in God and a final retribution, and you cut all the cords of conscience and moral obligation.

3. Good men have an important part to act as citizens. Is it their duty, then, to become noisy politicians?—to cherish angry passions, and mingle in the storms of party strife? No; but it is their duty to pray "for all in authority," and to "lead quiet and peaceable lives, in all godliness and honesty." What if the praying man undervalues his own usefulness, and is undervalued by the eager candidates for public honours? Perhaps the shepherd of Salisbury Plain did more to promote his country's wel-

fare than her first minister of state. But does the whole duty of Christian citizens consist in prayers for rulers, and quiet submission to the laws? Certainly not. For the right of *suffrage* they are accountable to their country and to God.

To bold contemners of God, to political zealots and madmen of all parties, I say nothing. But to those who fear God, I speak in His name to-day. Men of prayer! forget not your country. Mourn for its sins, pray for its rulers, obey its laws, cherish good-will towards all its inhabitants. Meekly, but inflexibly maintain the rights of conscience. Discourage party violence, the curse and shame of the land. Hold on, and hope to the last. Be calm in every emergency,—watch and pray, and wait for some heaven-commissioned hour of deliverance.

The Progress of the Righteous and the Wicked Compared.

By Rev. NOAH PORTER, D.D., Farmington, Conn.

"The path of the just is as the shining light, that shineth more and more unto the perfect day. The way of the wicked is as darkness; they know not at what they stumble."—Prov. iv. 18, 19.

A CONTRAST is here presented between the lives of the just and the wicked. The life of the just is compared to light, that beautiful emblem of truth, holiness, and joy; and the life of the wicked to darkness, the emblem of ignorance, sin, and wretchedness. While there is this contrast in the nature of the course pursued, there is in one particular a resemblance: they both are progressive.

It is my design to trace the steps of this progress in the lives both of the just and the wicked, and to present them to your view side by side, as an encouragement to enter immediately upon the one, and to avoid the other.

I. *At the commencement of both there are difficulties to be overcome.*

II. *These difficulties, by perseverance, are gradually diminished.*

III. *Similar, also, in some respects, are the means by which they both are advanced. They are alike subject to the power of habit.*

IV. *There is also this other point of resemblance in the paths of the just and the wicked, that as they approach their end, they afford clearer and more decisive indications of the eternal state to which they lead.*

Youthful travellers, the path of the just and the way of the wicked are before you. They open on the right hand and the left; they recede from each other continually, and will do so for ever. For you it remains to take your choice. Oh, enter now the path of the just. It is pleasant as the morning light, and as the morning light, it shines more and more unto the perfect day. Supremely delightful, even to angels, is the character of the youthful penitent. Delightful, too, are the persevering struggles of the penitent against the powers of evil for the mark of the prize of the high calling of God in Christ Jesus. Let this character be yours. Let this struggle be now commenced and ardently prosecuted. So every difficulty shall yield to your constancy, and every duty become easy and delightful in your course. Heaven shall rise in ravishing prospect on your view as you advance, and the light of an eternal day shall illumine before you the darkness of the tomb. But if you intend ever to enter that path, choose it now, for " the way of the wicked is darkness." Self-delusion, sin, and wretchedness mark its progress, and the blackness of darkness for ever are its sure and dreadful termination. Remember now, therefore, your Creator in the days of your youth.

Necessity of Divine Influence.

By Rev. GIDEON N. JUDD, Bloomfield, N. J.

"Not by might, nor by power, but by my Spirit, saith the Lord of Hosts."
—Zechariah iv. 6.

WHEN Cyrus, king of Persia, issued his decree, giving the captive Jews permission to return to their own land, and rebuild their city and temple, a pious remnant, under Zerubbabel, gladly availed themselves of the opportunity. Their enterprise, however, involved great difficulties. They were few in number, their city and temple were in ruins, and could not be rebuilt without great labour and expense, and they were surrounded by numerous and powerful enemies. The whole history of this work, as recorded in the books of Ezra and Nehemiah, is a complete verification of the text. Nor has its truth been evinced only in those events. The temple at Jerusalem was a type of the church of God. In the erection of this spiritual building, He has from the first employed, and His word assures us that He will continue to employ, instruments which in themselves are utterly powerless. By mere human might no soul ever was or will be converted, and no saint has grown, or will grow in grace. Without the special blessing of God, all efforts to introduce pure religion into pagan lands, and augment its power where it already exists, will be unavailing. This is more than implied in the text.

The import of this inspired passage we shall endeavour to place distinctly before you, by showing,

I. *The reality and importance of the means of grace.*

That means are employed in the conversion of sinners, and the increasing sanctification of the saints, are positions supported both by scripture and fact. And equally evident is it, from the same authority, that revealed truth is the chief instrument employed to produce these blessed effects. It is written on the pages of that volume, which was sent from above to teach the science of salvation,—" The law of the Lord is perfect, converting the soul,"—" Of His own will begat He us with the word of truth,"—" Being born again, not of corruptible seed, but of incorruptible, by the word of God, which liveth and abideth for ever,"—" I am not ashamed of the gospel of Christ, for it is the power of God to salvation,"—" Faith cometh by hearing, and hearing by the word of God."

The methods by which Divine truth is made to produce these effects, however, are exceedingly various. The dispensations of Divine Providence—both benign and afflictive—the religious education of children, Christian example and effort, the reading of the sacred scriptures, prayer, and the preaching of the gospel, are all employed in calling attention to divine truth, and in fastening it upon the conscience and the heart. By all these and other methods have sinners been roused from spiritual slumber, convinced of their exceeding criminality, and converted to God. And in the simple fact that these are Divinely appointed means, we have proof complete of their great importance. The same wisdom which devised, and benevolence which adopted, the stupendous scheme of redemption, have made the best selection of means for its accomplishment.

God could, indeed, accomplish His purposes of mercy without them. And were He disposed thus to employ His power, He could, without the labour of man, transform barren wastes and dark, untrodden forests into fruitful fields. He could, too, have raised the temple from its ruins, and restored His worship in its hallowed courts, without the instrumentality of His servants. And it is equally true that He can convert men, and mature them for glory, without means and instruments; but when and where has He thus employed His power? "Where no vision is, the people perish." Where have sinners been converted to God, but by the presentation of revealed truth to the mind, by means of the benevolent efforts of the pious, a religious tract or book, or the written or preached word? Was a moral wilderness ever converted into the garden of the Lord without the labour of the spiritual husbandman? And after having been thus transformed, has it flourished and brought forth the fruits of righteousness without religious culture? These blessed effects never have been, and never will be, produced by other means, because God will not bring His own institutions into disrepute. From this view of the reality and importance of the means of grace, we pass to show,—

II. *That they owe all their efficacy to special Divine influence.*

This is evident,—

1. From what the scriptures teach concerning the character of man by nature. They do not represent him as needing merely the urgency of those motives which are embodied in the system of revealed truth, and the common influences of the Holy Spirit, to subdue His rebellious will and fit him for heaven. They do not, indeed, deny that he may have a high sense of justice and honour, and possess humane and social affections in a high degree; but they do teach, in language which it would seem admits neither of denial or evasion, that his moral depravity is

entire. What will means, unaccompanied by the power of God, do towards prostrating the strong empire of sin in the soul? Can unparalleled deceit lead to holy ingenuousness?—desperate wickedness, to conformity to God's law?—enmity to His character, to love?—and death in sin, to newness of life? It is clear as a sunbeam, that the heart, unsubdued by Divine power, would resist all the motives to holiness which heaven, earth, and hell could furnish. Its renovation never has been, and never will be effected by human might; and only by special agency of the Holy Spirit.

2. That means are rendered efficacious only by special Divine influence, is evident from the fact, that the scriptures ascribe to God the entire glory of the sinner's salvation, and of the predicted triumph of truth and righteousness in the earth. The means selected by infinite wisdom for the attainment of these most important ends are, in the estimation of a vainglorious world, weak and contemptible. This Divine procedure, though foolishness in the eyes of men, is worthy of God. Had He chosen means and instruments for the accomplishment of His stupendous purposes of mercy, distinguished for what commands respect and veneration among men, the effect produced by the unseen efficient cause would doubtless be chiefly ascribed to them. That they are entitled to no share of the glory attached to the effects produced by them, the oracles of truth abundantly testify.

3. The scriptures most explicitly and forcibly teach that all the holiness consequent on the use of means is produced by special Divine agency. Take the following as a specimen of multiplied passages inculcating this truth. " So then, neither is he that planteth anything, neither he that watereth : but God that giveth the increase."

On these arguments we rest the proposition, that the means of grace owe all their efficacy to special Divine influence. With this truth, however, and indeed with every other which God has revealed, we have something more to do than merely to establish it by argument. It is adapted to make us holy ; nor can we innocently fail to apply it to this end. Let us then attend to some practical deductions from the one we have just considered. From it we learn,—

1. That the only hope in regard to the salvation of sinners is in the sovereign mercy of God. The means of grace to which multitudes trust, while they only abuse them, have no efficacy. They are, indeed, important. Without them the attainment of salvation is not to be expected. The enjoyment of them, however, is no certain evidence that those thus favoured will " inherit the salvation which is in Christ Jesus with eternal

glory;" for thousands, exalted to heaven by privileges, have sunk down to hell.

2. The subject we have contemplated suggests one important reason why the means of grace are attended with so little success. Too much reliance is often placed on them, and too little on God. Whenever this is the case, very little is to be expected from them. He will not give His glory to the instruments by which He works. When the necessity of special Divine influence to render means successful is overlooked, and reliance is placed on human power, He withholds His blessing, disappoints the misplaced confidence of His people, and rebukes their presumption.

3. From what has been said, we learn the great importance of giving due honour to the Holy Spirit. Since the means of grace produce no saving results unless accompanied by His special influence, our dependence on Him should at all times be felt and acknowledged. Nothing can more directly tend to arrest His sacred influences, than to withhold from Him the honour to which He is entitled.

4. The subject we have contemplated teaches us, that when the means of God's appointment are diligently used in humble reliance on Him, His blessing may confidently be expected. He may, for a season, withhold it in order to try the faith, and patience, and humility of His people; but in due time they "shall reap if they faint not." The diligent use of the means which He has appointed, in humble dependence on Him to render them efficacious, honours His wisdom, and benevolence, and authority, and power.

His word authorizes the belief that, when the means of His appointment are used, in humble reliance on Him, this influence will, to a greater or less extent, be granted. None, however humble their sphere, and apparently feeble their efforts to promote the cause of Christ, need despair of success. Let them diligently improve the talents committed to them, and confidently look to God for His blessing.

Sinners urged to a reconciliation with God.

By Rev. GIDEON N. JUDD.

"We pray you in Christ's stead, be ye reconciled to God."—2 Cor. v. 20.

IN the text, man's native alienation from God is assumed as a fact not to be disproved; and on the authority of this apostolic and inspired assumption, we shall proceed, in God's behalf, to urge the overture of reconciliation which it contains. That the reasonableness of this plea, and the importance of yielding to it, may be duly appreciated, we propose,—

I. *To state the ground of controversy between God and man.*

The ground of the controversy between God and His revolted creatures on earth is a claim for supremacy on the part of both. This, doubtless, many will be "slow of heart to believe," and others will unhesitatingly deny. It is a statement, however, characterized by the soberness of truth. God comprehends perfectly His own being and attributes, and the relations which exist between Himself and all mortal beings. Nor is it less certain that His unlimited excellences, and righteous supremacy over them, justly entitle Him to their highest love and cordial and unreserved obedience. These claims mankind by nature resist. They refuse to love God, to repent of their sins, to seek for pardon and eternal life through the atonement made by His beloved Son, and to subordinate their inclinations and interests to the honour of His kingdom. By doing this, whatever they may profess to the contrary, they practically declare that they will not have God to reign over them. Here the parties are fairly at issue : and the point in dispute is, whether the will of man or their Maker shall be done,—whether the right of infinite sovereignty shall be maintained, or sacrificed to the wishes of a proud, selfish, rebellious world.

II. *The terms on which this controversy may be settled next demand our attention.*

Parties at variance can be reconciled only in one of the three following ways.

1. Without rendering satisfaction for injuries done, or even investigating the grounds of the controversy, or the manner in which it has been carried on, the parties may agree to exercise mutual forgiveness, and ever after treat each other as friends.

2. Another way in which contending parties become reconciled is by mutual concessions and forgiveness.

3. Another method by which controversies are terminated among men, is for one of the parties to concede all, and make peace on terms proposed by the other. Thus, and thus only, can a peace be concluded between God and alienated, offending man. And let it not be forgotten that their compliance with the terms

III.—K.

of reconciliation He proposes must be *sincere*,—must be *unreserved*. Genuine reconciliation to God also includes unreserved submission to His will, together with a cordial approbation of His revealed method of saving sinners.

Having noticed the terms on which the controversy between God and man can be settled, we pass,—

III. *To urge a compliance with them.*

1. They are reasonable. God requires no more than is His righteous due,—nothing which a proper regard to His own honour as the supreme Ruler, and the best interests of the universe do not imperatively demand. Those to whom these terms of reconciliation are proposed are the sole aggressors. Their enmity to His character and government is wholly unprovoked.

2. We press the treaty by the consideration that the terms are immutable. When controversies exist among men, overtures of reconciliation are sometimes rejected in anticipation of their being made easier. But all hope of a change in the terms of reconciliation with God is vain.

3. We urge a compliance with them by the consideration of what God has done to prepare the way for overtures of pardon and peace. The necessity of such provision, previous to any proclamation of mercy from Him, did not arise from any implacability in His nature, but from His boundless benevolence. His unbending majesty as the moral Governor of the universe could not allow Him to make proposals of peace to the guilty, except through a medium which should put honour upon His violated law, and make Him appear venerable and glorious in the view of all accountable beings. This the good of the intelligent universe, which looks up to Him as the assertor of eternal holiness and order, demands. In order to open a channel through which His mercy might flow to our revolted race,—to constitute a medium of reconciliation between Him and them, He spared not His own Son, but delivered Him up for their offences.

4. A rejection of God's terms of pardon and peace is fraught with the most revolting impiety. The tendency of all the dispensations of His providence is to influence you to be at peace with Him. Thus to treat Jehovah, your Creator, Preserver, Benefactor, and King, who, at infinite expense, provided the way for your return to Him, is a crime which no finite mind can duly estimate. It is breaking asunder every bond of duty to your Sovereign. It is despising His infinite excellences, and the inestimable blessing of His friendship.

5. Your reconciliation is urged in the text and verses immediately connected with it, by considerations of amazing tender-

ness and interest. He places Himself before you in the attitude of a suppliant. In the text, he does not command, but beseeches you by us, to become reconciled to Him. And in whose stead do we deliver this message of infinite mercy and love? Instead of His beloved Son, the great Days-Man, who, by a mysterious union of deity and humanity, is fully qualified to act as Mediator between the offended Majesty of heaven and His rebellious subjects on earth.

6. That your everlasting destiny depends on the manner in which you treat the gracious overture of reconciliation. Nothing can possibly be gained by persisting in your enmity to God's holy character and service. It is an unequal controversy, perseverance in which must end in defeat and ruin. Your knowledge compared with His is ignorance; your wisdom folly; and your strength weakness. "Who hath hardened himself against Him and prospered?"

We have now delivered our embassage. We have placed before you the terms of reconciliation proposed by your offended God. On you now rests the fearful responsibility of deciding whether you will yield to the claims of duty; to the entreaty of infinite love, and be blessed with God's eternal friendship; or reject them, and sink beneath His frown for ever. No power in the universe can release you from the responsibility of becoming reconciled to God, nor can you offer a single valid plea in extenuation of the guilt of refusal.

And now, perishing fellow-sinner, what is thy decision? Soon thou must make it, or the power of doing so will be taken from thee for ever. The period of God's forbearance has its limits. The mediatorial hour hastens to its close. Soon the last lingering call of mercy will sound in thy ears; and if it die away unheeded, in thee will be verified the fearful threatening of insulted majesty and justice,—"Because I have called, and ye refused; I have stretched out my hand, and no man regarded; but ye have set at nought all my counsel, and would none of my reproof: I also will laugh at your calamity; I will mock when your fear cometh; when your fear cometh as desolation, and your destruction cometh as a whirlwind."

The Spiritual and Elevated nature of True Piety.

By Rev. CHARLES JENKINS, Portland, Maine.

"The way of life is above to the wise, that he may depart from hell beneath."—Prov. xv. 24.

IF we glance at the pages of the Bible, we shall perceive that spiritual religion is there presented as an abstract and elevated concern. Its one great and obvious feature, as there delineated, is its opposition, at once, to the predominant temper and bias of the native human heart, and to the controlling maxims and pursuits of the world. The Bible represents the subjects of saving piety as seeking present and endless felicity in a way far above "the common walks of virtuous life." Let our text be taken as an example of the brief, plain, and striking manner in which the Bible uniformly represents that religion which is pure and undefiled before God. "The way of life is above to the wise, that he may depart from hell beneath." Here, it is thought, are suggested certain views of an exalted piety, as exemplified in the principles, feelings, and aims of men, which it must be interesting and profitable to take.

I. *It is elevated in principle.*

It will be found that no one is better than his principles. As a man thinketh in his heart, so is he. Strictly speaking, no one can be called a person of principle, who is not decidedly religious according to the standard of the Bible. For that cannot be called with propriety *principle* in morals or religion, which has not a fixed character and invariable tendency. And none but the consistently religious have motives or grounds of action which are settled and uniform in their influence. I observe,—

1. That their religion is elevated in principle above the received maxims of worldly prudence. Such a prudence is actually nothing more than a selfish and time serving policy. It extends solely to interests of a personal and temporary nature.

2. It may be observed that the religion of the truly wise is

elevated in principle above the accredited standard of worldly morality. When the native human character is considered, and the slow progress which man, under the most favourable circumstances, makes towards any true sublimity of sentiment, it should not surprise us that the form of the world's ethics is low.

3. Let it be observed, that saving piety is elevated in principle above the authority of prevailing opinions. It might doubtless be safely assumed that a religion which is from God, would involve principles of action much more fixed and invariable than the opinions of erring and mutable man.

> 'Tis sweet to stand, when tempests tear the main,
> On the firm cliff, and mark the seaman's toil!
> Not that another's dangers soothe the mind;
> But from such toil how sweet to feel secure!
> Yet sweeter far on Wisdom's height serene,
> Upheld by truth, to fix our firm abode;
> To watch the giddy crowd that, deep below,
> For ever wander in pursuit of bliss,
> Amid opinion's ever-varying strife.

II. *The wise, who are in the way of life, are elevated in taste.*

There is a much closer connection between sound religion and good taste than is generally considered. The person of true piety, other things being equal, is better qualified to judge of merit in all the various departments appropriate to the exercise of taste, than one who is a stranger to the power of experimental religion. But when those in the high way of *life* are said to be elevated in taste, a *religious* taste is chiefly intended—a taste which is occupied in judging of, and relishing or disrelishing objects, as it respects their moral and religious qualities. In this respect I proceed to observe,—

1. That they who are eminently wise unto salvation, are elevated in taste above the mere external decorations of their persons or dwellings.

2. They who are decidedly in the way of life are elevated in taste above the desire of human applause.

3. That the elevated spiritual taste of such as are in the way of life renders them superior to the admiration of merely talented men.

4. Those who in some good degree are living up to the duties, privileges, and consolations of religion, are raised by their spiritual taste above the feeling of enthusiastic delight in the works of mere art, of taste, or of fancy. Religion, as it has been already remarked, more than anything else, elevates and corrects the

intellectual taste, and assists its decisions. But it does more, it gives a new taste and opens a new field for its exercise and gratification. This new taste relates to things as holy or sinful,— as possessing qualities of moral beauty or deformity, grandeur or debasement. Throughout the walks of literature, of art, and of fancy, ravishing beauties are mingled with disgusting deformities. Flowers lie thickly scattered over a mass of pollution. The heavenly-minded believer cannot, therefore, as he once could, range those walks with unmingled and enthusiastic delight. He had rather ponder some great truth of scripture, than gaze at the clustering beauties which adorn the most splendid page of human literature. He had rather contemplate any single feature of the inspired delineation of the New Jerusalem, than all that is grand and lovely in the efforts of genius and art.

III. *The way of life is above to the wise, in that they are elevated in pursuit.*

Their practice is no less sublime than their principles and taste. They are as much above the common walks of worldly men in the character of their efforts, as they are in the views and relish of their minds. On this topic I can only very briefly observe,—

1. That such as are in the way of life are elevated in pursuit above what might be deemed their worldly interest. The ground of their action, it has been observed, is the Divine glory in the purification and salvation of men. This is the predominant motive that prompts their efforts. The end of their efforts is the end of their faith, even the salvation of their souls. Heaven is the prize of their high calling.

2. They who are wise unto eternal life are elevated in pursuit above the present benefits of religion. They are less solicitous to find the way of wisdom the way of pleasantness, than to find it the way of holiness, and its end the fruition of God. It is things invisible for which they labour and endure, and not for things seen and temporal.

In view of all that has been said, I cannot but remark,—

1. That true religion, by which I mean that which is connected with the salvation of its subjects, is vastly more abstract, elevated, and holy than is generally supposed. Men think it what it is too commonly seen to be in the lives of its professors, and not what it is declared to be in the book of God.

2. Saving religion is above the conception of worldly minds.

3. Saving piety is above the reach of worldly accident and changes. Oh, how safe and blessed are the saints of God! Why

does not such a view of their condition constrain the wicked to strive to make it their own?

4. To present them with an additional motive to do this, I add, in conclusion, that all who are not with the truly wise, advancing in this elevated way to heaven above, are hastening their steps to hell beneath. There are but two great ways,—the strait and narrow way of life, and the broad way of death. These two ways conduct to two immensely different ends. The one is an eternal heaven, the other is an eternal hell. Fellow-sinners, we may judge which of these ends we are about to reach, by the way which we now pursue.

The Character, Conduct and Destiny of the Jailor and Felix contrasted.

By Rev. G. A. CALHOUN, North Coventry, Conn.

"Then he called for a light, and sprang in, and came trembling, and fell down before Paul and Silas; and brought them out, and said, Sirs, what must I do to to be saved?" &c.—Acts xvi. 29-34; also Acts xxiv. 25-27.

THESE passages of scripture contain each a concise account of the religious character and conduct of an individual; and my object in presenting both before you at the same time is, that we may contrast the character and conduct of the trembling jailor at Philippi, and those of the trembling Felix at Cesarea, and derive instruction from the contrast. In relation to the jailor and Felix, I observe,—

I. *They were both sinners.*

II. *They were both brought in an interesting manner within the reach of religious instruction.*

III. *They were both convicted of sin under the instructions which they received from the Apostles.*

IV. *They both resolved to engage in the concerns of their salvation.*

V. *The jailor resolved to delay no longer his immor-*

tal interests, while Felix put off the subject to a future period.

VI. *The jailor soon gave evidence of piety, while Felix aforded evidence of increasing hardness of heart.*

VII. *It is probable that the jailor is now in heaven, and that Felix is in the world of despair.*

From what has been disclosed in relation to the character and conduct of these individuals, we learn,—

1. That persons may resemble each other for a season, who in subsequent life, and in eternity, shall be vastly different.

2 The difference between embracing religion now, and resolving to embrace it at a future period, is very great. In the first place, the one yields to the suggestions of the Holy Spirit, and the other hesitates. In the second place, the person who embraces religion *now* ceases to be under the power of sin. But the convicted sinner, however many his tears and deep his distress, who delays making his peace with God, is still a slave of sin. In the third place, the person who embraces religion *now* may appropriate to himself the promises of the gospel. But there are no promises to him who resolves to give God his heart at a future period. And again, the person who engages in religion *now* may have assurance of heaven: while it remains fearfully uncertain whether the resolution of the other is ever executed.

3. There are periods in the life of all which appear to be solemnly critical, and of infinite moment. And may not the present be a period solemnly critical, and of infinite moment to some hearers? My friends, the Spirit of God may, at the present time, be nearer to you than ever after, if He is now resisted. The crisis with you may now have arrived, and the reception or rejection of offered grace to-day may settle your destiny for ever.

The Duty of Restitution.

By Rev. SHEPARD K. KOLLOCK, A.M., NORFOLK, VIR.

"Behold, Lord, the half of my goods I give to the poor; and if I have taken anything from any man by false accusation, I restore him fourfold."—LUKE xix. 8.

NOTHING is more obvious than the antipathy felt by a certain class of professed Christians against the preaching of morality, as if it infringed upon the great doctrine of justification by faith. If it be a cold, pagan, heartless, philosophic morality, detached from religion, and independent of its influence, let it be rejected. But if it be a morality founded upon Christian principle, and looking directly to the will of God as its rule, and the glory of God as its end, it is surely proper for the discussion of the pulpit, and suited to the state of man as a fallen creature. Men need to be reminded of the nature and indispensable necessity of Christian virtues, and to be often urged to the practical duties of the New Testament. The Saviour often preached such morality, and the Apostles inculcated it in all their epistles. It is enforced by the example of him who uttered the words which we have read to you,—" Behold, Lord, the half of my goods I give to the poor ; and if I have taken anything from any man by false accusation, I restore him fourfold."

The duty enforced by the example of Zaccheus is that of Restitution, or the act by which we restore to our neighbour that of which we have unjustly deprived him. Let us notice,—

I. *The foundation of the duty of restitution.*

1. It is founded on the very nature of justice; for justice consists in rendering to every one what belongs to him. If we had no scriptures to instruct us in the will of God on this point, still natural reason would sufficiently teach us that it is our duty to restore all that we have fraudulently acquired, or unjustly retained. Of all the human virtues, justice is first in importance. This is the cement of human society—the spirit which connects all its members—which inspires its various relations, and maintains the order and subordination of every part. Without it, society would become a den of thieves and banditti, hating and hated, devouring and devoured by one another. Among many nations, unvisited by Divine revelation, the duty of restitution has been often enjoined, and declared by the laws necessary for the well-being of society. Among the ancient Egyptians, Greeks, and Romans, it was demanded as a proper regard to the rights of

others, and the means of preserving them sacred and inviolate; and among the Mahomedans it is enforced with equal rigour.

2. Let us appeal to the Holy Scriptures. In the 22nd chapter of Exodus, in the 6th of Leviticus, and the 5th of Numbers, we find express ordinances on this subject.

3. Restitution is a duty so indispensable, that without it there is no salvation. At first view this assertion may appear harsh and uncharitable; yet its truth must be evident upon the least reflection. Tell me, can we be saved without repentance? No! "Except ye repent, ye shall perish," is the language of your Judge. But do we really repent of an injustice which we have committed, when we refuse to repair it? Tell me, can we be in a state of salvation, when we have no love to God, and no love to our neighbour? But the man who refuses to make restitution loves not God, for he despises His laws and tramples upon His authority; nor does he love his neighbour, for he voluntarily persists in wronging him, and withholding from him his rights.

II. *What is necessary for the performance of this duty?*

1. We must examine with care whether we have ever wronged our neighbour, and in how many modes we have done it. We cannot too carefully examine ourselves on this subject, nor be too much guarded against the thousand illusions which men form to satisfy their consciences. Allege not for your excuse, example—custom—the necessity of acting like others. All this is of no avail now in the sight of the Omniscient—will be of no avail hereafter at the bar of God. No matter what others do— it is true, and as long as there is a distinction between right and wrong, it will be eternally true, that whatever you have obtained from your neighbour by open violence or insidious over-reaching is his property—not yours.

2. Restitution should be prompt. Many persons know that they have the property of another, and content themselves with a vague intention of restitution, and by this means lull their consciences to repose,—"I will, at some future time, make restitution." But when? You as yet know not the time, and perhaps it may never arrive.

3. Restitution must be full and entire. Zaccheus does more than satisfy those whom he had wronged, for he resolves to restore fourfold. Fearful lest he should not fully recompense them, his generous heart makes the resolution, and his piety is ready instantly to execute it.

Such is the nature of this duty, and the manner in which it

should be performed. But how many are there in the world who, to elude the obligation, allege the most specious reasons. If I make restitution, I cannot maintain that rank in society, that style of living, to which I have been accustomed. Others refuse to make restitution, because they desire to bequeath their property to their children. Some are ashamed to make it. But surely it is rather a matter of commendation. In acting as did Zaccheus, you proclaim, not your shame, but your honesty—not your ignominy, but your fearless determination to comply with the dictates of justice and the commands of God. If the injury be private, let the restitution be private. Provided you do it effectually, you may be as prudent in the manner of accomplishing it as you please. But do it, in some way or other, as you desire peace of conscience, as you dread endless perdition.

In view of this subject, I remark,—

1. How small is the number of those who are saved! We have seen that the restoration of all which has been acquired by violence or fraud is indispensable for salvation. We know that thousands of frauds are daily committed, and yet how few acts of restitution do we witness!

2. What great discoveries shall be made at the day of judgment. Then the mask of hypocrisy shall drop, the cloak of religious profession shall be torn off, and the true character of those who sought and retained " the wages of unrighteousness " shall be fully exhibited. Then there will be seen many "painted sepulchres," blazing comets, "wandering and fallen stars, to whom is reserved the blackness of darkness for ever."

3. This subject teaches us the nature of true religion. It consists in benevolence to man as well as love to God, and assures us that without the former we can never exercise the latter.

4. This subject should lead us to avoid the very beginning of sin, and to pay the most scrupulous attention to the duties of truth and justice. Thus we shall be prevented from defrauding our fellow-men: thus, if necessity ever requires it, we shall be able easily to make full restitution. "He that is unjust in the least is unjust also in much," and incurs the condemnation of God as effectually as if he were guilty of the greatest injustice.

5. Show by your conduct, ye who have in any degree defrauded your fellow-men, that you feel the force of conscience and the truth of God; imitate Zaccheus, and make restitution. This discourse has presented you with a morality little suited to the taste of the age—with a doctrine terrible to many modern Christians. But after all, my brethren, the difficulty of the duty which I preach arises not so much from the nature of the

thing itself, as from the excessive attachment which men have for this world; from the feebleness of their faith, and the faintness of their desires for the things of heaven. How sweet the satisfaction to be able to say with the apostle, " I have wronged no man, I have defrauded no man."

The Christian's Duty to Prisoners.

By Rev. BERIAH GREEN, Hudson, Ohio.

"But I say unto you, love your enemies; bless them that curse you, do good to them that hate you, and pray for them that despitefully use you and persecute you; that ye may be the children of your Father which is in heaven," &c.—MATT. v. 44–47.

THIS passage presents one important point, in which Christians are required to rise above others. Every man has his objects of kind regard. Robbers and assassins love each other. And while upon all around them they wage a deadly warfare, they may defend each other's rights with the utmost decision of purpose, and energy of action. Much more do men of elevated morals and taste cherish, for the larger circle in which they move, a generous confidence and lively attachment. But Christian benevolence, while it strengthens and refines every amiable feeling natural to man, may also be expected to raise him to a higher, wider sphere of action. It will not permit him to confine his regards to a circle of friends. He may not think it enough to extend their circle, so as to admit the deserving and unfortunate. Christian principle will lead him to pity and bless such objects of want and woe as his natural feelings would prompt him to overlook or hate. This statement is clearly supported by the passage which stands at the head of this discourse. Those forms, then, of guilty, suffering humanity, which others regard with aversion or neglect, Christians may be expected to pity and bless.

Never, perhaps, does guilty, suffering humanity assume a form more likely to be overlooked or despised by the world at large than in the person of the imprisoned convict. But Christians may justly be expected to regard him with pity,—may be justly expected to make prompt and vigorous exertions to promote his welfare. This I argue,—

I. *From the character of Christians.*

1. A leading attribute of the Christian character is disinterested benevolence. Who that reads the Bible needs to be informed that "love is the fulfilling of the law"?

2 The friends of improvement in prison discipline expect the countenance and aid of Christians, from "the deep sense of personal guilt they habitually maintain."

8. Especially will the friends of improvement in prison discipline cherish this expectation, when they remember that in their own experience, Christians have full and delightful evidence that "the grace of God is of sufficient efficacy to work a radical and permanent reformation in the character of sinners, however deeply depraved." Christians will not regard the character of the foulest convict as ruined beyond the hope of reformation.

II. *That Christians may justly be expected to countenance and aid the friends of improvement in prison discipline, may be argued from the means of usefulness they are able to employ.*

III. *The commands of Jesus Christ bind His disciples to labour for the benefit of imprisoned criminals.*

IV. *The providence of God greatly encourages the expectation, that Christians will be forward to do what they can to promote the highest interests of the prisoner.*

Prison discipline, then, in order to be healthful and efficient, must be conducted on Christian principles. The principles, embodied in the character of the disciples of the Saviour, furnish the very agents which the discipline demands.

Difficulties of Old Age without Religion.

BY REV. STEPHEN H. TYNG, PHILADELPHIA.

"Woe unto us! for the day goeth away; for the shadows of the evening are stretched out."—JER. ix. 4.

THE subject which, from this text, I intend to commend to your attention, is an old age without religion. It is truly a painful subject, but one to which it is a matter of duty to call the attention of procrastinating man. In the remarks I shall make, so far as they are addressed to those who have not yet attained this period of life, the subject calls for the most serious admonition and warning. But in regard to those of my hearers who are already aged, or who are upon the verge of the declining years of manhood, it becomes me to employ the utmost tenderness of manner, united with the most ardent language of persuasion.

The points to which I wish particularly to direct attention are the *difficulties* and *sorrows* of old age without religion, without a vital union with Christ, and the comforts of His love. "Woe unto us! for the day goeth away, and the shadows of the evening are stretched out."

I. *That period of life, during which the Saviour grants to men the privileges of the gospel, is known under the appellation of a day of grace; a day in which He waits for the sinner's repentance, and is peculiarly ready to aid his efforts.*

The great object to be attained during the continuance of this day is reconciliation to God, and the consequent enjoyment of His love. They who seek Him early have the promise that they shall find Him; and if man be wise in the morning of this day of privilege, the way of return to God is filled with encouragement. In old age this reconciliation to God is rendered embarrassing and painful by this first difficulty, that "The day goeth away." The period of grace has almost come to its close. The aged sinner must necessarily reflect upon a long, long duration of mercy, which has passed by unimproved. Every privilege of the gospel has brought with it an individual responsibility. Not one of its advantages can have been enjoyed without a corresponding obligation to render an account thereof to the holy and heart-searching God.

"The day goeth away." It has been enjoyed, in the fulness of its privileges. It has been long allowed to endure for some of those who listen to me now. But since it has been utterly unimproved, it has tended only to increase the guilt and danger of the soul. For fifty years the Redeemer has called upon an individual present to turn to Him and live. For fifty years angels of mercy have watched for his conversion. For fifty years Divine Providence has crowned his ways with lovingkindness and tender mercy. How hard and difficult to arouse him to a sense of the privileges which he has yet remaining, and of the duty which is yet resting upon him! He thinks he would return, but he fears lest there should be no hope for his soul.

II. *The second difficulty which the text suggests, to prevent the spiritual return of the aged sinner unto Christ, is the short period of grace which is now left to him.* "*The shadows of the evening are stretched out.*"

Many years have passed by unimproved. But very few, at the best, are now left for his soul's salvation. As life passes away, the work to be done increases, in the same proportion as the time in which it is to be done is diminished. Death now stands at the door. The line which separates earth from hell has dwindled to a hair, and the aged sinner is tempted to yield to utter despair of escaping the ruin which is so close upon him. The difficulty which his own heart presents, as arising from this shortened period of probation, Satan uses as a temptation to him to be quiet and unconcerned under his load of sins. A spirit of deep and agonizing earnestness for his soul he cannot, and he does not wish to attain; and there is no opportunity for any slow work of grace.

III. *A third difficulty in the way of aged sinners, arises from the increased hardness of their hearts.*

When they were young, conviction agitated their minds. The solemn proclamations of Divine truth awakened their attention. Their eyes could weep under the preaching of the gospel. Their affections could be attracted by the inviting hopes and promises of the gospel, and they often felt strongly excited towards a life of holiness and peace. But now they have no such feelings.

They sit under the preaching of the word utterly unmoved. This utter hardness of heart,—the necessary accompaniment of age, and still more necessarily the effect of a long continuance in an unconverted state of character,—forms a serious difficulty in the way of the aged sinner's return to God.

IV. *The remaining difficulty to which I refer, as hedging up the aged sinner's return to God, is the pride of character which attends the advanced periods of life.*

The heart may be often moved, the conscience awakened, and the feelings roused in the bosom of the aged transgressor, and a vehement desire be felt to lay down this burden and find peace. But an assumed dignity and coolness of manner are drawn over a broken and bleeding spirit, because the acknowledgment of these awakened desires is so humiliating to the age and station of the individual. But there is no other course presented. To this humbling ground the sinner must be brought, or he will assuredly perish. Age furnishes no exemptions. So far from it, it requires still deeper abasement for the long continuance of guilt. This difficulty is now preventing, and has long been operating to prevent, the return of some of my aged hearers to Christ. They are convinced, as they listen to the gospel, of the importance of the course pointed out. They almost resolve to pursue it. But when they return to their homes, the acknowledgment to children, and domestics, and friends, that they have been all this time in the wrong, is so painful and repulsive to their minds, that they cannot yield.

Brethren, your time is short, your difficulties are many, your work is arduous, but it is not impossible; and would you set yourselves immediately about it, God would remove the difficulties, and give you success. Nothing is wanting in God, but there is much wanting in yourselves. O that you could be persuaded immediately to turn to Christ, who invites you, and promises salvation only upon your return. Aged friends, why will you not yield at once? Come out from ruin, and flee to the arms of Jesus. However painful and humbling the work may be, the humbling step is but one. Be willing to be abased in the Divine presence, and feel that though aged and respected among men, there is no respect of persons with God.

Sorrows of Old Age without Religion.

By Rev. STEPHEN H. TYNG, Philadelphia.

"If a man live many years, so that the days of his years are many, and his soul be not filled with good, I say that an untimely birth is better than he."—Eccl. vi. 3.

LONG life has been esteemed among all nations as one of the greatest and most desirable of blessings. In the earliest periods of the world, the number of years allotted to man as his season of probation was very great. Now that the days of men are comparatively so circumscribed, we can hardly imagine the appearance or the feelings of an individual, whose locks were the growth of nine centuries, and who had lived to witness many thousand immortal beings, as the lineal descendants from himself. Yet this was the first measure of human life. But the fallen nature of man transforming this lengthened period of trial merely into a more extended progress in iniquity—a more unfathomable depth of sin,—the Divine Creator has, in successive generations, cut down the opportunity of rebellion against Him, in the case of each individual, to less than one tenth of the period first granted to the human race. No longer like the oak, which is said to occupy three centuries in its growth, three centuries in the enjoyment of its maturity, and three centuries in decay, now, "we all do fade as a leaf." At the utmost ordinary limit, the days of man are threescore years and ten. And the wish for long life can hardly carry the mind beyond this period. But the fact that so very few ever attain to this utmost limit leads us to arrange our plans of business and exertion within a much narrower scope than that would allow us. In our worldly occupations, we are governed by the rule, that what we have to do must be done quickly. And yet how many are hoping to prepare for an eternal occupation, and to attain an inexhaustible knowledge, in the last flickering of human existence! In the business of this world men are wise. It is only in relation to eternity that they seem to be void of reason. The text leads me to consider,—

I. *The great object and purpose of human life.*

The great object of human life is that "the soul may be filled with good." It was for this object that man was placed in a period of earthly education; and it is for this alone that Divine forbearance lengthens out to gray hairs the life of man, to see if the hour will come when men will be wise, and think of the things which belong to their peace. The possession of an immortal soul forms a man's chief distinction from the brutes which perish.

That man's soul is filled with good who has found a reconciled God. There is none good but one, that is God. He who has received Jesus in his heart by faith, so that God dwells in him and he in God, has found the one great abiding good for man. The privileges of the gospel are bestowed upon us, and the voice of Jesus is calling us through our whole period of probation, that we may be led to seek salvation in that infinite atonement, which is offered as our only good. Any state, within the conception of man, short of the final and interminable agonies and despair of hell, is preferable to the state of an old man without religion.

II. *I am thus led to my second topic of remark,—the sorrows of the man who has passed through life, and "his soul is not filled with good."*

1. The first cause of sorrow in old age without religion, to which I refer is, that man has passed through a life, a reflection upon which gives him no comfort. So has the Divine Creator constituted the human mind, that man is compelled to look back continually upon his own conduct and character. Even if he would desire and endeavour to forget himself, he finds that he cannot do it. Past days and years rush involuntarily upon his recollection, and bring to him their load of joy or sorrow, and lay it down before him for his cool and inevitable inspection. We are always laying up something for our latter days, and according as we have sown shall we then reap.—[Instance Job, David, Paul, and Polycarp.] But what sorrow, anguish, and

self-crimination arise in the heart from the retrospect of a wasted life ? No beam of light is cast forth upon the mind from any act or feeling that recollection brings to view. Every hour rises up as an accuser of a guilty conscience. A remembrance of youth is a remembrance of convictions smothered, the Holy Spirit resisted, and a Saviour's love despised. The thoughts of a past manhood present an awful picture of a sinner, carefully building for himself an altar from the stones of the world, and immolating upon it, to the enemy of God and man, his immortal soul. The latter years, as they have collected upon each other, and are thrusting him so rapidly from the earth, seem only the gathered impetus of that stone of neglected grace which is now ready to fall upon his soul and grind him to powder. All the resolutions and plans which he made for life have gone by unfulfilled. Nothing but wretchedness can arise from a life which has been spent without Christ. Old age may be crowned with human glory, loaded with earthly wealth, and having every comfort which the intercourse of men can give ; but this reflection upon a murdered soul, a twice crucified Saviour, a miserable bargain with Satan, will tear the glory from a royal diadem, and turn the sweetest joys of earth into anguish and poison.

2. The second sorrow of an old age without religion to which I will refer is, that man is pressing forward to an eternity for which he has no preparation. The only preparation which any sinner can have for a happy eternity is to be found in the Lord Jesus Christ, clothed with everlasting righteousness, and receiving a free redemption through His blood. This eternity cannot be avoided. There is no discharge in this war. With resistless force, man is pressed onward to the valley of the shadow of death, and, whether prepared or unprepared, he must appear before the judgment-seat of Christ. This course is altogether inevitable. In youth, the thought of it seems to be easily removed, because the day of parting appears to be far off. The youth may live to be an old man, and, as he thinks, will then have time enough to take care of his soul. But when old age has arrived, the hour of death cannot be far removed. To-morrow and to-morrow he may be here; but ah, the awful hour is not far removed,—it cannot be,—when he must be carried, without hope or comfort, to the bar of an offended God. And while an eternity unprovided for is thus near upon him, he feels that it would have been better for him if he had not been born.

III. *Another sorrow of old age without religion is, that man has experienced the vanity of the world, and has nothing to supply its place.*

The false paintings of the world delude the young, and palm themselves upon them for realities. They love to be thus deceived. They make no opposition to the delusions practiced upon them by these enticing instruments of Satan. Wealth, and pleasure, and reputation seem to be proper and reasonable objects of pursuit, and in them the young vainly imagine that they can find satisfaction for their souls. But the aged have outlived these deceptions. I am addressing some, my brethren, who can tell me that they have tasted of every fountain which the earth can offer, and know that but miserable comfort is to be derived from them all. Mere sensual indulgence, whether of a light and giddy character, or of a deeper stain of pollution, can offer them nothing, for they have no feelings of desire to which such provisions are suitable. Money can do them no good, for it will require but very little to purchase for them a grave or a coffin, and soon these will be all they shall want. Their own characters can furnish them no consolation, though a thousand sycophants should praise their course of life; for they see that man judgeth by the outward appearance, but God looketh upon the heart. They are obliged often to sit down in a contemplation of their own past and future existence, and their minds present a perfect blank, so far as any source or object of comfort is to be found. The world recedes and disappears; its cisterns are all broken, its springs are dried, its flowers have withered, its joys have become entirely tasteless; and in the midst of all this wilderness of the soul, they can find no fresh springs of hope or peace.

Surely, then, the assertion of my text is proved to be established upon a true foundation. And every hearer who has come to old age in an unconverted state, has infinite reason to shake himself from the dust, to give up every thought about any other object, and to consecrate singly to this great purpose of his soul's salvation every remaining hour of life. I feel no sorrow in driving the aged who are without Christ to despair. When they do feel and care enough about the matter to despair, I shall have hope that the Lord is so overturning all their long-standing self-righteousness, that He may build for them a city which hath foundations, which shall be eternal in the heavens. It is not despair which is likely to injure them. They are perishing in lethargy, in cold and heartless unconcern, and the sooner they despair of accomplishing anything but eternal ruin in their present course, the better will it be for them. Now is your accepted time and your day of salvation. And may the Holy Ghost be pleased to apply to your hearts these solemn truths, to persuade you to improve it. Amen.

Motives and Means of Peace to the Churches.

By Rev. JOHN H. AGNEW, Newark, Delaware.

"Peace be within thy walls."—Psalm cxxii. 7.

THIS prayer of the sweet singer of Israel contains a sentiment which ought to be cherished in every Christian's heart, and often uttered in his petitions before the throne. It is of the same spirit with the final blessing and legacy of the dear Redeemer,—"Peace I leave with you; my peace I give unto you."

I. *Remark on the importance of peace in the kingdom of Jesus Christ.*

1. The triune Jehovah, the covenant God of the church, is the God of peace. How frequently, in the benedictions of the Apostle Paul, is He thus characterized,—"The God of peace be with you," Rom. xv. 33; "The very God of peace sanctify you wholly," 1 Thess. v. 23; "The God of peace make you perfect in every good work," Heb. xiii. 20; "God is not the author of confusion, but of peace," 1 Cor. xiv. 33.

2. Jesus Christ, the Head of the Church, and King in Zion, is the Prince of peace—the Lord of peace. At His birth as the Son of man, the choir of the heavenly host sang, "Peace on earth."

3. The Spirit, who inhabits the church as His temple, is a Spirit of peace, and refuses to dwell in the midst of noise, strife, and confusion. "The fruit of the Spirit is love, joy, peace, long-suffering, gentleness, goodness, meekness, temperance."

4. The constitution of the kingdom of Christ is one whose essential principles are peace. "My kingdom is not of this world. If my kingdom were of this world, then would my servants fight." The gospel is the gospel of peace. "Have peace one with another." "If it be possible, as much as lieth in you, live peaceably with all men." The kingdom of God is peace.

5. The church can only then show forth her beauty, and glorify her King, when her members are at peace with one another. The beauty of the church consists not in any external habiliments, or any system of observances, but in a meek and quiet spirit, which, in the sight of God, is of great price; in

the manifestation of kindness, tenderness, meekness, forbearance, peace.

II. *But if peace be so important, and so manifestly incumbent on the children of the Most High, it will be interesting to inquire, What means should be used for its cultivation ?*

1. Walk in the Spirit, and ye shall not fulfil the lusts of the flesh. If we place ourselves under the guidance of the "Peaceful Dove," and act in conformity with His suggestions, we shall be preserved from biting and devouring one another, and shall pursue the things which make for peace. And when a brother errs, we shall labour to restore such an one, in the spirit of meekness.

2. In contending for the faith, avoid the usual concomitants of controversy. The whole contest for the faith once delivered to the saints must be conducted without strife or vain-glory, and with the meekness and gentleness of Christ; so that the sanctifying power of the gospel may be manifest even in controversy, and win opposers from the snare of the devil.

3. In reference to differences of opinion among those who name the name of Jesus, and acknowledge His reign in their hearts, if they be of minor consequence, and not necessary to salvation, they must not be dwelt upon, as if of more importance than the vital and practical points of the Christian faith. On this subject there is doubtless much error in the practice of the Church; much that prevents the cultivation of peace, grieves the Spirit of all grace, and throws a cloud over the horizon of the Christian world. The Psalmist considered the prosperity of the Redeemer's kingdom to be dependent on its peaceful condition, and every righteous soul will, doubtless, respond to this call to "pray for the peace of Jerusalem." "For my brethren and companions' sakes, I will now say, Peace be within thee."

4. Peace will be promoted by not dwelling too exclusively on a single aspect of divine things, nor magnifying one particular doctrine above another of equal importance in the word of God.

5. In controversy, verbal or written, impute nothing to opponents which they do not allow, neither pervert their meaning, nor attribute consequences which they disclaim.

6. Abstain from censoriousness, and pride of intellect. These faults are intimately connected, and where they exist have a direct tendency to stop the current of the river of peace, which

makes glad the city of God. We must not be wise in our own conceits, and say, "We are the people, and wisdom will die with us;" thus assuming to ourselves a singularly correct judgment, wrapping around us the robe of self-complacency, and walking forth in self-important majesty, expecting the world to follow in our wake.

In view of results so desirable, we cannot but reflect, how unholy the flame which burns in the Christian's heart, when he cherishes any dispositions opposed to the peace of Jerusalem. Oh! how should the church humble herself before God, and, weeping tears for past offences, pour forth the fervent prayer, "Peace be within thy walls, and prosperity within thy palaces. For my brethren and companions' sake, I will now say, Peace be within thee." Truly, "they shall prosper that love thee, O Jerusalem!" When, oh! when shall it be said of Zion spiritual, "She is beautiful, the joy of the whole earth, her walls salvation, her officers peace, her exactors righteousness!"

Evidences of True Conversion.
By Rev. CHARLES WALKER, Rutland, Vermont.

"And Zaccheus stood and said unto the Lord, Behold, Lord, the half of my goods I give unto the poor; and if I have taken anything from any man by false accusation, I restore him fourfold And Jesus said unto him, This day is salvation come to this house."—Luke xix. 8, 9.

WHATEVER might have been the views and feelings of this man,—whether mere curiosity, or some better motive prompted his desire to see Jesus,—it is evident that the instructions of the Divine Teacher had a powerful effect on his mind, and produced a striking change in his character and prospects. There can be no doubt that he had hitherto been a worldling. Love of money and desire of gain had been his ruling passion. But from the time he received Jesus as a guest into his house, his whole character was changed. He became a new man. He believed in Christ, and showed the sincerity of his belief by a sacrifice of his former inclination and habits. He adopted voluntarily a course of life which, considering his former character, must have been the strongest effort of self-denial. His avarice gave place to liberality. A benevolent spirit entered his bosom and crowded out selfishness.

I. *When the gospel is cordially received and fully embraced, it subdues a man's ruling sin.*

II. *Evidence of Christian character is to be sought, not so much in what a man says, as in what he does.*

III. *On the disposal of property, there is a wide difference between the opinions of men and the instructions of Jesus Christ.*

The Importance of Domestic Happiness.
By Rev. SAMUEL MILLER, D.D., Princeton, N. J.

"Thy tabernacle shall be peace."—Job v. 24.

MAN was made for society, and the earliest form of society was that of the family. The all-wise Creator had scarcely made the first parent of our race before He said,—" It is not good for man to be alone ; I will therefore make a help-meet for him." And to show the importance and permanence, as well as the close and endearing character of this connection, He added, " For this cause shall a man leave his father and mother, and cleave unto his wife, and they twain shall be one flesh."

As domestic society was the first that was formed, so it lies at the foundation of all other, and enters more deeply into the order, the purity, and the happiness of our world than a volume could display. It does more to cement civil society, to create the tenderest relations, to soften the heart, to refine, polish, and harmonize the children of men, than all the laws which human wisdom ever formed.

The importance of domestic happiness, then, is to be the subject of the present discourse. It is to this bless-

ing to which Eliphaz refers in the words of our text,—
"Thy tabernacle shall be peace." The word "tabernacle" signifies a family tent, or movable dwelling. Such dwellings formerly were, and indeed still are, exceedingly common in Arabia, where Job is supposed to have resided, and in many other parts of the Eastern world. The term here may be considered as designating, by a very common figure, not only the tent itself, but also the family inhabiting it.

I. *The inestimable importance of domestic happiness appears from the unavoidable intimacy and extent of its influence on human comfort.*

It is the wisdom of every one who wishes to establish his happiness on the firmest basis, to study to make his own dwelling, as far as possible, the abode of harmony and love. He who finds not comfort here will probably find it nowhere. The absence of this blessing will be like a worm, constantly gnawing at the root of his enjoyment; while he whose domestic happiness is well established, will seldom fail to experience its benign influence in all the walks of life, and in the discharge of every public and private duty.

II. *That it is a blessing equally attainable by all classes of persons, and which may be enjoyed, not occasionally only, but every day that we live.*

Some of those attainments which we most covet, and which enter in no small degree into the elements of personal comfort, can be reached only by a select few of our race. But the happiness arising from a well-ordered and affectionate domestic circle may be enjoyed by all classes of the children of men, in all situations of life, at all seasons; nay, it may be said to be most rich, sweet, and productive, when separated from the false pleasures of an ensnaring world, and left to its own resources.

III. *By the multiplied and wide-spreading mischiefs which daily result from its absence.*

If the mere privation of present comfort were the only evils resulting from domestic discord and strife, the mischief, though serious indeed to each individual, would not be so deep and vital as we often witness. But this, in a multitude of cases, is but a small part of the evil. In how many melancholy instances have domestic feuds and alienations driven husbands from their homes to the haunts of vice, tempted wives to violate their plighted allegiance, impelled children to take refuge among strangers from the miseries of their parental abode, and betrayed all into habits as degrading and destructive as they were criminal! When home is attractive it will seldom be deserted; but if it be uncomfortable, it is an instinct of nature to fly for relief to some other society.

IV. *Its essential and unavoidable influence on the church of God.*

The family has been called "the nursery of the church." In fact, every Christian family is a little "church" within itself. We have the authority of holy scripture for this language.—(Col. iv. 15; Philemon 2.) And as the character of any aggregate body is necessarily formed by the character of its parts, so the visible church of Christ will never fail to be such as are the families that compose it. If peace, order, and love reign in every dwelling, or in a majority of them, peace, order, and love will reign in the church.

V. *The more general and perfect domestic happiness is, the more pure, harmonious, and happy will be the community at large.*

Communities are made up of families. And as the whole is equal to all its parts, in the science of numbers and quantity, so it is equally plain that, in the department of morals, the whole body will ever be found to bear the character which is generally borne by its component parts.

It is plain, then, that every patriot, as well as every moralist, and every Christian, ought to prize domestic happiness as a most important matter, in which the state, as well as the church, has a deep interest; as a matter which lies at the very foundation of all social order; as a precious attainment, on which are suspended the intellectual, moral, and spiritual welfare of our children, and the real comfort of every form of human society, to an extent which nothing but the most ample experience can fully appreciate.

From the view which has been taken of this subject, we may see,—

1. The perfect infatuation of those who undervalue the happiness of the domestic circle, and are constantly seeking enjoyment elsewhere.

2. It is evident that this is a species of enjoyment for the se-

suring of which it is worth while, as well as necessary, to take unwearied and constant pains.

3. How much reason have those who are favoured with a good degree of domestic happiness to rejoice and be thankful! Highly favoured of God! You enjoy a treasure. Prize it highly, improve it carefully, guard with the utmost care against everything that may mar or diminish it, and pray without ceasing that it may be maintained unimpaired.

4. Important as domestic happiness is to all the children of men,—to the high and the low, the rich and the poor, the bond and the free,—it is evident, from the foregoing statement, that there are some to whom it is of peculiar importance, and who, of course, ought to labour after this blessing with a peculiar care. They are those whose station in society renders their conduct most conspicuous, and their example most influential: such as ministers of the gospel, public men of all classes, the wealthy, the learned, and, in short, all who occupy elevated places among men, and whose habits, whether they will or not, cannot fail of being noticed and spoken of by multitudes.

The Means of Domestic Happiness.
By Rev. SAMUEL MILLER, D.D.

"Thy tabernacle shall be in peace."—JOB v. 24.

AN attempt was made, in the preceding discourse, to unfold the importance of domestic happiness. We have seen that its relations and its value are incalculable; that its importance is deep and vital to ourselves, to our children, to the church of God, and to the community at large; that all have a deep interest in securing and maintaining it; and that those who undervalue and neglect it are among the most infatuated of mortals.

But another inquiry arises, no less interesting and practical: How shall we attain this blessing? What are the effectual means of securing domestic happiness? To the consideration and answer of this question, let us now direct our serious attention.

I. *If we desire to secure domestic happiness, we must make a high estimate of its value, and labour without ceasing to attain it.*

The family, like the heart, is liable every day to go wrong, and will assuredly go wrong, unless it be guarded with the utmost vigilance. Such are the infirmities and sinfulness of our nature, that the social machine will never work well when left to itself. We cannot safely intermit our watchful care of it for a single hour. And this watchfulness must extend to every member of the household, from the head to the youngest child and domestic; to every interest of the household, great and small, temporal and spiritual. And, after all, this watchfulness must be conducted under the deep impression that it will be ineffectual without the Divine blessing.

II. *We cannot expect the reign of domestic happiness in any household, without the prevalence of sincere and ardent domestic affection.*

Let the tenderest mutual affection be cultivated by all the members of the family. Let the utmost care be taken to guard against everything adapted to impair its strength, or suspend its exercise. "Love suffereth long, and is kind; love is not easily provoked, thinketh no evil, beareth all things, believeth all things. Love covereth a multitude of sins." "Better is a dinner of herbs where love is, than a stalled ox and hatred therewith."

III. *The habitual government of the temper in the several members of the family is essential to domestic happiness.*

In every family occurrences will arise to try the temper. In this depraved world, where we have all our failings, we ought to expect this, and to make all our calculations, and set a guard over our spirits accordingly. Now, when anything is said or done, either by mistake or carelessness, or by a sudden temptation, that tends to give offence, or to produce irritation,—unless it be met by a spirit of forbearance and self-government, unless there be such a curb placed on the temper as will guard against irritation, and prompt to that "soft answer which turneth away wrath,"—there must ensue heart-burnings, hard thoughts, and a state of feeling wholly inconsistent with domestic harmony and love.

IV. *If we desire to cherish and secure domestic happi-*

ness, it is important that all domestic intercourse be marked by habitual and mutual respectfulness.

Amidst the intimacy and familiarity in which members of the same household live with each other, they are extremely apt to lose sight of that constant manifestation of respect which can never be abandoned without harm.

V. *Habitual prudence is another important means of securing domestic happiness.*

Prudence is practical wisdom. Without this, no society, from a family to a nation, can continue a day in comfort. Even domestic affection and amiable tempers cannot prove effectual where childishness and indiscretion reign.

VI. *Another important means of attaining domestic happiness is a close adherence to regularity and order in the management of domestic affairs.*

There must be system and regularity in our tabernacles, if we would desire them to be at peace. Every member of the household must know his own station, and perform his own duty. When domestic affairs are thus conducted, there will be tranquillity and comfort. Order begets neatness, neatness comfort, and comfort love.

VII. *The last means of domestic happiness which I shall mention, and which may be said to embrace all the rest, is, the reign of pure and undefiled religion.*

All the means which have been hitherto mentioned may be in a good degree possessed, and if religion be absent, there is no security that the tabernacle will be in peace. A venerable divine of the last age was accustomed to say, "A family without religion is like a house without a roof, exposed to every storm." Never was there a more correct and weighty maxim. Where the principles of genuine piety have no place, domestic affection, amiable tempers, prudence, mutual respect, and the strictest order may be maintained, and yet all be in vain, for they may all vanish in a day; and even while they last, there are important sources of domestic enjoyment over which they can exercise no control. There are exigencies in domestic history in which they are all highly important as auxiliaries; but none of them, nor even all of them combined, furnish the essential element of the blessing which we seek. This is to be found only in the religion of the gospel.

Nothing has so powerful a tendency to refine and strengthen domestic attachments as real religion. The ties of grace are the purest and the strongest on this side of heaven; and where to the bonds of natural affection these are added, they become endearing and precious in the highest degree.

The view which has been taken of this subject suggests a variety of reflections which are worthy of our serious regard.

1. The first reflection is, that all the means which are necessary for securing and extending domestic happiness are equally conducive to individual enjoyment.

2. It is an obvious reflection, from what has been said, that, if we desire to derive all those benefits from religion in our families which it is adapted to produce, it must be constantly kept in view, and made a prominent object in all our domestic affairs.

3. Another reflection suggested by what has been said, and of no small importance, is this: How easy it is for a single unhappy member of a family to destroy its peace!

4. We are led to reflect, from all that has been said, how little reason we have to be surprised that many families, respectable, affluent, and placed under many outward advantages, enjoy so little real happiness. The reasons are various, but any one of them is quite sufficient to account for the fact.

O ye who desire to invite and retain this blessing under your roofs, but have hitherto failed of realizing your desire, try the means which have been suggested. Fairly, and in good faith, make the experiment.

The Humiliation of Christ.

By Rev. RUFUS W. BAILEY, South Carolina.

"Therefore, being by the right hand of God exalted, and having received of the Father the promise of the Holy Ghost, He hath shed forth this which ye now see and hear."—Acts ii. 33.

ON the memorable day when this text was uttered, the church experienced a revival of religion. The multitude had listened to Him who spake as never man spake; yet they were unmoved. An eventful stillness had succeeded the eventful scenes of the crucifixion. The disciples were first scattered and perplexed, then assembled with one accord in one place, and engaged in prayer,—"that prayer which opens heaven." So it proved. Eminent displays of God's power soon appeared among the disciples. This was noised abroad, and soon brought together a great multitude, to whom Peter preached the gospel.

Then it was the gospel was attended with "the demonstration of the Spirit and of power." The multitude, who just now mocked, were pricked in the heart, and called on Peter and the other apostles to guide them. The Apostle, in his preaching, ascribes these wonderful displays of power in the physical, intellectual, and moral revolutions there effected, to Jesus of Nazareth, whom the Jews had crucified, but whom the apostles now declared to be the Son of God, the true Messiah, the Maker of worlds, the only hope and Saviour of men. These positions he proved to the Jews by the most unequivocal evidences, drawn from their own scriptures, and finally from His resurrection, of which the apostles themselves, and a great many others, were witnesses.

Much of the plan of redemption is distinctly comprised in this single sentence. We are led to consider in this text the *humiliation* of Christ, His *exaltation*, and the *Trinity employed* in the work of man's salvation.

The humiliation of Christ, distinctly set forth in the discourse of Peter, is more than implied in the text itself; for when it is said, He is exalted, we cannot comprehend the term except as we contrast it with humiliation, or a state inferior to that He now is declared to occupy.

The humiliation of Christ, which we propose to consider in this discourse, may be embraced under three inquiries.

I. *What was the humiliation of Christ?*

Not the act of humiliation which becomes the sinner; for He

knew no sin, and therefore could never have the sense of guilt, which prompts to humility. But it was a descent from greatness, a stooping from dignity, which may consist with the greatest purity, as it is often the exhibition of the most disinterested benevolence.

From what, then, did the Saviour stoop? Here we are brought directly to inquire what He was. On this point it is not now my design to multiply all possible proof, but merely to assert the supreme claims of Christ to Divine honour, in order to illustrate another point—the humiliation of Christ in executing His office of Mediator. It is this Being, thus exalted, and clothed with supreme majesty, "who was found in fashion as a man, and took upon Him the form of a servant, and became obedient unto death, even the death of the cross." But it is impossible for us to see what Christ has done, until we have a correct view of His character. We can never perceive His true humiliation, until we measure the distance He has stooped. On the cross, where Jesus of Nazareth was nailed, and poured out His lifeblood, we behold the Maker of worlds, the Sovereign of the universe, the Former of our bodies, the Author of our spirits. Do you know of any deeper humiliation than this? Can you conceive of any greater disparity of circumstances? Here is a place to which we should tread softly and frequently.

II. *What was the object of this humiliation?*

When God had made the world, and fitted it up for the accommodation of man, He created a holy race to inhabit it. They abused His mercies, lost their love for their Benefactor, and wandered away from Him. It is after this rebel race that Christ is reaching. He came from heaven to seek and save the lost. To effect our salvation, it was necessary the penalty of the law should be met; and to remove this difficulty in the way of pardon, the Saviour consented to receive the expression of Divine wrath upon Himself. His humiliation was necessary to the work He undertook, and the object was accomplished in His sufferings and death.

III. *The influence of this humiliation, therefore, or the effect of it is,—*

1. The removal of all insuperable objections to the sinner's salvation.

2. The exhibition of the Divine attributes in a manner and to a degree they would never otherwise have been seen.

3. The humiliation of Christ furnishes a subject peculiarly calculated to affect and soften the heart.

4. In the humiliation of Christ, God's hatred of sin is eminently displayed.

5. In this event, God has shown His exceeding great love to man.

6. In the humiliation of Christ, we have an example for imitation.

7. The effect of Christ's humiliation is to deepen our impression of the grace of God.

Come then, my soul, here take thy privileged and chosen seat; here employ all thy contemplations,—here rest that weary anxiety, which seeks in vain for peace and hope in sin. Come, sinners, from the various pursuits and perplexities of life, sit together at the feet of Jesus, and learn of Him. Contemplate Christ crucified, Christ the mighty God, the equal Son, and crucified to save us from wrath.

The Exaltation of Christ.

By Rev. RUFUS W. BAILEY.

"Therefore, being at the right hand of God exalted," &c.—Acts ii. 33.

THE exaltation of Jesus in His Mediatorial character was the necessary result of His humiliation. He had assumed our nature, been tempted in all points like as we are, felt our infirmities, suffered an ignominious death on the cross, and had risen from the tomb. After this, and while surrounded by a multitude of His disciples, he was parted from them, and received up into heaven.

To those who conversed with Him after His resurrection, and who were now the eye-witnesses of His ascension, the evidence of His Divinity was complete. But it is the design of the Saviour that the testimony of competent witnesses to this fact shall be confirmed by standing evidences of His presence and power through every age of the church. In accordance with His promise, and in the execution of His purposes of grace, He sent the Spirit in the work of conversion soon after His ascension. And while the multitude were under the influence of the Divine visitation, Peter boldly preaches Christ crucified, demonstrates to the Jews from their own scriptures that He was the Messiah, appeals for further confirmation to His miracles wrought in their presence, certifies to His resurrection and ascension, and adduces the obvious manifestations of Divine influence at that time on the multitude as a standing testimony of His presence and power. "Therefore," he says, "being at the right hand of God exalted, and having received of the Father the promise of the Holy Ghost, He shed forth this, which ye now see and hear."

The divinity of Jesus, proved in His humiliation, is demonstrated also in His exaltation. For we may consider Him exalted,—

I. *In the place He now occupies.*

He was united in glory with the Father before the world was. This glory was beheld in Him while on earth, full of grace and truth. He was received up into glory when He ascended, exalted above men, being appointed Head of the church and Heir of all things,—above angels, as it is written, "far above all principality, and power, and might, and dominion, and every name that is named, not only in this world, but also in that which is to come, made so much better than the angels as He hath by inheritance obtained a more excellent name than they," where He will continue to be, preparing for the reception of the saints, until He shall come again to judge the world ; for all judgment is committed into His hands. Christ exalted as the Sovereign of the universe, the Creator, Preserver, and Judge of all; original, underived, omnipotent, independent ; who supports the pillars of the universe, and can safely keep whatever is committed to His hands. He is exalted as a Saviour, having accomplished the redemption of sinners.

II. *Christ as a Mediator is exalted in His own moral perfections, illustrated in the plan of redemption.*

These perfections are inherent, and depend not for their existence and excellence on anything that has been, or can be done. But in the plan of redemption, circumstances were furnished for their public and eminent display. They shone through the man Christ Jesus, and illuminated His character in the days of His flesh. They furnished an example in practice, and inspired a code in morals, such as philosophy has exhausted its powers in vain to create. Exalted to His seat in heaven, He sheds His glory through all the place, and enkindles in all His worshippers a flame of love, admiration, and joy. And having received gifts for men, He diffuses through this dark world the light and grace, which roll a flood of dazzling glory through heaven and eternity.

That which gave offence on earth will constitute the glory of the Saviour in heaven. The purity of His character, and the strictness of His moral law, and the justice and spirituality of His kingdom will there be His glory. It is the holiness of God, which secures the love and homage of all holy beings. Their song is, "Holy, holy, holy is the Lord God of hosts." This is the standard of pre-eminence with the inhabitants of heaven. The holiest being there will be the happiest, and accounted the most worthy.

III. *We contemplate Christ as exalted in the execution of His Mediatorial office, and in the praises of the redeemed.*

By virtue of His atonement He saves sinners; not by works of righteousness which they have done, but by His own grace. And, sensible of their dependence on that grace, their song will always be,—"Not unto us, not unto us, but unto Thy name give glory."

The company of the saved will be a great company, and their habitual employment will be acts of praise and homage to Him, who has redeemed them out of every nation, and washed them in His own blood. The scriptures say this company will be innumerable. Every one, who shall stand and bow there, will be a trophy of victorious grace, saved by Christ. Not one will take any merit to himself, or ascribe any part of the work of his redemption to any but to Jesus of Nazareth. They will constitute, therefore, a standing and shining monument of His benevolence and power. Each was an heir of hell, and all that makes him differ from those, "the smoke of whose torment ascendeth up for ever and ever," he owes to the grace of Christ.

Glorious thought! that Christ is still exalted, and we are under discipline for heaven. Yes, He is still at the right hand of God, exalted to be a Prince and a Saviour. Still it may be repeated, He has "received of the Father the gift of the Holy Ghost."

Thanks be to God, we may still add, "He has shed forth that which ye have seen and heard."

From the wide field of instruction furnished by this subject, two or three reflections deserve particular consideration.

1. How humble ought Christians to be, under a sense of their dependence, and with the example of Christ, their great Master, before them!

2. We see the safety and dignity of those who trust in Christ. He is exalted. "He is able to save to the uttermost *all* that come unto God through Him, seeing that He ever liveth to make intercession for them." We, then, "have a strong consolation, who have fled for refuge to lay hold of the hope set before us in the gospel." The exaltation of Christ ensures the safety of every believer.

3. There is one other consideration, which I would not fail to suggest. It is the manner in which all that has been said must affect the finally impenitent. When, as impenitent sinners, you stand in judgment, your condemnation will not proceed on the evidence that you have stolen, or lied, or profaned God's holy name, or holy day. These, if they exist, are minor offences. They are all merged in one great, damning sin,—the rejection of an offered Saviour. "This is the condemnation, that *light* has come into the world, and men have loved darkness rather than light."

It becomes my duty, then, again to offer for your acceptance this Saviour from sin, once humbled, now exalted and glorified. To you are the words of this salvation sent. The Saviour, now exalted, condescends to plead with you. Our God is a God of mercy, but not of mercy only. Opening His everlasting Book, I read,—"He whets His glittering sword, and His hand takes hold on vengeance." I see—"dark clouds are His pavilion round about." I hear—it is the voice of mercy still, but of mercy long abused, and the very next accent may be the thunder of that voice which calls you to judgment—oh, "Kiss the Son, lest He be angry with you, and ye perish from the way when His wrath is kindled but a little."

The Trinity employed in Man's Redemption.
By Rev. RUFUS W. BAILEY.

"'Therefore, being by the right hand of God exalted,'" &c.—Acts ii. 33.

MUCH of the plan of redemption, in its executive process, is set forth in this single text, leading us directly to consider,—

I. *In our text the salvation of the sinner is set forth as the work of the Trinity.*

We plainly see that the doctrine of a Trinity in the Godhead is taught in the holy scriptures. Here are the Father, and the Son, and the Holy Ghost, three Persons employed in the work of man's salvation. The Father gives to the Son, and does not receive the gift. The Son receives the gift from the Father, and does not make the gift to the Father. The Son sends the Holy Ghost, and is not sent to Him. The Holy Ghost is sent, or, as our Confession of Faith has it, "proceeds from the Father and the Son," and does not send the Father nor the Son. Can any distinction of persons be more plainly expressed?

Again, when the law as to be repeated to Israel, the Lord said, "Hear, O Israel: the Lord thy God is ONE Lord." And so God is properly, essentially, and absolutely ONE only living and true God, infinite, eternal, and unchangeable, having an existence in a Trinity of persons; mysterious, like all His attributes; co-equal, co-eternal, and essentially the same in all Divine perfections.

When man was originally formed of the dust of the earth, it was the result of Divine counsel in the Trinity,—"And God said, let Us make man." When man had violated the Divine law, and was found wholly destitute of that *love to God* which that law required, his redemption was the result of Divine counsel in the Trinity.

II. *We are to consider more explicitly the part which each person in the sacred Trinity performs in the work of man's redemption.*

The law has been made and prescribed to man by the ONE only living and true God—Father, Son, and Holy Ghost. This law, having been wilfully and wickedly violated, God, as the Maker and Executor of the law, must exact the penalty of temporal and eternal death. If mercy is extended, justice must not be disparaged, nor truth violated, nor the depraved and rebellious heart remain in its enmity and pollution.

Here, then, the Father represents the law, preserving the faithful administration of justice. The Son represents the sinner, meeting in Himself the penalty of the law, and thereby providing for the dispensation of mercy. The Spirit executes a Divine work on the heart of the sinner, which illustrates to his experience the Divine attributes of justice and mercy, and prepares him to receive pardon under a full conviction of utter unworthiness and ruin.

Nor are here conflicting interests. The whole disposition of the Godhead is in favour of the administration of justice, of mercy, and of truth. The Father loves mercy as well as justice, and can never urge the latter to the prejudice of the former. Christ loves justice as well as mercy. The Holy Spirit aids the dispensation of neither at the expense or exclusive of the other. Yet the Father performs a work in the plan separate from the Son, and which the Son does not perform. The Son performs a work which the Father does not perform. The Holy Spirit performs a work separate and different from both. And yet whatever is performed by the Father, or the Son, or the Spirit, is properly or strictly the work of God, harmoniously approved and sanctioned in the Divine mind. Is justice asserted? It is God. Is mercy dispensed? It is God. Is a sinner saved? It is God who does it.

III. *We are now to consider the necessity of this Trinity to the work of man's redemption.*

We should speak with great caution and respect when we undertake to say what God cannot do, or what it is necessary for Him to do. We do not see how this work could be performed without this Divine Trinity. If the claims of the law are to be asserted, who will assert them but God? God must execute His own law. It can be safely intrusted in no other hands. Like its Author, the Divine law is immutable. All else is liable to change, and therefore can furnish no parallel. If an atonement, or satisfaction to that law is to be made, God only can make it. Who else can do it?

Again, if the sinner is to be saved in heaven, it is necessary he should be holy. A work of regeneration must be performed in his heart. Who can do this but He who made the soul, who intimately understands its nature, who can Himself control it, and turn it as the rivers of waters are turned? He only can enter into its secret chambers, analyze it, reveal its secret and hidden lineaments to its own view, control, new-create, and sanctify it. None but God can do this.

Surely to the accomplishment of this plan the Trinity is necessary. All other theories are inadequate, imperfect, and unsafe. They take some part of the work from the hands of God, and commit it to a creature, subject to the direction of fatal imbecility, ignorance, or doubt.

IV. *We have still to contemplate the beauty and harmony of the doctrine.*

Its harmony is exhibited where mercy and truth have met together, and righteousness and peace have embraced each other. Here are clashing interests, but no discord. When eternal ruin hung over the fate of man under the administration of the violated law, this plan of redemption was matured in the council of the Divine Trinity. The Father consented to deliver up the only begotten Son to the operation of the law, a substitute for sinners; the Son consented to yield His life a ransom; and the Holy Spirit became the efficient Agent in illustrating this plan to the minds of sinners,—dark, ignorant, and lost; and in gaining the voluntary consent of these perverse minds to the truth.

The beauty of the doctrine appears principally in its adaptation, and actual efficiency to produce its end, and that end one of the highest glory and benevolence. It saves sinners,—saves them from the curse of the law. We say, then, with the chief Apostle,—" Without controversy, great is the mystery of godliness: God was manifest in the flesh, justified in the Spirit, seen of angels, preached unto the Gentiles, believed on in the world, received up into glory."

The Earth filled with the Glory of the Lord.

By Rev. SAMUEL MILLER, Princeton, N. J.

" And the Lord said, I have pardoned according to thy word: but as truly as I live, all the earth shall be filled with the glory of the Lord." —Numbers xiv. 20, 21.

THE practice of confirming a declaration with an *oath* is of very early origin. And although the multiplication of oaths is a great evil, and the act of taking or administering them with lightness an aggravated sin, yet *they* are, undoubtedly, in great error who maintain that all swearing, even on the most solemn occasions, and on the call of judicial officers, is unlawful. "An oath for confirmation," says an inspired Apostle, "is an end of all strife." Accordingly, in the sacred history, we find many examples of holy men, on various occasions, employing this form of asseveration. But, what is much more decisive still, we find the High and Holy One Himself repeatedly adopting it to confirm both His promises and His threatenings.—Heb. vi. 17, 18.

These words were spoken on a very distressing, and, to the eye of man, a very discouraging occasion. When the twelve men who had been sent into the wilderness of Paran to spy out the land of promise, brought back their report, the mass of the people were almost overwhelmed with alarm and discouragement. Moses, however, interceded for the people in a most touching strain of importunate prayer, and he prevailed. "The Lord said, I have pardoned them according to thy word; but as truly as I live, the earth shall be filled with the glory of the Lord."

In giving the most ample interpretation to the language of our text, we are certain that we do not go beyond the spirit of holy scripture.

I. *The import of the promise before us.*

This import, expressed with so much solemnity of asseveration, is large and precious. "As I live, saith the Lord, all the earth shall be filled with the glory of the Lord." Glory is the manifestation of excellence. The glory of God is that display of His most blessed character and will which opens the way for His intelligent creatures to know, to love, and to obey Him. This glory is exhibited in various ways. It shines in all the works of creation. All the works of God, we are told, praise Him. Again, the glory of God is manifested by the works of His providence. But, above all, is the glory of God displayed in the work of RE-

DEMPTION; in the great plan of love and mercy by a Redeemer, which was first revealed to the parents of our race immediately after the fall; which was more and more unfolded in the ceremonial economy; and which reached its meridian brightness, when the Saviour, the blessed "Sun of Righteousness," rose upon a dark world. In this wonderful plan of salvation, the glory of God shines with its brightest lustre. Here all His perfections unite and harmonize, and shine with transcendant glory. Now, when the gospel, which proclaims this plan of mercy, shall be preached and received throughout the world; when every kindred, and people, and nation, and tongue shall not only be instructed in its sublime doctrines, but also brought under its benign and sanctifying power, then, with emphatic propriety, may it be said that "the earth is filled with the glory of the Lord." As the highest glory of which an individual creature is capable is to bear the image of his Maker, so the highest glory of which our world at large is capable is to be filled with the holy and benevolent Spirit of Him who is the brightness of the Father's glory, and the express image of His person,—is to have the knowledge and love of the Saviour reigning over all the populations of our globe, "from the rising of the sun even unto the going down of the same." Such appears to be the import of the promise before us. Let us next inquire,—

II. *What reason have we for believing that these scenes of glory will one day be realized ?*

First of all, and above all, our hope is founded on Jehovah's faithful and unerring promise. This is, undoubtedly, the chief ground of confidence. Hath He said, and shall He not do it? Hath He spoken, and shall He not make it good ? Jehovah is not a man that He should lie, nor the son of man that He should repent. Heaven and earth shall pass away, but one jot or one tittle of all that has gone out of the mouth of Jehovah shall not pass away until all be fulfilled. Let us attend, then, to some of the promises on this subject with which the word of God abounds. Take the following as a small specimen of the "exceeding great and precious" catalogue found in the inspired volume,—Psalm ii. 8; lxvii. 2; lxxii. 17; Isaiah xl. 5; Hab. ii. 14; Zech. ix. 10; Mal. i. 11; Phil. ii. 10, 11; Rev. xi. 15.

2. But further, our confidence that the religion of Christ will, one day, fill the whole earth with its glory, is confirmed by the consideration, that this religion is, in its nature, adapted above all others to be a universal religion. Its doctrines, its worship, and its system of moral duty are all equally adapted to univer-

sality. It teaches that God has made of one blood all nations of men to dwell on the face of the whole earth.—Acts xvii. 26. That He is no respecter of persons, but that in every nation, he that feareth God and worketh righteousness is accepted of Him. —Acts x. 34, 35. That He is alike related to the children of men, as their Creator, Preserver, and Benefactor; and that the high and the low, the rich and the poor, the monarch and the slave, all stand upon a level in His sight, and have all equal access, if penitent and believing, to the throne of His heavenly grace. Surely this character of our holy religion is adapted to confirm our confidence that it will, one day, as Jehovah has promised, gloriously fill the world; and that, literally, in Christ "all the families of the earth shall be blessed."

3. I have only to add, under this head, that the present aspect of the world furnishes much reason to hope that the accomplishment of this promise is drawing nigh. It cannot be denied, indeed, that, on the principle of worldly calculation, there is much in the present condition of mankind to distress and dishearten. More than seven parts out of eight of the whole population of our globe are still sunk in deplorable darkness and corruption. How many of these professors of religion we may calculate upon as probably real Christians! Ah, that is the question on which the humble, enlightened believer, though he may hesitate and weep, will forbear to attempt an estimate! What a little remnant, among all the multiplied millions of mankind, have any adequate or saving knowledge of the religion of Christ! O what a moral charnel-house does our world appear! What a valley of "dry bones!—exceeding dry!" "Can these bones live?" Yes, they shall live! The mouth of the Lord hath spoken it. And even NOW, amidst the darkness and misery which brood over the greater part of the earth, there are appearances, everywhere, which promise the approach of better days. I know not that there is, at this hour, a single portion of the globe to which the enlightened and prudent missionary may not obtain some degree of access, unless it be some portions which bear the Christian name, but are under the spiritual despotism of "the man of sin, the son of perdition, who exalteth himself against all that is called God." He who "sits as Governor among the nations," seems to be spreading a natural preparation, if I may so express it, around the world, for the preaching of the gospel among all nations. He seems to be slowly and silently laying a train for mighty movements in time to come. He seems to be showing us how easy it is for Him to incline the hearts even of His enemies—from worldly motives—not merely to permit the gospel to enter their territories, but to invite its ministers to come in

and proclaim their message. Never before was so large a portion of mankind accessible to the evangelical labourer.

Contemplate, further, the singular progress of various forms of improvement throughout the civilized world, all of which may be considered as bearing on the great promise contained in the the text. Behold the intercourse between distant parts of the globe increasing every day with a rapidity, and to an extent beyond all former precedent! Think of the endless improvements in the means of conveyance from one part of the world to another. Consider the wonderful improvements in the art of printing. And, to me, it appears worthy of special notice, that there are so many indications that the English language,—the language of those parts of the world which are most favoured with gospel light,—will probably, ere long, become the prevailing language of the whole world.

III. *What is our present duty in relation to the promise before us?*

1. Undoubtedly our first duty is to believe the promise. This is the very least that can be demanded. Unbelief "makes God a liar," poisons the very fountain of Christian confidence, cuts the nerves of all spiritual exertion, and tends to discouragement and despondency.

2. Another duty incumbent upon us, in relation to this promise, is to labour and pray without ceasing for its accomplishment. They are undoubtedly guilty of an unwise and criminal perversion of God's word who infer, because He has promised a specific and rich blessing, and will certainly bring it to pass, that therefore they may repose in a state of entire inaction and unconcern respecting the event. There is no piety, my friends, in that confidence which neglects prayer, and which does not add to prayer diligent effort to attain that for which it prays. Show me thy faith by thy works, is a maxim equally of reason and revelation. God's kingdom is a kingdom of means.

3. A third duty, in relation to the promise in our text, is, that in labouring for the spread of the gospel, no adverse occurrence, however painful, ought to discourage us, or at all to weaken either our confidence or our efforts. With that promise, we may meet the most distressing difficulties without fear. When Stephen, the first martyr, was stoned to death by an infuriated mob, to whom he came with a message of love, "devout men," we are told, "carried him to his burial, and made great lamentation over him." But, mark the event! The persecution, though not so intended by the persecutors, became the means of sending many ministers of the gospel away from Jerusalem, in vari-

ous directions, and thus of extending and building up the church of God, instead of effecting its destruction, as the malignant adversary had confidently expected.

4. A further duty, in reference to the promise before us, is, that we pray without ceasing for the power of the Holy Spirit, to render all the means which are employed for its accomplishment effectual. When we recollect the extent and difficulty of the work to be done, how many millions are yet in darkness and misery, how hard and full of enmity the human heart, and how obstinately the warnings and entreaties of mercy have been resisted, we may well despair of human wisdom and strength, and look to Almighty power for success. It is not by might nor by power, but by my Spirit, saith Jehovah, that means are attended with a saving energy.

5. If so great a work as evangelizing the whole world is promised, and is certainly to be accomplished, then our plans and efforts for promoting this object ought to bear a corresponding character; that is, they ought to be large, liberal, and ever expanding. We ought to consider it as our duty to devote to this object our utmost resources, and to engage the co-operation of all, over whom we exert an influence.

Let us, then, with one accord, rouse ourselves, and endeavour to rouse others to new zeal, and larger enterprise, in spreading the knowledge and glory of the Lord. Every heart, every tongue, and every hand that can be stirred up to engage in this great work, from infancy to old age, is needed. And remember, that the more thoroughly any of the children of men can be excited and consecrated to this work, the richer the benefit they gain for themselves.

The Importance and Means of an able Ministry.

By Rev. BAXTER DICKINSON.

"A workman that needeth not to be ashamed."—2 Tim. ii. 15.

THE public ministry of religion is of Divine appointment. Is has always been God's leading instrumentality in maintaining the cause of truth, piety, and salvation, and it is to endure "to the end of the world." In the arrangements of Christ for setting up His kingdom on earth, this institution is very prominent. He selected the men, trained them under His own eye, sent them forth to preach, and gave them instructions for perpetuating the holy order.

A characteristic, first in importance, beyond question, is decided godliness. For the absence of this, nothing can atone. Scripture demands it. The nature of the office demands it. The Christian teacher should have the fruits of the Spirit in strong, vivid, and prominent exercise. He must be "a man of God ; full of faith, and of the Holy Ghost—rooted and grounded in love."

But while this is indispensable, other qualifications are also essential. The Head of the Church would have an *energetic*, as well as honest and devoted ministry. And hence the necessity of looking to its intellectual, as well as religious character. It is obvious there are many causes now tending strongly to lower the ministerial character, and thus to abridge its influence and usefulness. These I need not even name. They are, most of them, alas, too familiar. The danger will be obviated, if the church but duly respect herself and the honour of her King, and thus, with proper feeling, insist on the qualifications which God Himself requires in her pastors. It cannot, then, be amiss, at such a time, and on such an occasion, to dwell on—

I. *The importance of an able ministry.*

1. That such a ministry was designed of God for men, is clearly manifest from scripture precept. "The priest's lips should keep knowledge, and they should seek the law at his mouth." "Till I come, give attendance to reading." "Neglect not the gift that is in thee." "Meditate upon these things." "Study to show thyself approved unto God, a workman that needeth not to be ashamed."

2. From the express provision God has made for training and supporting it.

3. All the most important movements of the church have taken place under the instrumentality of able men.—[Instance

Moses, Aaron, Paul, Luther, Calvin, Wesley, Whitfield, and Edwards.]

4. A ministry of vigorous character is to be expected from the language of prophecy relative to the glory of the latter day.

5. From the strength and number of the forces to be encountered and overcome.

6. A ministry of strength is manifestly called for by the grandeur and importance of the objects to be gained.

7. The all-absorbing and imposing character of worldly objects and improvements calls loudly for an efficient ministry,—such a ministry as, in the name and power of God, may arrest attention, and turn off the eye from beholding vanity. We live at a period of great enterprise, and in a land affording scope for bold experiment in every direction. At such a crisis, what but new energy in Zion's watchmen is to save her and her children from being ingulfed in that general tide of worldliness, which threatens to drown millions in perdition?

The ministry is also a profession, and needs for its success the respect and confidence of the community. But to secure these, it must have an elevated intellectual character. It must keep pace with the general progress of society.

8. A ministry of great strength is called for by the prospect of unwonted excitements in the civil and religious world. A moment's view of the world will, at once, reveal to the eye abundant occasions for excitement. They are seen in the organizations of civil society. They are seen in the conflicting systems of religion. They are seen in the spreading sway of infidelity, superstition, and lawless violence. Before men can universally be brought to concede to each other their rights, and to God His dominion, immense changes, of an exciting character, must obviously take place.

At such a crisis, we need, for Zion's sake, a ministry of unwonted wisdom, foresight, and power. We need, in the holy office, men who can stand amid high excitement, without being thrown off their balance,—men who can look at the raging tempest with a calm and courageous heart. We need men enlightened into all truth and duty,—men of enlarged and liberal views, as well as of inflexible integrity and firmness. We need a ministry above all selfish considerations and party bickerings; that can keep its eye and hand steadily upon the "ark of God," come what may. Which suggests one other consideration, viz.:

9. This elevation of character in the ministry will contribute to union among all the truly faithful. And who that looks over our Zion, with anything like an angel's love, or an angel's pity, must not desire such a result?—"that they all may be one."

This is indeed practicable; for the Saviour has enjoined it, and fervently prayed for it.

With these views of the importance of an able ministry, we are very naturally excited to inquire,—

II. *By what means may such a ministry be secured to the church and the world?*

1. Candidates for the holy office must set for themselves a very high standard of ministerial character. They must settle it as a first principle, that qualifications enter into every call to preach the gospel,—that "no man taketh this honour unto himself, but he that is called of God, as was Aaron,"—a name signifying a mountain of strength.

2. To select the most promising spirits, even in childhood, and train them in faith and prayer, with the hope and trust that God will call them to the office. Let, then, the hearts of pious fathers be turned anew to their children; and let the devout mother regard her most promising son as peculiarly God's property. And let those who have no such bright offspring, without grudging, or envy, or partiality, adopt the most suitable objects of intellectual training for God. Let them go and select from the Sabbath school, or the obscurest hamlet. Let them place the child of genius and promise under a pious and able instructor, and follow him daily with their prayers, and with full faith that God will sanctify the offering for Christ and His church.

3. To select proper locations for theological study.

4. Competent pecuniary support.

5. For securing such a ministry as is demanded by the age, let there be cherished a spirit of humble, fervent, believing prayer. If the church has ministers of a proper character, she will receive them from God. His promise is, "I will give you pastors after mine own heart." "He gives some, evangelists; and some, prophets; and some, pastors and teachers." In all the efforts of the church, then, to increase the number and strength of the ministry, let her remember that "promotion cometh not from the east, nor from the west, nor from the south,"—that "except the Lord build the house, they labour in vain that build it."

Sure Means of Spiritual Prosperity.
By Rev. BAXTER DICKINSON.

"And now, brethren, I commend you to God, and to the word of His grace, which is able to build you up, and to give you an inheritance among all them which are sanctified."—ACTS xx. 32.

THE Apostle Paul, when he uttered this benediction, was at Miletus, a town on the western coast of Asia. He had planted many churches in different parts of Europe, and particularly in the Grecian states; and he was now on his way to Jerusalem, from which he had been absent a number of years. Arrived at Miletus, he sent for the elders of the church of Ephesus—a church not far distant,—on which he had bestowed much labour and concern, and for which he still cherished a strong affection. The elders came at his invitation, and the interview was one of great interest. The Apostle could stop but a short time, for he must, if possible, be at Jerusalem at the feast of Pentecost. He availed himself of the occasion, in reviewing his labours among them, glancing at his prospects, and giving suitable counsel and exhortation. In this connection he uttered the benediction before us, closed with prayer, and departed amid the cordial salutations and tears of the brethren, who all accompanied him to the ship.

Coming before you for the last time as your minister, I have been led by my feelings to adopt this parting benediction as the theme of discourse:—"And now, brethren, I commend you to God, and to the word of His grace, which is able to build you up, and to give you an inheritance among all them which are sanctified."

I proceed, as proposed, to some suggestions with reference to your future prosperity.

I. *You cannot too soon have a stated, evangelical, and devoted ministry.*

II. *Another thing important to your welfare, is a spirit of uniform and elevated piety in the church.*

III. *You will need also a temper of mutual concession and forbearance.*

IV. *Let me urge a steady and zealous regard for the religious improvement of the young.*

V. *Let me urge a generous support of the benevolent movements of the age.*

VI. *Let me urge you to cultivate, habitually, the spirit of prayer.*

With this brief review of our connection, and this notice of a few things deemed specially important to your spiritual welfare, I now leave you. Ye, brethren, are peculiarly our joy and our crown. Be ye steadfast, unmoveable, always abounding in the work of the Lord. Forgetting the things which are behind, reach forth to those which are before.

But it is matter of pain and grief that, in closing this ministry, I see many still far from righteousness,—without God and without hope. As respects your salvation, my humble efforts seem to have been all in vain. Possibly they have proved only a savour of death unto death. Some of you have, at times, been alive to your guilt and ruin, and earnestly resolved to seek salvation. But your goodness was like the morning cloud and the early dew,—soon passing away. Others of you have, from month to month, and year to year, been but little, if any, affected by the gospel. Ah! dying fellow-sinners! give heed for this once, I entreat you, to the parting voice of your friend. Begin this day the great work of salvation. Engage in it with your whole heart and soul. It is not a vain thing for you, because it is your life. I tremble, I shudder, to think of the bearing this ministry may have had on your immortal destiny! Spare me—O spare yourselves the anguish of an eternal separation!

My eye instinctively glances forward to that great day, when, with assembled worlds, we shall all meet again. Live, live, my immortal and beloved hearers, in steady prospect of that day! Live for God, for a dying world, for heaven, for eternity! FAREWELL!

The Sinner's Desperate Depravity.

By Rev. DANIEL A. CLARK, New York.

"Behold, thou hast spoken and done evil things as thou couldest."—Jer. iii. 5.

THIS passage evidently teaches the doctrine, that men are as depraved as they can be in present circumstances. The charge is made by the infinitely Holy One, and can be fully substantiated against every member of the unregenerate family. The justice of the charge may appear from a consideration of the following positions,—

I. *That God, in His providence, has surrounded the sinner with many circumstances operating powerfully to modify human character.*

Among the circumstances which illustrate the position, I mention,—

1. Education.
2. Human law has a similar effect.
3. The law of God.
4. The troublesome supervision of conscience has greatly modified human character.
5. The whole gospel, the law drawn out into offensive interference with the sinful pleasures and follies of men, has modified human character beyond all calculation.
6. All the gospel institutions.
7. The desire of heaven has the same effect.
8. The fear of hell, also, holds back many from the commission of crime.
9. The expectation of a judgment has the same effect.
10. Public sentiment is a great preventive of crime.
11. The domestic affections produce the same result.

Thus we have recounted some of the circumstances which modify the human character. These are, indeed, of vast importance. They result in what we term civility, good morals, &c., all bearing kindly upon the present condition of man. They all speak the wisdom and kindness of God,—they are so many golden chains let down to earth, to modify its moral corruptions. We ought, then, to thank God for these modifying circumstances, and pray that He would put these chains all on, and keep them on, till even the vilest and most obdurate shall yield to His infinite love. We ought to view men in more hopeful circumstances, in proportion as God shall hold them by these moral bonds. For, while a young man respects the Sabbath, and is obedient to his parents, there is more hope of him than afterwards. While he is afraid to swear, we may hope that he will begin to pray. While he dare not avow open infidelity, we may hope, if we do our duty, that he will yet believe revealed truth to the saving of his soul.

II. *By these circumstances every sinner is actually restrained in his wickedness, and held back in his downward career. In proof of which we observe,*—

1. Men are uneasy under these circumstances, which shows them to be restraints.
2. Men are constantly trying to alter their circumstances.
3. When men at length alter their circumstances in any of these respects, they often show out a worse character.
4. When these restraints are all removed, men are uniformly far more wicked than if they had not been imposed.

III. *That every sinner does make the attempt, and succeeds as far as God will let him, to sunder these ligatures that would hold him fast to reason, hope, and heaven.*

Let us trace his steps, and see his ravings.
1. See how he breaks over and breaks through the restraints of education.
2. Human laws.
3. The law of God.
4. Supervision of conscience.
5. The institutions of the gospel.
6. From all thoughts of heaven or fear of hell.
7. Through all the restraints of public sentiment.
8. And the domestic affections.

If in nothing else, he has shown a character bad as language can describe, or actions prove; he has given a climax of the whole in his attempts to sunder all such ties, and cut himself lose from God, and from the whole family of kindly influences that would save his soul from death.

Such is the obstinacy, the rebelliousness, the ingratitude of the sinner. Must he not, then, be born again—have a new heart and a new spirit—or never enter into the kingdom of God?

Perdition Dreadful.

By Rev. WILLIAM T. HAMILTON, Mobile, Alabama.

"Gather not my soul with sinners."—Psalm. xxvi. 9.

THE sacred Scriptures make known to us not only the certainty of a future state, not only that it will be a state of final retribution to the good and the evil respectively, but also, that at death we enter forthwith on these rewards. In the New Testament, this point is placed beyond the reach of doubt; for, to the dying thief our Lord declared, "This day shalt thou be with me in paradise." And Paul says, "I desire to depart, and to be with Christ, which is far better." And in another place, we read of those who now, "through faith and patience, inherit the promises." Neither was this great truth kept hid from the Old Testament church, is as plain from the translation of Enoch and of Elijah, without seing death, and from the phraseology sometimes employed by the sacred penmen of the Old Testament, when recording the death of good men. Thus it is said, "Abraham gave up the ghost, and died in a good old age, an old man and full of years, and was gathered to his people."

This interpretation appears the more probable, from the manner in which the Old Testament writers speak of the wicked at their death. Thus we read, Job xxvii. 19, "The rich man shall lie down, but he shall not be gathered." And, in view of the obduracy of the Jews, Isaiah writes, "Though Israel be not gathered, yet shall I be glorious in the eyes of the Lord." From all which it is apparent, that to saints in the Jewish church it was made known that at death, each one, approved of God, should join the society of the blessed; while from the privilege the wicked should be debarred.

The passage before us, moreover, intimates that at

their death, the wicked will be associated together. "Gather not my soul with sinners." This prayer expresses the utmost earnestness of desire for separation from the wicked, and for exemption from their portion after death. Why, then, is fellowship with the wicked after death so greatly to be deprecated? It is so,—

I. *Because they will constitute a community exclusively evil, in which not one holy, or virtuous, or good being will be found.*

The designation applicable to them all, without exception, is *sinners*. In one vast assemblage will be convened all the wicked, all the abominable, and the vile, that have ever lived upon the face of the earth.

To the truly pious mind, associations, even for a short period, with the abandoned and the wicked, is productive of exquisite pain, in hearing their blasphemies, witnessing their violence, their clamour, and their excesses. Nay, to any person of common sensibility, it must be a very painful necessity that compels a temporary companionship with the grossly wicked, giving way to their vicious propensities, their boisterous passions, and their debasing appetites. What individual here, but would feel it to be one of the severest of punishments to be compelled to pass a month in no society, night or day, other than that of the inmates of a penitentiary; to hear their blasphemies and their ribaldry, their filthy witticisms, malicious raillery, empty and polluted conversation; to witness continually their low cunning, and to endure their loathsome familiarity? What, then, must it be to pass a life so degraded, so heart-sickening?

Were the devout and the godly all withdrawn, the sanctuary closed, and the voice of the preacher heard no more, vice would reign triumphant over the land; and our lovely villages, and flourishing towns, would speedily exhibit only a counterpart of the wretched cities long since merged in the depths of the Dead Sea. How appalling, then, must be the prospect of being entirely secluded from the good, associated with none but the wicked, and with all the wicked of every class and degree of turpitude, and with the father of lies, and with his fiendish hosts, in one horrid community! If such be their prospect, who will not exclaim with the Psalmist, "Gather not my soul with sinners." But consider,—

II. *Not only will the society be composed wholly of the*

wicked, but their evil passions, uncontrolled, will be the source of constant wretchedness.

All experience shows that tastes long fostered, habits long indulged, become fixed, and exert a powerful influence over the whole man, even against his better judgment and his sober wishes. What is there to warrant the idea that propensities cherished and obeyed through life, will be lost in death? What authorizes the expectation that the soul, merely by a separation from the organ of its communication with the material universe, will lose its peculiar and distinctive characteristics? The mechanic, or the artist, is a mechanic or an artist still, when he has laid aside his tools; he has the same knowledge of his art, the same love for its exercise. In like manner, the soul must be the same still; as ambitious, or irritable, or proud, or selfish, when it has laid aside the body (which is only the soul's instrument for acting on material objects) as before. The wicked, therefore, will carry their evil passions still in their bosoms, to the world of spirits; and, if so, they bear with them eternal fires of wretchedness to consume them.

What an amount of misery is sometimes inflicted on a large and amiable family by a single vice of one member! What would be the condition of that family, of which each member should be the slave of some one odious propensity, and all clashing, in their pursuits one with another? It would be wretchedness intolerable! What mind, then, can conceive the depth of misery that must pervade a vast community, of which each member is vicious,—a slave to vile, ungovernable passion; where generosity, kindness, forbearance, and moderation are wholly unknown; where selfishness reigns uncontrolled in every heart; where each one is stung with fierce passions, and intent on his own gratification, regardless of all around him; whom he hates and despises, and by whom, as he is well aware, he is himself as heartily despised and hated. Is this the fellowship of the lost? Then "gather not my soul with sinners."

III. *They lie under the curse of Almighty God.*

God is the great fountain of light, and joy, and gladness, to the intelligent universe. 'Tis His smile that lights the sun, and gilds the landscape with beauty. 'Tis this that sends the sweet thrill of joy through the bosom of youth, alleviates the toils of manhood, kindles the fire of domestic comfort and domestic love, and soothes the cares and alleviates the sorrows of declining age. If God frown upon us, the heavens are hung with blackness, the earth sickens, vegetation languishes, business fails, labour is fruitless, commerce decays, and pestilence and death desolate the abodes of men. 'Tis God's smile that fills the heart of the contrite with peace, renders the sanctuary a banqueting hall to the soul, pours a flood of transporting radiance into the Christian's closet, nerves him to successful combat with spiritual foes, gives him strength to walk steadfast in the narrow way, dispels even the darkness of death's gloomy vale, and opens to the view of the dying saint the glories of the heavenly inheritance.

But where sinners are gathered, the favour of God never beams. They are left to the wretchedness of their own vices, unmitigated by one smile from God, unsoftened by one token of His favour or of His pity. Not only so: they are not merely deprived of His favour,—they are not merely left to the uncontrolled dominion of their cruel and tormenting passions,—but they are made to feel the weight of His positive anger, the bitterness of His tremendous curse. It is, I admit, a distressing and overwhelming reflection, but the scriptures distinctly present it before us, and represent the doom of the wicked by the most appalling imagery. They are consigned to a fiery lake, prepared, originally, for the devil and his angels. They are cast into outer darkness, tormented in flames, without the possibility of obtaining the least mitigation of their sufferings, which extort from them incessant weeping, and wailing, and gnashing of teeth: while the worm that never dies ceases not its gnawings within!

Wrath—how intolerable! To be cast where all that is loathsome and repulsive in character shall surround you; where fierce passions shall rage in a continual tempest within; where the hand of the Almighty shall kindle fiery torments within you; where your breath shall be blasphemy, your drink tears, your only music groans and lamentations! Shall any of us sink under this tremendous curse? God, in mercy, forbid it! "Gather," oh, "gather not my soul with sinners!" be the earnest cry of each of us.

IV. *To aggravate the curse, memory will still live, and conscience never fail to perform her dread office.*

We are, indeed, fearfully and wonderfully made; and not more so in our corporeal frame, than in our intellectual and moral conformation. How important, for instance, is the single faculty of memory. Without it, accountability were out of the question, punishment and reward alike impossible. Let a man be entirely deprived of memory, and he becomes conscious only of the sensations of the present moment; the past and the future are to him equally a blank. For how should he, who retains no recollection of the past, either pleasant or painful, know what to-day may yield pleasure or inflict pain ? How, then, shall he plan for the one, or guard against the other ? What idea could such a person form of punishment or of reward ? Place such a being in heaven, and after millions of ages spent there, he would be no happier than at the moment of his admission ! Thrust him down to hell, and he at once tastes the sum of his misery in the first pang; with its endurance, it is for ever buried in oblivion. The past is forgotten, and is no more; the future is unseen, unanticipated, and is not. In the passing instant his consciousness and his very being are wholly concentrated. Take away memory, and, it is plain, conscience expires with it, and remorse becomes impossible.

But, memory we have, and memory we shall for ever retain.

1. This is plain from the nature of the case: memory is an original faculty, inherent in the mind, and indestructible as the mind itself.

2. It is plain from the charge urged home by the Judge of all the earth, on the consciences of the wicked arraigned at His bar,—" I was an hungered, and ye gave me no meat : I was sick, and in prison, and ye visited me not."—(See the close of Matthew, chapter 25.)

3. It is plain from the conversation between the father of the faithful and the rich man tormented in hell,—" Son, remember that thou in thy lifetime receivedst thy good things, and likewise Lazarus evil things."—(See Luke, chapter 16.)

Could the condemned outcast but believe himself blameless ; could he only believe his punishments heavier than his desert, it would surround him as with a panoply, and shield him from the fierceness of Divine wrath. But this it is that fans the fires of hell, and pierces with ten thousand barbs the sufferer's panting heart,—he knows he is reaping but the just reward of his doings. Heaven's glories beheld in the distance, and the echo of celestial hosannahs heard in hell's dark caverns, shall only rouse conscience to proclaim,—" Atoning blood flowed for us too ; a heavenly portion was offered to us too, but we spurned it for the momentary pleasures of sin." All hell quakes at the confusion ! its fiery billows rise, and roll, and rage, and break upon the ear,—" Ye knew your duty, but ye did it not." And quivering lips and hollow groans reply,—" We knew our duty, but we did it not. Our doom is just." The terrors of a guilty conscience who can bear ! Merciful God, " gather not my soul with sinners ! "

V. *They know their doom is unalterably fixed; escape, relief, change, and death, are alike hopeless.*

On this subject reason utterly fails, analogy can furnish no clue to guide, and collected wisdom of all created beings were incompetent to decide what should be the duration of punishment inflicted on incorrigible rebels against heavenly majesty,—on the daring despisers of God's offered mercy. But this impenetrable mystery the Infinite Mind has vouchsafed to clear up. The compassionate Saviour Himself has said,—"The wicked shall go away into everlasting punishment; into hell, where their worm dieth not, and the fire is not quenched."

Appalling though the prospect be,—inscrutable though the reasons be that render such a decision necessary,—to doubt it were folly, and to deny it worse than madness, since the Son of God asserts it. This it is that forms the crowning point in the wretchedness of the damned,—their woes shall never end! Those fires will never die out; that worm will never cease its gnawings; that frame—lacerated in every fibre, quivering in every muscle, and bleeding with anguish at every pore, will never sink exhausted. Respite there is none, relief none, change is hopeless, escape impossible, and death—oh! 'tis a living death; the soul grappling in one eternal struggle with the monster death,—bleeding in intensity of agony from his envenomed darts,—is ever fainting, ever dying—but never, never, *never dead!* Were annihilation possible after countless ages had rolled away, the gloomy anticipation might yield some relief—lend some support to the soul against its tide of sorrows; but annihilation is hopeless—it is impossible; for God has pronounced the curse eternal. His breath fans the fire—His almighty arms sustain the sufferer to endure it. Eternity!—an eternity of wretchedness!—how unspeakably awful! Such an eternity, so filled up with suffering, awaits the impenitent. What, oh, what then shall it profit me, if I gain the whole world,—its highest honours, its finest treasures, its richest enjoyments,—and then lose my soul! God of mercy, "gather not my soul with sinners!"

From the pit, whose horrors we have been contemplating, there comes up the voice of admonition. Ten thousand groans commingle in the sound; ten thousand sighs waft it to our ears —he who is living in sin, impenitent, unsanctified, is fitting for a place in this horrid society. Remember, He who has said drunkards, and liars, and the unclean, shall not inherit the kingdom of God, has testified also,—"He that believeth not shall be damned."

Dying sinner! "behold the Lamb of God,"—the bleeding

Saviour. Forsake the paths of folly, break off your sins by repentance, and surrender your whole heart to Jesus Christ, who is mighty to save. Believe on Him. That faith will purify your heart; and the entire change it effects in your character, and your emotions, will give assurance of acceptance, while you pray, "Gather not my soul with sinners." Amen.

The Example of Christ in Self-denial.
By Rev. IRA TRACY.

"Let this mind be in you, which was also in Christ Jesus."—PHIL. ii. 5.

IN the example of Christ we have a perfect pattern for our imitation; a pattern which we are bound to imitate in all cases where our situation is like His. Let us, then, for a few moments, look at—

I. *What He did for the benefit of sinners.*

1. He left the honours and enjoyments of heaven. He was King of kings, and Lord of lords.

2. He endured the company of the degraded and wicked.

3. His labours were incessant and painful. He went about doing good.

4. He came among those by whom He knew He should be despised and rejected. Take the history of His life on earth, and observe the treatment He received, and received, let us remember, for the good of others. See the Saviour of the world cradled in a manger, because the inn was occupied by those considered more honourable! Hear the proud Pharisee saying,—"Behold a man gluttonous, and a wine-bibber, a friend of publicans and sinners." See Him before the Jewish Sanhedrim. They all condemn Him to be guilty of death. They then begin to "spit in His face, and to buffet Him." Others cover His face and smite Him with the palms of their hands, and contemptuously ask, "Who is he that smote thee?" See Him next led away to stand, like a felon, before the Pagan governor. Here again listen to the slanderous accusations against Him; and hear the infuriated cry,—"Away with Him! away with Him! Crucify Him! crucify Him!" And by whom was He thus depised, rejected! It was by those whom He most tenderly loved. He saw His enemies,—the enemies of God,—degraded and perishing

in sin, and His pity was moved. For our sake He could bear to be crowned with thorns, and spit upon, and called a vile imposter.

5. He bore our sins in the garden and upon the cross. The self-denial, the condescension, the insults of which I have spoken are as nothing, when compared with the sufferings of Gethsemane and Golgotha. It was in the garden that he began to drink of the bitter cup,—the wrath of God against sin. See Him retiring with the three disciples, and beginning "to be sore amazed, and to be very heavy." His soul is exceeding sorrowful, even unto death. He lifts up His voice in prayer,—"Father, if it be possible, let this cup pass from me;" but the burden is not removed. Again and again He pleads, and no relief is granted; nor can there be, without the loss of a world. But the salvation of the world is an object so dear to the Sufferer, that He will not relinquish it. The rage of hell and the frowns of heaven can be borne, rather than we should be left to perish! All this, however, is but the beginning of His sorrows. An ignominious death, and the entire desertion of His Father's countenance are yet to be endured. "They took Jesus and led Him away. And He, bearing His cross, went forth. And when they were come to the place which is called Calvary, there they crucified Him. And at the ninth hour, Jesus cried with a loud voice, saying, 'My God, my God, why hast thou forsaken me?' And He bowed His head, and gave up the ghost."

Such are some of the self-denials and sufferings to which Christ submitted for the good of others. Keeping this example in view, and remembering that, if the same mind be in us which was also in Him, we shall do as He did, so far as our condition permits.

II. *In what respects our situation, in relation to a world of sinners, is like that of Christ.*

1. As Christ saw mankind perishing and without a Saviour, so we see millions of our fellow-men in the same condition—perishing, and without a Saviour.

2. As Christ knew that the salvation of the world depended upon Himself, so we know that the salvation of the heathen depends, under God, upon us who have the gospel.

3. As Christ could not effect the salvation of the world without self-denial, so we cannot save the heathen without it.

4. As Christ knew that His labours and sufferings would not be in vain, so we know that if we, with the same spirit of obedience to God and benevolence to men, deny ourselves, and

give the gospel to the heathen, it will be the means of their salvation.

5. As Christ saw a sufficient reward in the joy set before Him, so we shall be abundantly rewarded for all our efforts in this cause when we come to see the fruit of our labours in heaven.

If, then, "the same mind be in us which was also in Christ Jesus," we shall make the greatest possible efforts for the salvation of the world.

The Love of Home: its Influence on Religion and Character.

By Rev. AMOS BLANCHARD, Meriden, N. H.

"Wouldest thou be spoken for to the king, or to the captain of the host? And she answered, I dwell among mine own people."—2 Kings iv. 13.

THERE is a sweet and touching simplicity in the answer of the woman of Shunem to the question of Elisha. This reply evinced a mind unsophisticated in the ways of the world; without ambition in respect to its honours and distinctions; averse to change; and which found in the common and every-day duties of life, and in its own social and domestic circle, ample scope, not only for the exercise of its sympathies and its charities, and the kindly play of those affections which are essential to the formation of virtuous character, but also the highest degree of human happiness. There is great force in the proverb, "Home is home, though ever so homely." It is founded on the great law of Divine Providence, which instituted the domestic institution, divided the race into families, and implanted in the human bosom the love of home, of kindred, and of country. The love of kindred, of home, and of country is essential to the best interests of religion, the highest style of virtuous character, and the production of the greatest amount of happiness enjoyed in our present state. This will appear, if we consider,—

I. *The peculiar fitness of the family state for the early development and perfection of the natural affections.*

II. *That home is the best school for early mental training. There is a most important training for the mind before it receives any from the formal processes of education.*

III. *If we consider the influence of family discipline in regulating and restraining the passions. The constitution of the family implies subjection to their parents on the part of the children.*

IV. *If we consider the influence of home in the formation of habits of useful industry.*

Toil and effort is the price of everything good and great. The mind cannot be educated without study, nor the body remain sound and vigorous without exercise. The law of labour, therefore, is not only essential to our existence, but also to our happiness. Now, to the end that the law of labour may be cheerfully and sweetly obeyed, habits of industry must be formed in early life.

V. *The love of home, of kindred, and of country, calls into exercise some of the highest and noblest qualities of our nature in behalf of their well-being and prosperity.*

Aside from religion, the brightest page in the annals of our race, is that which is connected with the love of home, of kindred, and of country. Home is, or ought to be, the sacred spot where the heart has garnered up its choicest earthly treasures. It is there that virtuous character is formed. Now our country is our home, in a wider sense. The very things, therefore, which endear home to us, bind us with strongest cords to our country. Hence, next to our homes, our greatest sacrifices and self-denials will be in behalf of our country. This rouses to high activity our mental powers,—this tasks to the utmost our physical energies. We lay our time, our wealth, and even life itself, on the altar of patriotism.

> "Breathes there a man with soul so dead,
> Who never to himself hath said,

> This is my own, my native land,
> When home his footsteps he has turned
> From wandering on a foreign strand?
> If such there be, go mark him well,
> To him no minstrel praises swell.
> High though his titles, proud his name,
> Boundless his wealth as wish can claim;
> Despite his titles, power, and pelf,
> The wretch concentrated all in self,
> Living shall forfeit fair renown,
> And doubly dying shall go down
> To the vile dust from whence he sprung.
> Unwept, unhonoured, and unsung."—*Scott.*

VI. *This home-feeling affords a soil congenial to the growth of piety, as exhibited in love to God, and our neighbour.*

The love of home and kindred is not religion. Patriotism is not religion. They may exist in a high degree, perhaps, though not in their purest form, in the absence of religious principle. Still, it may be doubted whether true religion is ever found to exist in a heart where the love of home, of kindred, and of country is wanting. The truth is, where the character is wanting in this respect, it is generally wanting in every other. He who is deficient in regard to domestic duties, will always be deficient in regard to his duty to God.

We learn from this subject,—

1. The importance of cultivating the love of home and of country. This subject points out,—

2. One great source of national degeneracy and corruption. The want of this home feeling, and the wide prevalence of a mercenary spirit, produces a constant desire of change, leads to indulgence in ruinous excesses, and to the perpetration of great crimes. A floating population can never long be either moral or religious.

3. The cause of that discontent, which makes so many in our churches dissatisfied with their condition, producing such constant removals, as to reduce many churches, once flourishing, to a state of weakness and dependence.

Piety in the Aged.

By Rev. LEWIS H. REID, Fayetteville, N. Y.

"And she was a widow of about four-score and four years, which departed not from the temple, but served God with fastings and prayers night and day."—LUKE ii. 37.

THIS is recorded of Anna the prophetess, who, like the aged Simeon, was waiting of the consolation of Israel. Like him, she was eminently devout, manifesting her piety in a faithful attendance upon the services of the temple, and in fastings and prayers, continually. Three verses furnish all that we know of her history; and yet, who would not prefer to have such a memoir of himself written, than the volumes which set forth the exploits of a Napoleon or an Alexander? The subject which the text naturally suggests is, *piety in the aged.* In considering this subject, it is worthy of note that,—

I. *Piety in the aged confirms and illustrates the promise which God has made of long life to those who fear His name.*

II. *Piety in the aged crowns those who possess it with especial honour.*

III. *Piety in the aged commends religion to others.*

IV. *Piety in the aged furnishes a beautiful illustration of the maturity and ripeness of Christian character.*

"The path of the just is as the shining light, that shineth more and more unto the perfect day."

1. A general inference from the considerations offered is, that we should imitate the pious aged. If we would obtain the promise of long life ourselves, enjoy an honoured and useful old age, and come down at length to the grave like "a shock of corn fully ripe," we must follow in the steps of those of whom we have been speaking.

2. How thankful should the children of pious and aged parents be.

3. The departure of aged Christians from our midst reminds

us who remain, that the ranks before us are thinning out, and that we are pressing up to the fore-front of the line. We should see to it, then, that we have their piety, and can honour their place.

Importance of Prayer for the Conversion of the World.

By Rev. JUSTUS DOOLITTLE.

"Thy kingdom come."—Matt. vi. 10.

THAT it is natural for man to pray, all history furnishes evidences. The universal prevalence of supplication offered to idols and spirits in heathen countries, and the experience of all, in times of sudden and imminent danger, or of alarming sickness, prove it. Prayer is also a revealed duty. The Bible gives important instructions in relation to its nature and right performance. It teaches us that there is only one Being to whom prayer, as a religious act, may be addressed, and instructs us, in various passages, in regard to the different objects for which prayer should be offered to that Being. The text illustrates these remarks, inasmuch as it brings to our notice that Being, and is itself a prayer for a specific object. That Being is the only true and living God, and the text is a prayer for the coming of His kingdom on the earth.

This discourse will be devoted to the consideration of the importance of prayer for the conversion of the world. I remark that the importance of such prayer is seen,—

I. *In the fact that Christ directs His disciples to make it.*

II. *In the good influence it exerts over those who offer it in sincerity and in earnest.*

III. *In the encouragement it affords those who have consecrated themselves to labour in person for that object.*

IV. *Prayer is the only effectual means of bringing down God's blessing upon us.*

Will you not, when you daily visit the closet, plead in greater earnest, and in the exercise of a more active faith, in behalf of a lost race, than you have ever yet done? When you bow in the social circle, and in the weekly prayer meetings of the church, will you not supplicate, with a becoming importunity, for the prevalence of God's spiritual reign among all the nations of the earth? At your evening and morning family devotions, will you not remember the heathen in their deep degradation and sinfulness, and offer a sincere and fervent petition for their rescue? In the sleepless watches of the silent night, and often while engaged in your usual pursuits, abroad or at home, will you not elevate your soul in a voiceless prayer to God, in the short but comprehensive request, "Thy kingdom come"?

The Leaven of the Kingdom.

BY REV. J. M. SHERWOOD, BLOOMFIELD, N. J.

"The kingdom of heaven is like unto leaven, which a woman took and hid in three measures of meal, till the whole was leavened."—MATT. xiii. 33.

THIS parable contains the statement of a great principle or law, which exists and operates both in the kingdom of nature and of grace. It is the law of silent, unconscious growth, development, and assimilation. This law has many wonderful illustrations in the natural world. The growth of the vegetable kingdom,—what is it but a standing miracle of the power of God! An acorn is dropt into the earth. That acorn, little as it is, contains the germ of a mighty growth. It dies; but from its mouldering ashes there shoots forth a thing of life, which, without hands, and without any visible means or agencies, grows to a trunk of great size and height, and flings out its brawny arms towards heaven, and strikes deep its roots in the earth, and stands forth in the pride and greatness of its strength, to attest for ages and centuries the power of that hidden life which the acorn contains.

The instance cited in the text is no less remarkable. A handful of "leaven" is hid in three measures of meal, and the woman goeth about her business. That leaven contains a latent principle or power, which is sure to work a great change in that mass of meal which conceals it. Quickly the process of fermentation begins; the parts nearest to the leaven are first affected; the work of agitation goes on silently but rapidly; the mass begins to expand and rise; the living spirit extends its quickening influence until its own life is imparted to the whole, and the desired change has been wrought in it. If it were not for the commonness of these things, they would excite the profoundest interest and wonder. The power of God is as really displayed in them as in what are called miracles.

Now to these marked developments of a hidden and expansive life in nature, Christ compares "the kingdom of heaven." There is an instructive analogy between the natural and spiritual world in the operations of this very law. There is a latent life, a silent unconscious power in Christianity, that works out the purposes of God in a manner truly wonderful. God has chosen to regenerate this world on the same principle that "leaven" operates in producing its wonderful change,—the law of silent, unconscious, expansive, all-permeating, and all-prevailing moral influence. This law has signally characterized the entire history of "the kingdom of heaven" in the world.

I. *We have a signal illustration of this law in the history of God's revelation to man.*

The Bible which contains it is the consummated and grand result of a long series of supernatural communications, and of immensely varied and innumerable agencies, spread out over a period of four thousand years. Unlike the Koran, the Shaster, the Mormon Bible, and the sacred books of other spiritual delusions, the record of our faith did not drop down out of heaven entire and complete. There is a singular and infinitely corroborating providence connected with its formation and its history.

The germ of this entire revelation was the solitary promise which God gave to the first parents of our race when their sun had set in hopeless darkness. It was a little "leaven," and it worked a blessed change. Time added to it. Other promises followed. "The kingdom of heaven" was set up. The regenerating principle was implanted. The revelation gradually grew in the range of its doctrines, in the variety of its topics, and in the clearness and certainty of its discoveries and teachings, as the mind of man was fitted to receive and profit by it. The trial, the growth, the experience of four thousand years sufficed to complete the great and difficult work. The rays of scattered light were now all brought into a single burning focus; the coming of Christ was the explanation and the fulfilment of all that had gone before: the Old Testament had found its counterpart, its living life, its consummated development in the New, and the world had now reached mature age; it was in a condition favourable to receive "the whole counsel of God."

What an outgrowth of that original promise, which kept from absolute despair the first guilty pair of our race! The world cannot now go back. The "leaven" of progress and regeneration is fairly lodged in it. And it must work. It is working. We see and feel the far-reaching effects of its silent power. The regenerating, overcoming, all-assimilating process is going forward continually,—faster than it seems to the eye of outward observation.

II. *The history of the Christian church furnishes another illustration of the doctrine of the text.*

How small and feeble were its early beginnings! To the eye of human reason and judgment, how utterly inadequate was such an agency to the work of regenerating this fearfully corrupt world! Jesus Christ has been crucified by His own nation and church, as an imposter. His disciples are so few in number, that a small "upper room" holds them all. They are friendless, without learning, without influence, simple-hearted, destitute of policy, and singularly wanting in all the elements and means of earthly power and success. And that little, feeble, obscure band of hated and despised men constitutes "the kingdom of heaven!" And all the world is against them. But the "leaven" of God's power and wisdom, and of the Holy Spirit's regenerating influence, was wrapped up in the simple faith of those men, and hid in their renewed hearts. The power to work, change, regenerate, was in the "leaven," not in man.

How quickly and how powerfully that "leaven" worked in the first ages of the church, we are all informed. It began at Jerusalem, as soon as the scene of the crucifixion had closed. It began with the murderers of our Lord. It thence spread to other lands and other nations.

The history of missions to the heathen in our own day is furnishing a remarkable commentary on the words of our text. The gospel has never worked as other powers work, to bring about its results. Its laws are peculiarly its own. It has never begun with the mass, but with individual men. Deep in the heart of individual man it hides the "leaven," or wraps it up in some principle of faith, or some new idea or experience, which some obscure person or agency is made to "hold forth," and there it is left to work its way to the outward life,—to gather strength to itself noiselessly and unconsciously,—to quicken heart after heart, carry captive mind after mind, and work its way down to the foundations of things. "The power of God" is hid there, and it will surely work its way to conquest and dominion.

III. *The history of opinions or doctrines, originating in, or essential to the kingdom of heaven, is a third fruitful source of illustration.*

Take the great Reformation under Luther. He finds an old and long-neglected copy of the Bible. He reads, wonders, admires, weeps, prays, wrestles, and rises from his knees a new man!—master of a new principle!—a new idea has taken possession of him!—a new life courses through all his veins! The "leaven" of evangelical doctrine is there, and in it the power of God, destined to work the most signal reformation that the world had witnessed since apostolic times.

At a later period Cæsar and Anti-Christ combined to put down the spirit of religious liberty which was rising in Europe. In Scotland, a noble band of men entered into a "solemn league and covenant" to defend that principle, cost what it would. They resisted with blood. They flung their banner to the breeze, and, in the name of the God of liberty and Lord of the conscience, battled as for life. Long did the carnage rage. Their solid mountains trembled under the shock of hostile armies. But that principle was a part of the "leaven of the kingdom of heaven." Live it would,—triumph it did. It gained a footing on its own free soil. It passed the Tweed. It infused itself into the Commonwealth of England. It finally, after many struggles and bloody conflicts, moulded the constitution of Britain into what it is. It took firm root in that land, and has made that people eminently prosperous, and the most influential for good of any on earth. That principle was the characteristic principle of the Puritans. The Pilgrim Fathers brought it here. It was the precious freight of the Mayflower.

IV. *The history of individual conversions strikingly illustrate the principle of the text.*

How wonderful is the way that God usually brings about His purpose in this particular. Seldom are sinners converted in a sudden and violent manner, like Saul of Tarsus, or the thief on the cross. No man can lay his finger on the beginning of the kingdom of God in his soul; or on the particular agency which converted him. A serious thought, an unconscious impression, a casual word, a providential visitation, may be the "leaven" which the Holy Spirit hides in his heart. Unseen and unobserved, there that leaven works. This is the way that God usually converts men.

We name three concluding remarks, out of many, which this subject suggests.

1. We are not to despise "the day of small things" in regard to "the kingdom of heaven."

2. We see in this law the reason why God makes such a selection of the subjects of His grace.

3. We infer hope for the world from our subject. The "leaven of the kingdom of heaven" is hid in it. That leaven will work, and nothing can hinder it. It is the hidings of God's power, and nothing can withstand it; and all the world shall one day confess its all-subduing agency, and come under the sway of its dominion.

The Unknown Depths of Depravity.

BY THE REV. A. B. VAN ZANDT, D.D., PETERSBURG, VA.

"And Hazael said, But what is thy servant a dog, that he should do this great thing? And Elisha answered, The Lord hath showed me that thou shalt be king over Syria."—2 KINGS viii. 13.

"KNOW thyself!" was the concise maxim of ancient wisdom, but like many others, it is a maxim more easily uttered than obeyed. The true knowledge of ourself is indeed the most difficult of all human attainments; it is, in fact, altogether beyond the reach of human attainments. A man may know something of himself, even as he may know something of external nature, and of his fellow-men. But in both cases there is a limit beyond which he cannot go,—there are hidden depths which he cannot penetrate. Especially in regard to his moral character, man is to himself an "unknowable individual." There are latent tendencies in his own heart, which may remain wholly unsuspected, until revealed, by an unlooked-for combination of circumstances, which shall call them into activity. It is on this account that men are so apt to misjudge themselves, and so prone to regard as harsh and unjust, the scriptural account of human depravity. They exclaim with Hazael, "Is thy servant a dog, that he should do this great thing?" Now, we would not needlessly disturb this self-complacency,—we certainly would not do it by any exaggerated representations of the inherent evil of the human heart. Nothing would be gained for the cause of truth and godliness, by painting the devil himself in darker colours than he wears, even if it were possible to do so.

It is, therefore, of the first importance that every man should at least so far know himself as to be sensible of his own guilt and danger. Without this it is in vain that we speak of the remedy; for without this, there will be no application to the great Physician of souls. It is not, then, in unkindness, but in love, that we lift the covering from that abyss of sin, the human heart.

In considering the facts of this brief history, there are three points worthy of attention:—

I. *Hazael knew that he was a wicked man, and that his tendencies were wicked.*

It is not improbable that his ambition had already suggested and entertained the purpose of the foul murder of Benhadad, which he afterwards committed. Perhaps this thought was in his mind when the prophet told him that the king's malady was not mortal, but that he should nevertheless die.

II. *But though consciously guilty, Hazael did not know how wicked he was, and to what lengths of crime the evil tendencies would carry him.*

It was not a hypocritical affectation of horror when he replied to the prophet's prediction, "But what! is thy servant a dog, that he should do this great thing?"

III. *But we notice that though honest in his recoil from the predicted atrocities, yet, as the event proved, he was capable of doing all, and more than all, that the prophet had said.*

The latent evil was in his heart, though as yet undeveloped in this precise form and degree. It needed only the fitting circumstances of power, passion, and opportunity to make him, in fact, the "dog," the ravenous beast of prey, which he supposed Elisha's prediction to imply. The devil was in possession, and though he had not yet turned out every lingering remainder of conscience and sensibility, yet he had it all in subjection, and could afford to take his time in bringing his deluded victim to the last degree of degradation and crime.

Perhaps you are ready to say,—"What have we in common with such a man? How can his character illustrate our own?" As to his deeds you have nothing in common, and as to the prominent points of his character you have nothing. I am not preaching to blood-stained murderers, or exterminating tyrants. But there is an important point, because it is the radical point in which his character and yours unite, and do actually become one. You look upon the man and his deeds, and you find in your hearts no sympathy with his crimes, but with instinctive aversion you brand him, in his own epithet, "a dog!" But I would have you look beyond his deeds to the source and spring of all his crimes, and then say, if you find no corresponding fountain of iniquity within your own breast. Say not, in your indignation, "Is thy servant a dog that he should do these things?" lest, in so saying, you only help to complete the resemblance, and point the moral which we seek to enforce.

Let us look at the facts:—

1. Hazael knew, when he uttered these words, that he was a wicked man, and that his tendencies were wicked. So do you, and so does every unrenewed man know the same. You may have no meditated murder upon your conscience, or any other deed of darkness to make you quail under the eye of a fellow man. But you have the guilt of long-continued and daring sin upon your conscience, and there is an eye before which you shrink abashed, and there is an accuser, sometimes sterner than the Hebrew prophet, whom you cannot confront.

2. But again, Hazael was a much worse man than he supposed himself to be, and capable of committing crimes at the prospect of which he shuddered. And so are you, and so are all unregenerated men far more wicked than they suppose, and capable of an excess of sin from which, under other circumstances, they would shrink with horror. The truth upon this subject is, no man knows himself until he is tried, every man finds himself more susceptible to the power of temptation than he had supposed, and any man, unrestrained by the power of Divine grace, has no security that he shall not be carried away to the last extreme of vice and crime. "The heart is deceitful above all things, and desperately wicked: who can know it?" "Let him that thinketh he standeth, take heed lest he fall."

3. And in intimate connection with this is that other fact, that every heart in which God does not reign is under the dominion of the devil. He may not, as yet, have exterminated all its sensibilities. The sinner may never, in this world, become altogether a devil, but the latent evil is there, and it only waits its development to make him all that his inexorable master would have him to be.

The Speed of Life Impressing Probation.

By Rev. TRYON EDWARDS, D.D., New London, Conn.

—"O Lord, by these things men live, and in all these things is the life of my spirit."—Isa. xxxviii. 16.

THESE are the words of Hezekiah,—a part of his reflections after his miraculous restoration from sickness, when the fifteen years had been added to his life. Reviewing his sickness, and recognizing in it the hand of God, he felt that the Divine dealings, as sanctified, were promoting his spiritual good; that they had wrought out, and were still working out in him, and for him, their intended design,—the intended result of probation. As the physical system lays hold of its proper food, and makes life out of it, so was his heart enabled, by grace, rightly to lay hold of his afflictions so as from them to make to itself spiritual life,—life eternal. And in this sense it is that he exclaims, in all the fulness and certainty of personal experience,— "O Lord, by these things do men live, and in these things is the life of my spirit."

The burden of his monody is not so much the severity of his sufferings, as the brevity of his days,—the swiftness of their flight; and even his afflictions, keen and trying as they were, seem most to have impressed him, because they made him so deeply feel that his life was speeding like the wind. This, then, is the thought on which I would fix in the passage before us, and to which I would ask your attention, *that the speed of life impresses our probation.*

In endeavouring to illustrate this thought, let us notice,—

I. *The fact that life is fast speeding away.*

On this point it is needless long to dwell, for it is a truth that is often pondered by the thoughtful heart, suggested as it is by the many changes of life, and especially by the opening and closing of successive years. Every one has at times felt, and sometimes deeply felt, with Hezekiah, in the context, that his life is departing, and that he is going to the gates of the grave; or with Moses, that he is carried away as with a flood; or with Job, that his days are swifter than the weaver's shuttle; that his life is as the wind,—that as the cloud is consumed and vanishes from sight, so his years are fast passing away. Other wings may weary and droop in their course, but the wings of time, with their calm, steady beat, seem but to gather strength by exertion, and to bear us with a mightier sweep the nearer we are to eternity.

II. *That it deeply impresses our probation.*

1. It rarely allows us to complete the plans in which we are engaged. Who is there that has not found this so in his own experience, that from youth up has not formed many a plan, neither unwise nor inconsiderate, which he never even began to execute? Who that has not felt "what mockeries were his wisest plans, his best resolves;" that

> "Upon each beckoning scheme
> No sooner do we fix our hope, than still
> Time bears us on, leaving each still undone,
> Adjourned for ever!"

2. By the rapidness of its flight it keeps us always in effort. And as every toilsome struggle, and conflict, and effort is probationary, both in the discipline it gives, and the state which it indicates, the speed of life which throws them upon us, loudly proclaims, and deeply impresses our probation.

3. By its rapid progress, it gathers more thickly about us the changes, and trials, and admonitions of life. The swifter the speed of life, the more trying appears its disciplinary work, because it compresses that work within proportionally narrower limits; and thus, in its pathway of sadness and tears, it the more loudly preaches of probation, and the more solemnly impresses it.

4. It so soon hurries us away from earthly scenes, and that, too, in the full vigour and activity of all our powers and faculties. How often is the statesman cast down in the full maturity of his talents and influence; and the man of business, just as he is qualified, by long practice and success, to enter on the largest plans; and the Christian student, or minister, when, by the thorough discipline of years, he is just giving promise of being able, with polished intellect and ripened piety, richly to

serve his generation by the will of God! The votaries of honour, the servants of usefulness, the idols of affection are cast down, and those who stand as pillars of the state totter and fall in their full strength. Each seems but just ready, by long experience and the full training of his powers, to lay hold on some long-sought prize, when he is summoned to the narrow house, and to all that is beyond it!

Leaving the subject to your serious reflections, I close with a few remarks which it suggests.

1. If the speed of life is always admonishing of probation, then it should also admonish us of our coming retribution. Every day that passes,—every rising morn, and beaming noon, and closing night,—every beating pulse, and heaving breath, and striking hour, and ticking moment, should be speaking to us of eternal things,—of those endless states of joy or woe on which so soon we must enter.

2. It should lead each one of us seriously and habitually to prepare for it. As retribution is the necessary result of probation, and takes its character entirely from it, we should improve the whole of the latter in diligently preparing for the former. The great principle of God's word is, that the whole of probation is the season of preparation for retribution; and that what is to follow death will depend, not on the act of dying, but on the life we have lived before we came to it.

3. It is no wonder that this world does not satisfy the soul. Every thing in our moral nature, and in the structure of our earthly state, proclaims that we were made for immortality, and we cannot be fully satisfied with any thing short of it. You may keep from utter starvation by feeding on the husks of time and sense; or in part slake your thirst at the impure fountains of sin, though it will be like drinking from the poisoned cup, which satisfies for the moment, to destroy in the end. But when you pass to eternity, and there find even these streams cut off, and these husks torn from you, then will you not hunger for ever, with no bread to feed you, and thirst for ever, without one drop of water to cool your tongue? Will not these desires, ever gathering strength, and never, never satisfied, be the unquenchable flame, and the undying worm to you?

4. If time is so fast flying, and life so fast speeding away, then your probation will soon be ended, and your retribution soon begun. Now you have Sabbaths, and sermons, and communion seasons, and all the means of grace, each, by the love of Christ, appealing to you, and each waiting, like some commissioned angel of mercy, to bear you to the skies. Soon will

all these means be gone. The flight of time will have borne them away as on the wings of the wind. And then results—*results*—RESULTS—will be all that remains to you for ever! Now means are yours, and possibilities yours, either for life or death,—for heaven or hell. But soon unchanging certainties shall come,—results which must be the atmosphere of your endless existence,—the robing of your spirit for ever! See to it,—oh, see to it, through the offered grace of Jesus, that they are such, that in them you shall rejoice, and not mourn to endless ages!

The Duty of Children to Honour their Parents.

By Rev. DAVID DOBIE, PLATTSBURGH.

"Honour thy father and thy mother; that thy days may be long upon the land which the Lord thy God giveth thee."—EXODUS xx. 12.

THE Apostle Paul has called our attention to the fact that this is the first of the ten commandments with a promise attached to it; and he urges the fact of the promise as the reason why children should be careful to obey it. The promise is a long life. Is it not remarkable, is it not worthy of the attention of all children, that such a promise is attached to this commandment? Does it not show that God places a high value on obedience to parents, and that even children are under His government; their actions noticed, their obedience rewarded, and their disobedience punished?

Before entering on the specific design of this discourse, which is to show what it is to honour father and mother, and to insist on the duty of children towards their parents, it may be proper to make a few remarks on the commandment itself.

First, this commandment is not intended solely for those who are commonly called children.

A second remark is—that this commandment is given in favour of all parents. This is a remarkable fact.

A third remark, very obvious, is, that here is a commandment for all children.

I. *What is it to honour parents?*

1. To honour parents is to obey them in all that is right, when they require it.
2. To honour parents is to do what is right, whether they require it or not.
3. To honour their parents, children must have respect to their feelings in reference to the choice of companions or of a profession.
4. To honour their parents, children must endeavour to act on all occasions so as not to make their parents ashamed of their conduct.

II. *Insist on the duty which this commandment enjoins on children.*

1. The first motive which we mention why children should honour their parents is, that by so doing, they will obtain the blessing of God.
2. That obedience to this commandment is the only way to secure peace of conscience.
3. That parents are the nearest and dearest friends of their children on earth.
4. God requires them to do it. This is the highest and most solemn of all considerations.

Do it with all your heart. Do it because God requires it. Do it on all occasions, and at every sacrifice of personal feelings. Seek grace from God day by day, that you may keep this commandment without fail or fault. Take pleasure in honouring your parents; for God is well pleased with all children who thus obey His will; and your obedience of this precept in regard to your earthly parents, will teach you the higher obedience of your Father in heaven. Obedience to God will become the law of your life. You will love all that is good, and learn to do all that is right. And your life on earth, being prolonged to a happy old age, you will then be prepared, through the mercy of God the Saviour, and through the sanctification of the Holy Spirit, for the service of God in glory, where your life will never end.

Christ a Moral Painter.

By Rev. W. W. NEWELL, Syracuse, N. Y.

"And He spake many things unto them in parables."—Matt. xiii. 3.

ATTRACTED by the teachings of Christ, great multitudes are gathered to hear Him. To avoid the throng, Jesus enters a little boat upon the calm sea. How impressive this scene. Here sits the great Teacher, the Master of all doctrine, and logic, and science. The crowded shore waits and listens. What an opportunity to display the depth of His intellect, and the vastness of His resources. He opens His mouth, and behold, according to His custom, the simple comparison. He abounds in imagery and metaphor. He descends to fields and gardens, to the woman sweeping her house, to the hen gathering her chickens. And this from heaven's greatest intellect, and earth's greatest preacher. Even the style of Christ's teaching is sufficiently important to engage the attention of His followers. I ask your attention to the subject of "Christ a moral painter."

Notwithstanding the Divine authority of Jesus, He did not confine Himself to the mere announcement or proof of a doctrine. But by means of words, He often presented to His hearers a moral picture. He flashed upon the mind's eye a whole scene of truth, with such vividness and power, that it could not be well perverted or forgotten.

My brethren, our business is to co-operate with Him, who "came to seek and to save that which was lost." And yet there are congregations among us that cannot, at the end of a year, recall one single living scene of truth. Formalities and common places in the pulpit are an abomination. Mere beauty of conception and language is frivolous. Simply profound and great sermons are the curse of any age. Is it not time that we rise above such preaching, and imitate the pointed, emotional preaching of the Lord Jesus Christ?

I. *Some reasons for the use of moral painting in sermons.*

1. It imitates the style of Christ's painting, and is a part of His gospel. We cannot preach the gospel without presenting the illustrations of Christ from the pulpit. Why should we not, like Him, lay the great world around us under tribute to the cause?

2. Moral painting meets a want in our nature. It appeals to man's perceptive faculties. God has met this want in the natural world.

3. Moral painting adds point and force to the argument. If it is said that stern reasoning is alone appropriate to the pulpit, I answer that reasoning and illustration are both essential. A mountain of reasoning might neither increase his convictions, nor move his heart. He wants the burning image to move his feelings. Pictures of truth appeal to the fervid part of our nature, and reach the heart. No truth is effectual without God's Spirit. But we are to present that which is best adapted to move men.

4. I have only time to urge the use of moral painting from the example of men, who have deeply moved the human heart. Poets have used it. Homer, Dante, Milton still live. The naturalness and brilliancy of their pictures will render them immortal. Advocates have often gained their cause by some touching scene of truth. Orators have used this instrument with thrilling power. Cicero had his Cataline and his Gracchus, Demosthenes had his Philip. His picture of that man was terrific. "The Athenians saw his black, deceitful heart. They heard him thundering at their gates. They saw themselves enslaved, chained, murdered, and the very slaves cried out, War with Philip."

And shall the children of this world be wiser than the children of light? Shall Christians reject this power? The wisest and most successful have used it. Inspiration is full of it. Think of the gospels, of Peter's pentecostal sermon, of Paul's remarkable conversion. The vividness and grandeur of Chrysostem's images explain his magic power. He dealt in living, breathing truth. What but this power enables us to talk of the immortal Bunyan? We track the foot-prints of his poor Christian from the slough of despond, clear up through the gate of the celestial city. What but this faculty made Whitfield the prince of preachers? So with Edwards and Payson. There is nothing that requires such imagination, taste, judgment, originality, emotion, and prayer, as the logical argumentation, and the forcible illustration of truth.

II. *The kind of moral painting to be used.*

Discredit has been brought upon this style of preaching. But we are not to abandon moral painting in sermons, because by some it has been badly done, and by others over done. A good thing is not to be abandoned because it has been abused. Great condensation is essential to a good picture of truth. Nothing can be more distasteful in a sermon than a long diffuse story. The parables of Jesus are brief and pointed. Above all, sacred truth should be illustrated with deep emotion. Christ's gospel is a weeping, thrilling message of glad tidings to the perishing. No other presentation of truth is gospel. If coldly uttered, it belies the beating heart of Jesus, and caricatures His yearning message.

When the heart is struggling to convince and move, it seizes some illustration that will flash conviction at once upon the soul. This makes moral painting so natural and appropriate to the pulpit. The preacher crushed with the love of Jesus, and the burden of souls, warms, and moulds, and dignifies, and makes effectual the simplest incident. How did Jesus make the brooded chickens so effective? He stood gazing down upon that doomed city. He saw those millions who might have been sheltered, sinking in agonized struggles, under the wrath of God. And He wept. Those tears of the Son of God have elevated that hen and her gathered chickens into a deathless and celestial picture. Like Christ, my brethren, should we give vent to a tearful heart. The vastness of our work is enough to make an angel weep. But with Christ's help it can be done. And he will do it best who determines under God that he will do it,—whose whole heart is fixed on doing it,—whose crushed spirit bows before God, and laying hold of some promise, cries with an importunity that will not be denied,—" Oh Lord, give me these souls"!

God does not promise heaven to the faithless preacher. His doom, of all others, will be most terrific. " What scene is this," says Griffin, " that I behold in hell? A lurid shape, more scarred with thunder than the rest, around which a crowd of dreadful beings, with furious eyes, and threatening gestures, are venting their raging curses. It is an unfaithful pastor. Those around

him are his wretched people. My soul turns away, and cries,—
'Give me poverty,—give me the curses of the wicked,—give me the martyr's stake,—but oh! my God, save me from the doom of the unfaithful minister.'"

The Great Sin.
By Rev. WILLIAM WARREN, Upton, Mass.

"Thou shalt not commit adultery."—Ex. xx. 14.

SIN has no excuse. And yet there is no form of iniquity but seeks to hide itself under some flimsy pretext or covering. One sin excuses itself on the ground of original propensity; another of temptation. This sin sets up the plea of law; that, of custom or fashion. Now, vice excuses itself on the ground of interest, honour, or example; now of appetite, pleasure, or passion.

The seventh commandment forbids every form of sensuality in act or thought. It requires the government of the sensual passions. It throws the sanction of heaven over the purity and chastity of the race. It forbids improper words and looks, indelicate acts, seductive arts, and all indecent modes of dress and exposure. It excludes the use of books, prints, and pictures, that excite the passions and debase the morals. It discountenances those vile exhibitions and disclosures upon the stage or otherwise, that tend to corrupt the imagination and undermine the moral principles.

I. *The most fearful denunciations of Scripture are against it.*

II. *Nature protests against it.*

Her voice is the voice of God; her laws, the laws of God. Nature protests against this great wickedness in the form of prostrate health, and a ruined constitution: of loathsome disease and entailed distress and degradation inherited by innocent offspring. And who can bear the burden of a condemning conscience, the tooth of corroding remorse, or the pointed finger of disgrace, detestation, and self-loathing? Infamy and fearful forebodings are the price paid for forbidden pleasure.

Pure enjoyment grows on the path-side of noble pursuits. It meets you always in the highway of duty. He that triumphs over temptation is a prince among men. There is far more joy in self-conquest than in yielding to sin. He who gains a victory over himself, sits upon a throne of power and enjoyment.

There is no violation of law against which God has hung out so many beacon-warnings as here. There is no sin that has so many signs exhibited in terror from every window of the soul. If God made one tree more sacred than the rest, and threw around it His strongest interdictions, can we wonder that in the paradise of morals there should be one trait, one tree, one virtue, more guarded and sacred than the rest.

III. *Sensuality breaks down the moral principles.*

The moral principles may be termed the masonry of the mind. They are the strong foundations of an enduring character. Nothing can be substituted for them,—nothing beautiful or valuable can long survive them. But they cannot long stand the shock of allowed crime.

Among the obvious effects or signs of this sin are a loss of the moral judgment, the absence of self-control and self-respect, a prevailing scepticism, and moral recklessness. Nor is this all. An incapability of domestic contentment follows; a loss of power to fix the affections, a destruction of the natural attachments, the absence of moral discernments, of respect for superiors, for authority, or the throne above.

IV. *Sensuality does violence to the virtues.*

The virtues are outposts of the character, mortised into the foundations of principle. They are the outward, the active, the ornamental in the life. But they cannot long survive the wreck of the moral principles, any more than the sails and colours of a ship can float after the deck has gone down. As the tassels crown the corn, or the bow the shower, so the virtues the character. But licentiousness sends a mildew upon all the field of virtues. As nights of frost strike the glory of the forest, nights of forbidden pleasure put upon the moral verdure the imprints of death. Sincerity fails, honour withers, truth and right are prostrate, friendship, affection, humanity, and patriotism perish.

V. *This sin ruins others.*

The seventh is the only commandment whose violation necessarily involves others in guilt. But this sin is one of temptation, and seeks companionship in crime. Happy is he who can say, I have corrupted no one,—I have defrauded no one. What reflection more cutting than to feel that we have been the cause of another's ruin.

VI. *This sin leads to every other.*

Like seeks like, tempts like, has an affinity, a charm for the same. Emphatically true is this of sensuality, when it becomes the master passion. It is lenient towards every evil, licenses every iniquity, and stimulates every vile habit. A slight allowance here is like the letting forth of waters, the embankments of moral principle, the fortifications of bold virtue, are swept away, or struck down. All soon becomes a wreck.

I would not forget the example of Christ here, how He ate and drank with sinners! Every thing depends on motive and faithfulness. When we can imitate Christ in these we may go anywhere, and do anything. I would do no injustice to the falsely accused, nor abandon those whom the deep waters of repentance have cleansed. No, let the worthy and well-intentioned be welcomed to our sympathy; and let us cast none away who will "go and sin no more." Say not the verdict against fallen woman is too severe. Say, rather, that against fallen man is too light. But to return from this digression.

VII. *I will now proceed to remark that this sin frustrates the great end of human life.*

It corrupts the body, perverts the habits, enfeebles the mind, unhinges the conscience, and renders the great objects of life insipid and tasteless. Who can undertake anything valuable, or patiently pursue any noble end without moral principle? Surely, there is no post of honour, or responsibility, or circle in life, for which this vice does not disqualify man. I have spoken of the effect of licentiousness in this world, but I have to add that a fearful future is before the wicked in the world to come. There is no habit that so benumbs the conscience, fetters the purposes, and destroys the recuperative energies of the soul as this. It makes the moral nature like the tinder, in which the sparks of temptation catch, and the fires of eternity kindle and consume. Oh, it is virtue's ways that are ways of peace. Take them, follow them, if you would not die. Ten thousand times I tell you to take them, keep them, follow them, if you would escape the lake that burneth. Think not that there is a loss in this. No! the gain is a thousand-fold here! But even if there were loss in self-restraint and self-conquest, who would not be willing to plant his joys here, in order to harvest them for ever.

With one or two words I close.

1. Beware of beginnings. The time to stop in crime is before commencement. Young friends, your safety lies in never taking the first step.

2. Give it no allowance in your meditations or imaginations.

3. Be sensitive and watchful against the first and least temptation. Put from you all books and pictures that have a licentious bearing. Fly from everything that endangers virtue or defiles the heart.

4. Avoid bad associates. Distrust them who prefer the night to the day; the lower to the higher pleasures; the dance and the frolic to the higher duties and aspirations of life.

5. Avoid every incentive to vice in dress, in fashion.

6. Attend to the words of wisdom. How much are such words worth! Oh, how many have said, *too late*. How have I hated instruction and despised reproof! Worlds would I give for the innocence I have lost, and the chance I once had to be saved!

7. There is but one course of safety: it is to give your hearts to Christ. Enter wisdom's ways. Come under the attractions of the cross. Then temptation will lose its charm, and your tastes and attachments will be pure. And when the hand of icy death feels for your heart-strings, and closes for ever life's warm currents, you will be safe,—you are blest!

The Religion of Common Life.

By the Rev. HOLLIS READ, Craneville, N. J.

"Ye shall know them by their fruits."—Matt. vii. 16.

THE passage furnishes a criterion by which to judge of men's hearts. Though endowed at present with no organs of sense, or mental faculties, by which to enter the secret chambers of the soul, and note what is passing there, yet there come out thence trusty messengers bearing unerring testimony to what is within. Would you know what is in man, you must see what proceedeth from him. A sweet fountain does not send out bitter waters, nor a good tree bear corrupt fruit. The deliberate, habitual actions of a man are the index of his heart.

Would we know the Christian, we must contemplate him in the relations in which he is placed, and see how he discharges his duties there. For religion is not merely the performance of a specified round of duties, but a principle, giving energy and character to his whole conduct. Its most indubitable evidence is to be sought in the manner of discharging the duties and meeting the events of life.

I. *We will look for the Christian in the hard-working man, his bodily powers taxed to the utmost, and his mind absorbed in his daily labours.*

How, in this situation, can he honour God and adorn a good profession? It must be in the mode of discharging his duties. The husbandman, for example, may plough, sow, and gather his harvest, religiously or irreligiously. There is all the difference of right and wrong, in the motives with which he pursues his daily avocations.

A man may work religiously, as well as pray, exhort, or give sincerely and with religious affection. Indeed, this is nearly the only way by which a large class of Christians can, in existing circumstances, develope their religious characters. The whole manner in which they discharge duties which do devolve on them,—whether on the farm or in the workshop, in the kitchen or in the parlour, by the wayside or the fireside,—these are their testimonials to the genuineness of their religion, as well as direct and effectual means of doing good. We must look for the reason of one's hope in the circumstances in which we find him. He must be a doer of the word in the sphere in which Providence has called him to act. Religion is abundantly a practical thing, equally, perhaps, capable of being exemplified in every condition and occupation in life.

II. *A further illustration of piety may be found in the adverse circumstances of life.*

Sin has brought into the world a fruitful progeny of woe. The path of life leads through shades as well as lights. It is called the "vale of tears,"—a state of suffering, rather than of doing or of enjoying. The whole tissue of life indicates it to be a state of trial for a better condition of existence. Who has not taken note of the unlooked-for movements of Providence in his own individual history? How have his schemes been frustrated, his pleasant dreams proved delusions, and prospects fair and promising been in a moment blasted.

We must watch the Christian along the path of life's common occurrences, would we have a fair picture of the inner man. There he is acting out the principles of his inmost soul. Nothing is real magnanimity—genuine patience and resignation to an all-controlling Hand—which does not preserve a Christian temper amidst the lesser evils and ills of life. Some of the most lovely growths of virtue, the most luxuriant and fruitful plants of piety, have lived, grown, and flourished all their days in the vale of tears. The thorns and briers of adversity could not choke them, nor impede their progress onward and upward to the skies.

III. *In men's commercial dealings.*

The whole duty of man has been summed up in this narrow compass,—"Do justly, love mercy, and walk humbly." To do justly is a work of mighty magnitude. For God has purposely made man's social and commercial relations such, that the discharge of their consequent duties involves a rigid test of moral character.

I know not whether poverty or riches affords the severest test of character. Each has its peculiar temptations, the one to oppress, the other to murmur and defraud. The rich are tempted to overlook what is due to the poor; the poor quite as much what is due to the rich. God has placed both in their respective conditions, to see how they will perform their respective duties, and act in their allotted spheres. Each condition may be equally important. For the difference between the highest and lowest,—the richest and poorest,—is too trifling for observation when viewed from the heights of eternity. Yet immense consequences are suspended on the manner of discharging the duties of either condition.

Would we know what is in man, we must choose our post of observation, not where we can see him only in his Sunday habiliments, or laced in the stays of a religious profession, but along the paths of his every-day life.

IV. *Would you further trace the lineaments of one's Christian character, follow him into his social and domestic relations,—take passing note of the company he keeps, the books he reads, and the pleasures he most relishes.*

See how he acts the part of friend and neighbour, of partner in business, or companion by the way, of an associate in pleasure, or a fellow-labourer in the field,—follow him as he performs the offices of parent or child, brother or sister, husband or wife. True religion sanctifies and blesses all these relations, and helps to a better performance of their duties. Heart-religion makes man better in whatever relation you find him,—better about his fireside, in his field, in his workshop,—a better member of society, more firm when right, more yielding when wrong, more indulgent to the foibles of others, more sensible of his own, and ever solicitous that if the society in which he lives be not happy and prosperous, harmonious and efficient, the sin shall not lie at his door.

And would you further apply the touchstone, inquire of the inner man what pleasures are there the most cordially relished, what book serves best to beguile a leisure hour, what company is the most congenial to your taste? In things like these you may discover an index of the heart, perhaps more accurately detect the ruling passion of the soul than in things more commonly regarded religious. Would you know a man's real character, you must see him at home, where he acts out himself—must follow him into the affairs of common life.

The subject affords an occasion for the following remarks:—

1. We err in supposing we are acting a less important part because a less conspicuous one. It is as important, and generally more difficult, to suffer the will of God than to do it.

2. Because we are to look for a portraiture of religion in the common toils, cares, afflictions, and intercourse of life, this affords no excuse for the neglect of duties more directly religious. Men live right because their hearts are right.

3. The subject enforces the duty of acting well our part where we are. Our circumstances are, no doubt, best suited to develop and form our characters. God knows what kind of discipline we need to mature and fit us for heaven.

4. Finally, we infer the fearful and lasting influence of the events of this life. Time is the parent of eternity. Our eternal destiny is suspended on the character we form amidst the common scenes of life. Every particle of time is big with eternal consequences. Every single, and in itself insignificant, event goes to determine our eternal destiny. How solemn a thing, then, it is to live! We often hear it said, "it is a solemn thing

to die." And so it is; but a more solemn thing to live in such a state as this, for it is life, not death, which forms our character—which fits us for heaven or hell.

Preciousness of the Soul's Redemption.

BY REV. RICHARD S. STORRS, D.D., BRAINTREE, MASS.

"For the redemption of the soul is precious, and it ceaseth for ever."—
PSALM xlix. 8.

THE carelessness of mankind at large, on the familiar subjects of death and eternity, is equally surprising and alarming;—*surprising*, because the world dwindles to a point in comparison with the immensity of worlds around us; and all its joys and sorrows, when weighed in the balances of the sanctuary, are lighter than vanity;—*alarming*, because earth alone is the theatre on which preparation is made for unseen worlds; and neglect of that preparation is followed by consequences at once fearful and irreparable.

The soul's redemption is the subject before us. As presented in the text, it naturally divides itself into four parts, viz. :—

I. *The object of this redemption.*
It is the redemption of the soul.

II. *The nature of this redemption.*

1. He is redeemed from the guilt or power of sin. By nature he is a child of disobedience, and a child of wrath. Carnally-minded, he is at enmity with God. Redemption breaks down this unhallowed dominion of sin, delivers the soul from bondage, and sets it at liberty, enlarges its vision, elevates its aims, diffuses through it the warmth of celestial fire, brings it into communion with the spirits of just men made perfect and with God Himself, and says to it authoritatively,—"Go and sin no more."

2. He is redeemed from the shame of sin. Is there not degradation and shame in wearing the yoke of a master, hurled from

heaven, and scathed by the lightnings of God's wrath?—in turning away from the glory ineffable, and plunging into the deeps of the pollution of selfishness?

3. He is redeemed from the sufferings consequent on sin in the future world. Even here his deliverance begins, and advances, amid tears, and prayers, and bitter self-condemnation; but it is perfected only when this mortal puts on immortality. Redemption secures the soul's deliverance from the torments of pride and envy, jealousy and malice, revenge and despair,—from the gnawing of the worm that never dies, and the fury of the fire that never shall be quenched.

And more than this, it elevates the soul to a participation in the glory and felicity of heaven! It introduces it to the presence of God, where is fulness of joy, and gives it a throne on the right hand of Jesus, with a kingdom and a priesthood that shall never fail.

III. *The quality of this redemption.*

It is precious.

1. In the expense at which it is effected. "Ye know that ye were not redeemed with corruptible things, as silver and gold, but with the precious blood of Christ, as of a Lamb, without blemish and without spot."

2. In the fact that it magnifies the Divine law. That would be no salvation, which should cost the sacrifice of a single principle in the government of God. Heaven would be annihilated, God dethroned, the whole fabric of the moral universe be dissolved, and no sound but of discord and war be heard throughout God's works. By the sacrifice of Christ these evils are avoided. No compromise is made with rebels. Precious indeed is that redemption, which defends the government of God from reproach, while it secures peace and consolation to the penitent believer. Precious!—because it encircles the throne of God with transcendent glories, showing its foundations to be immovable, and at the same time pouring a flood of light into the habitations of men, and creating new and boundless joys throughout all ranks of holy intelligences.

3. In the perfect adaptation of the plan to the circumstances of men, this preciousness yet further appears. Wretched and miserable as we are,—poor, blind, and naked as heaven sees us to be,—we may yet come boldly to the throne of grace, and obtain mercy, and find grace to help in time of need. How perfectly adapted, then, to our circumstances of poverty and helplessness!

4. In the unfading glories which it pledges, redemption is

precious. We need an angel's wing, an angel's eye, and more than an angel's experience to enter fully into that blessedness which remains to the redeemed of the Lord hereafter. None but glorified saints, not the noblest spirit of heaven who never fell, can fully understand the raptures of those who sing day and night, without ceasing, "Worthy is the Lamb that was slain; for He hath washed us in His own blood, and made us kings and priests unto God for ever."

IV. *The closing up of this redemption,*—" *It ceaseth for ever.*"

There is a time when the overtures of mercy will cease to be made. There are those infatuated by sin, and led captive by Satan, who will not listen to the voice of the preacher, pleading never so wisely,—who are engrossed with the cares and pleasures of this life, and resolved to have nothing to do with thoughts of eternity, and who, cutting themselves loose from restraints to enjoy what they can, risk the future on the uncovenanted mercy of God. For them, persevering in their folly, there is no redemption.

Nor does one ray of hope break in upon the darkness that wraps up the sinner who has rejected the redemption of Christ, either from the world he has left behind him, or from heaven above him. No voice of mercy greets him. No angel of the covenant comes near, with whom he may wrestle for a blessing; and no Lazarus leaves Abraham's bosom to convey a drop of water to cool his tongue, tormented in the flame. For him there is no Saviour now, no Comforter, no heaven, no glory, no happiness, no hope! Fallen spirits are his only companions, and fawning tempters are become his tormenters. Despair broods over his heart. He sinks. He dies—*for ever dies.*

For ever? Oh, yes,—for ever, and for ever! Sinner, reflect while not too late, that when thy season of probation shall be passed, when the offers of redemption cease to vibrate on thine ear, and the gates of thy prison-house are shut upon thee, thou shalt never come out till thou hast paid the uttermost farthing.

The Resurrection of the Body.

By Rev. JONATHAN BRACE, Milford, Conn.

"Marvel not at this: for the hour is coming, in the which all that are in the grave shall hear His voice, and shall come forth; they that have done good, unto the resurrection of life; and they that have done evil, unto the resurrection of damnation."—John v. 28, 29.

THE doctrine of the resurrection was one peculiarly dear to the primitive saints. They dwelt upon it with more frequency and interest than Christians of the present day are wont to do. The expectation that their weary, earthy bodies would spring pure and immortal from the tomb, supported them in all times of persecution, and comforted them in all seasons of tribulation. So animating was this doctrine to them, that their heathen and infidel enemies did all in their power to disprove it, and when they could not disprove it, did all in their power to prevent it from taking effect. Hence, in some instances, hewing the bodies of the saints in pieces, they cast them into rapidly rushing rivers, in hopes that they would be thus so mutilated and scattered as to make the future re-union of the several parts impossible. The resurrection of the body is, indeed, a doctrine which faith alone can grasp and appropriate to the strengthening of high and holy purposes in the soul.

In discoursing upon the resurrection of the body, I observe,—

I. *That it is possible.*
II. *That it is probable.*
III. *It is certain.*

We come now "to the law and to the testimony," in accordance with which, if any doctrine speaks, it speaks with clearness, and should speak to conviction. The Bible on this subject is full and explicit.

IV. *To the purpose, or object of the resurrection.*

1. One object may be to make a signal exhibition of Jehovah's power.

2. Another object of the resurrection may be to perpetuate the human species. The human race, composed of matter and mind, blending together the material and spiritual, form, as we may believe, a distinct class of beings.

3. But the great object of the resurrection,—paramount to all others, and which may be called *the* object,—is to bring the united body and soul, the entire man, before the judgment-seat of Christ. It is, that the actions of all the actors that have ever lived may be manifested, and their final allotments determined; that sentence may be pronounced upon every action, every family, and every individual of all the posterity of Adam, according to their works.

V. *The time and mode of the resurrection.*

The precise hour, or day, of this sublime occurrence, we cannot tell. Nor we only. No angel can mark it with certainty. It is not for them, any more than for ourselves, to know the times and seasons which Jehovah has reserved to Himself. We only know that it is not a final act, but immediately precedes the judgment; and that it will come unexpectedly, as a thief in the night. The mode, or manner, will be inconceivably amazing and glorious. There will be a visible appearance of Jesus Christ. "The dead in Christ shall rise first."

VI. *To the character of the bodies raised.*

As this is a matter of pure revelation, we must keep close to the inspired word. This is very copious and clear. The qualities of the glorified bodies of believers are drawn out with minuteness in 1 Cor. xv. 35-44.

Such is the destination of the Christian's earthly, frail, perishable body,—such the lovely and effulgent characteristics with which it shall be stamped. I say the Christian's body, for this description has reference to no other. We know not what odious deformities the bodies of the wicked will bear,—what hideous expressions the curse of sin will give them. We only know that they will be so disfigured as to "rise to shame and everlasting contempt." This is the language which inspiration employs with reference to them, and there leaves them! Such is the scriptural account of the resurrection of the body. Marvel not at it. Jehovah has pledged His word that it shall be, and the hour is rapidly hastening on when it will be all real.

In application of the subject, we observe,—

1. That it is extremely consoling to all the true friends of the Redeemer.

2. But while this subject affords special consolations to believers in the Lord, it should carry fear and trembling to the impenitent. Oh what scenes of horror will then open upon the impenitent! My impenitent hearers, are you prepared? Have you made ready for, have you thought of, the morning of the resurrection? Very soon will you be laid in the grave,—are you prepared to be summoned from it? Flatter not yourselves with vain hopes. Those only will be raised in glory, who undergo a moral transformation in this world. Those only will come forth to the resurrection of life hereafter, who come forth to the resurrection of regeneration and piety now. Awake, then, now, from a death in trespasses and sins, and Christ shall give thee life.

My friends, you may harden yourselves against this appeal, but when the earth is heaving, charnel-houses rattling, and graves opening, how will it then appear to you? You may now close your ears to the truth, but to the shout of your descending Judge you cannot close your ears. You may refuse to hear and obey the gospel, but the archangel's trump you must hear, and its summons you must obey.

The Sources of the Blessedness of Christians.

By Rev. RICHARD S. STORRS, D.D., Braintree, Mass.

"But ye are come unto Mount Zion, and unto the city of the living God, the heavenly Jerusalem, and to an innumerable company of angels," &c.—Heb. xii. 22–24.

THE Apostle would comfort his brethren in the faith. Their afflictions were manifold. The lusts of the flesh annoyed them. The world was in arms against them. Satan desired to have them, that he might sift them as wheat. Dangers girded them round on every side, and often they saw only destruction before them. Nothing would comfort them more than a lively perception of the blessings of their condition, as united to Christ by faith, and sanctified by His Spirit. To those blessings the Apostle refers them. The language he employs is so elevated, as to seem descriptive of the state of believers after death. But the context clearly requires its application to Christians in the present world. All will acknowledge it the duty of the Christian to live above the world, and hold himself consecrated in body, soul, and spirit to Christ; nor is it more his duty than his privilege. Real blessedness attends him when faithful to his holy vocation. Nor can this blessedness be better understood than by attending closely its sources, as developed in the text.

I. *It is a blessedness of Christians that God has here established a church, and provided the means of its perpetuity and enlargement.*

This church is often spoken of under the name of Zion, a name originally applied to "the city where our Lord was crucified." It was named also "the city of the living God," because the worship of Jehovah was here alone maintained, and His special presence betokened, by the visible glory, called the Shekinah, hovering over the mercy-seat. And because the worship offered here had respect to the Lamb that was slain, and is now adored by the hosts of heaven, it was also called "the heavenly Jerusalem."

"Mount Zion, the city of the living God, the heavenly Jerusalem," well fortified, and splendidly built, is placed in striking contrast with the rugged mountain of Sinai, rising in the midst of the desert, a misshapen pile of unsightly rock, scathed by the lightnings, and beaten by the storms of heaven.

II. *It is a further blessedness of Christians, that they are surrounded by invisible beings, whose office it is to minister to the heirs of salvation.*

III. *The blessedness of Christians consists also in their union with each other.*

They are come "to the general assembly and church of the first-born, which are written in heaven."

IV. *It is the blessedness of saints on earth that they have communion with saints in heaven.*

They are come "to the spirits of just men made perfect."

V. *It is a further blessedness of Christians that they have freedom of access to the eternal throne.*

They are come "unto God the Judge of all."

VI. *Another blessedness of the Christian is that he ever has a prevalent intercessor at the right hand of God.*

Let the subject be pondered, prayed over, and inwrought into the framework of our spiritual constitution. God has not only established a church, but planted us within its enclosures, and done to His vineyard all that He could have done in it. He has assigned to the angels of heaven the duty of watching over us, and aiding our conflicts with sin and hell; He has united us with each other, and with all Christians on earth, by bonds that neither life nor death can break; He has given us the privilege of holding communion with friends who have fallen asleep in Jesus, and with the spirits of all just men made perfect; He has authorized the utmost freedom of access to His throne, at all times, and under all trials; and, to complete the whole, has announced His only-begotten and well-beloved Son to be our continual Advocate, when charged with guilt, either by our own consciences, or by the great enemy of the soul.

Beyond these, what blessing can we ask? Any other than a grateful heart,—a heart more perfectly subdued to the love of God, and the faith of Jesus? If we are Christ's, all things are ours; the world, things present, things to come, God with all His riches, heaven with all its glories,—all are ours!

True Element of Ministerial Devotion and Success.

By Rev. J. DE FOREST RICHARDS, Chester, Vt.

"For I determined not to know anything among you, Jesus save Christ and Him crucified."—1 Cor. ii. 2.

SUCH was the earnest, unimpassioned resolution of a devoted, self-denying apostle and minister of Christ. And almost no other man, in any age of the church, has laboured so successfully, as an ambassador of the Lord, in the great work of reconciliation. The full proof of his ministry, and the secret of his success, are found in the text and its connection. Christ crucified was the beginning and the end of his ministry. Here is discovered, in this great apostle, the lock of his strength. Cut this from him, and he becomes like another man.

Hence we derive this important sentiment :—The knowledge of Christ, the true element of ministerial devotion and success. This is illustrated in the life and ministry of Paul.

I. *Let us inquire, What is it to know Christ in the sense of the apostle in the text.*

To know Christ as an humble believer, is rightly to understand His character; to appreciate His divine excellence, and His infinite value as the only Saviour of man; to have experimental acquaintance with the way of salvation, by faith in the blood of His atonement. Thus to know Him is life eternal.

The preacher must know all this by actual and personal experience; and he must be able to declare the same to the comprehension of others. It is his chief business to reveal the knowledge of Christ in all His fulness, as the Saviour of lost men; and to preach Him in all the sublime doctrines He inculcates, the precious promises He makes, the threatenings He utters, the immortal hopes He inspires, and all the infinite blessings He has to communicate.

II. *Let us, in illustration of our subject, remark the high standard of devotedness on which Paul resolved, in the words of the text, not to know any thing save Christ.*

Let us, for a moment, look at this earnest apostle in the attitude in which he is here presented to our view, and we shall discover a spectacle of the morally sublime seldom equalled. Having received from the lips of Christ Himself his commission, he has started on a tour of missionary enterprise. We find him in a foreign land, fleeing from the violence of persecution, destitute and unattended. Spending a few days at Athens, he comes to Corinth, and has already entered the thronged metropolis; and, "pressed in spirit," he lifts up his voice, scarcely heard amid the din of that bustling, thoughtless, pleasure-seeking populace, whose very tutelary deity was the goddess of lust, and declares his first message, "testifying that Jesus is the Christ." In Him is salvation for the chief of sinners. I am come to proclaim to dying men salvation from death and hell. My business is most urgent. My commission is imperious. Delay may be fatal to you; for soon the door of mercy will be shut, and heaven will seal your doom for ever. Therefore I am determined not to know anything among you save Jesus Christ and Him crucified.

III. *What were the motives which urged Paul to such self-denial and singleness of devotion in preaching the knowledge of Christ ?*

We shall find them all drawn from one and the same source. They may all be traced up to Christ on the cross, as the fountain head. The love of Christ constrained him. Here is discovered that silent, yet mighty spring and moving power which controlled every act and purpose of his life.

1. His first motive was obedience to Christ as his Lord and Master. He had been ordained by Christ Himself as a minister of reconciliation.

2. Another motive was gratitude to Christ as his Redeemer and Saviour.

3. The arduousness of the work to which his Lord had called him was a motive to great self-denial and earnest devotion.

4. His estimate of the value of man's salvation, was another strong motive which impelled him to zealous effort and self-sacrifice in preaching Christ crucified.

5. Another consideration which animated the zeal of the Apostle, and urged him forward with singular devotion to his work was the certain success and grand results of preaching Christ.

6. Paul, amidst his devoted labours and sufferings, kept his eye fixed steadfastly on his final reward. "I press towards the mark for the prize of the high calling of God in Christ Jesus."

Concluding remarks :—

1. From our subject we learn what is the best kind of preaching. It is that which savours most of Christ.

2. We learn that it is no part of a minister's duty to seek to please men. If they are pleased with the truth, it is well. But how can a minister of Christ turn aside from a full and faithful exhibition of the gospel, to suit the wishes of those

whom the truth will not please? That preaching is not always the most profitable which is the most pleasing, or the most applauded.

3. We see in the light of our subject the great value and importance of the gospel to sinners.

This gospel, my hearers, is as important for you as it was for Paul and the Corinthians. Brethren in the ministry, we see the greatness and the dignity of our calling. It has its trials, and its far-reaching responsibilities; and it has, too, its great reward.

Acquaintance with God.

By Rev. EDMUND B. FAIRFIELD, Hillsdale, Mich.

"Acquaint now thyself with Him, and be at peace; thereby good shall come unto thee."—Job xxii. 21.

WHEN an ancient philosopher was asked, "Who and what is God?" he requested a day to frame his answer; but at the expiration of that he had only become the more deeply perplexed, and prayed that he might have yet another day. And when that had passed, he asked for still another. And having thus secured in succession various extensions of time, he finally replied that the more he had pondered the question, the more perplexed he had become; and the more involved in mystery the nature and attributes of Deity appeared.

And thus with every man who would attempt with his own short ladder to scale the loftiest heights, or with his own scanty plumb-line to fathom the deepest depths of the Divine nature. "Canst thou by searching find out God? Canst thou find out the Almighty unto perfection?" But there is a kind and degree of acquaintance with God which the soul of man may attain to, and to that the text exhorts us.

I. *Acquaintance with God.*

The thought is inspiring, the very conception is ennobling, and the reality transcendently glorious. How may it be obtained?

1. Through His works. The sculptor reveals himself in the statue; the artist in his picture; the mechanic in his mechanism. And the whole universe, whose maker and builder is God, is but one continuous and glorious revelation of the Great Architect:

2. We become acquainted with God through His providential government of the world. His kingdom extendeth over all.

3. We become acquainted with God through the human soul.

4. But especially do we become acquainted with God through His written word. But let me be understood. It is the Bible of which I speak—not systems of divinity—not confessions of faith. Here we have the only true, full-sized portrait that God has ever given us of Himself.

5. We become acquainted with God through His Son Jesus Christ, who was God manifest in the flesh, and in whom dwelt all the fulness of the Godhead bodily.

6. But besides the external embodiment of Himself in His Son, we have given to us the invisible and omnipresent Spirit, who shall take of the things of Christ and show them unto us,—who can come to the inner temple of the soul, and there present to the spiritual eye a spiritual God.

II. *What are the results of this peaceful acquaintance?*

"Acquaint now thyself with God, and be at peace; thereby good shall come to thee." What good? I reply,—

1. Great mental enlargement. The greatest conception of human intelligence is the idea of God. No other thought so fills the entire spiritual vision. And a constant association with that thought, as it lives in the soul, expands the mind as no other can. We are affected by the character of those with whom we associate. And he who lives and walks with God, possesses a mental elevation corresponding immeasurably with the nature of Him with whom he is thus brought into association. The best of all knowledge is the knowledge of God; the greatest of all sciences is the science which acquaints us with God.

2. But the heart is enlarged as well as the mind. Its sympathies are wider, its charities are broader. All creatures are seen as the creatures of God. Acquaintance with God inspires confidence in His government. Taken into the inner sanctuary, we see the hand that moves the universe. Without we see the

working of the mighty machinery; within, the power that guides it. And all the events of life pertaining to ourselves, however mysterious they may be, can awaken no distrust of God.

The sorrows of life are easily borne, for he endures them as seeing Him who is invisible. The sympathy and the supporting arm of God make the burden light. The loss of some earthly good may be a trial; but it is a light one, and but for a moment. And,

> "Why should the soul a drop bemoan
> That has a fountain near."

All that he loses, or can lose, is but a drop from the ocean. Such an one is at peace with the universe. He who knows God is at peace with death. For God's dominions extend over the waste domain of even the king of terrors. He is blest with the most glorious companionship. He is never alone,—never unbefriended. In the desert, with no mortal eye to cheer or pity, God is with him.

Learn,—

1. How perfect an antidote for unrest of soul does the text present to us. Acquaint now thyself with God, and be at peace. This is peace; not fictitious peace, but true, substantial, positive, permanent; as enduring as God its eternal source.

2. The great end of all God's dealings and doings is to make us acquainted with Himself. He writes His name upon every cloud and upon every star, paints it upon the rainbow, utters it in the thunder, whispers it in the summer breeze; He speaks to us from the written page, and with the still small voice of the inward monitor; He comes to us with the voice of the prophet, the apostle, and the living preacher; speaks to us through His Son; speaks to us by His Spirit; comes in rebuke; comes in melting tenderness; comes in the falling shower; comes in the sunbeam; comes in the dew-drop. Every disappointment of earthly hope, every loss of earthly good, every calamity, every bereavement, every prosperity, every adversity, every dashing wave of sorrow, every gilded wave of joy, every pain of body, every burden of the heart, every ill, every sorrow, every sin, still speaks in the ear of man,—" Acquaint now thyself with God, and be at peace; thereby good shall come to thee,"—*and thereby only.*

Life's Changes and Lessons.

By Rev. T. S. CLARKE, D.D., Franklin, N. Y.

"And the king said, Is there not yet any of the house of Saul, that I may show the kindness of God unto him? And Ziba said unto the king, Jonathan hath yet a son, which is lame on his feet."—2 Sam. ix. 3.

THE lessons of life are sometimes fearful, but always instructive to him who believes in the all-pervading providence of God. Of these lessons, the chapter containing the text is very suggestive.

I. *We have here a vivid illustration of the mutability of worldly greatness.*

About thirty-four years before the event here recorded, Saul received his appointment, as the first king of Israel, under circumstances prophetic of a splendid and prosperous reign; the events which led to his election,—his majestic personal appearance,—his sacred anointing,—his receiving another spirit from God,—were circumstances full of promise for the future. He had a rich kingdom, a powerful army, a numerous family, and the manifest favour of heaven. Yet, at the close of thirty-four years from this time, where is Saul,—what is the condition of his family? He has forsaken the Lord, who had so signally befriended him in his early manhood; he cuts the thread of his own life, and goes unbidden and unprepared to the bar of God. Where is his family, about which so lately were gathered all the luxuries and the pride of life? They were scattered at first here and there, till at length only one individual of the royal race of Saul is found, and he is a pauper and a cripple.

But while these sad changes are going on in respect to Saul, we have another individual presented in this chapter, whose history illustrates,—

II. *The efficiency of the favour and blessing of God in the way of well-doing.*

This individual was David, living at first in Bethlehem, the youngest of seven sons, and, for that reason, perhaps, chosen to keep his father's sheep; and, though his occupation was humble, affording but few, if any, facilities, as one would think, for rising in the world, yet he seemed determined to do with his might what his hands found to do. It was thus that he started in life, "seeking first the kingdom of God, and His righteousness," and then making it his commanding object to take lessons in the line of self-improvement, and to reach the highest excellence in the little sphere he was called to fill. Little did he think, while practicing with the sling and the stone, and waking to ecstasy the living lyre, and settling his mind in the great principles of truth and righteousness, what an influence these exercises would have on the success of his after life. The starting point of success is being faithful in that which is least. Let our young men, therefore, be of good courage, and trust in the Lord, and do good, and He will surely bring it to pass.

III. *We have also, in this chapter, an instance of a truly magnanimous spirit, exhibited by David towards the house of Saul, his bitterest enemy.*

An example which we shall do well to gaze at till it finds its counterpart in our own conduct. His magnanimity in the case before us rose far above any former precedent. For when firmly seated on the throne, and his enemies on every side subdued, he bethought himself of the house of Saul. "Is there yet any that is left of the house of Saul?" Why does he ask? Is it that he may put them out of the way? That they may not disturb the succession of his own family to the throne? O no; but it is that he may "show the kindness of God to them." Now it is refreshing to see such a spirit.

Any one, even a man of the smallest capacity, can be mean, cruel, unmerciful, and revengeful, for this is natural; but it requires a large heart, triumphing over all selfish considerations, not only to forgive a powerless enemy, but to bring him in his necessities into our own houses, and to permit him to sit, as we would a friend, at our own table. It has been well said, that to do good to those who love us, is natural; to do evil to those who do us good, is devilish; but to do good to those who do us evil, is godlike. It is imitating Him who "causeth the sun to shine on the evil and the good, and sendeth the rain on the just and the unjust."

IV. *We have also in this chapter an example of genuine and disinterested friendship.*

We mean by friendship the attachment of kindred hearts and minds,—an attachment steady and abiding through all the changes that occur in our mortal life. Such a friendship never existed in greater purity and ardour than between David and

Jonathan. Here is proof of a friendship far from common, that neither the lapse of time, nor great personal prosperity had been able to cool. It often happens, from a variety of causes, that the friends of our youth are forgotten. Yet these early friendships, as we calmly and thoroughly recur to them in our thoughts, have power to move the soul to its lowest depths. "Every man for himself," is the doctrine of selfishness,—a doctrine that gains strength, as life goes on, unless we take care to cultivate tenderness of feeling.

We honour David, therefore, the more for making himself an exception to the general course of human practice. In the height of his prosperity, he thought of Jonathan, his early and devoted friend; and the recollection did more than merely draw out the exclamation, "Alas! my brother!" It led him also to ask, "Is there yet any that is left of the house of Saul, that I may show him kindness for Jonathan's sake?"

V. *In the facts alluded to in this chapter, we see a remarkable interposition of Providence in behalf of the fatherless and afflicted.*

Jonathan, it will be remembered, was slain before he reached the prime of his life. He left a son, by the name of Mephibosheth, unable to take care of himself, for he was lame on both his feet. It was doubtless true, also, that, in the downfall of Saul's house, his property went down with him. But where, amidst all this confusion, do we find Mephibosheth, fatherless and lame, and probably without such an order of intellect as to command general respect? He was first taken up by Machir, who afterwards became a very useful friend to David. But as if this were not enough to illustrate the interest which God feels in behalf of the fatherless and afflicted, He also touched the heart of David, and thus this child of misfortune was introduced into the palace, and invited to eat meat during the rest of his life at the king's table.—Ex. xxii. 22; Ps. lxviii. 5.

VI. *We notice also the advantage attending a pious ancestry.*

There was nothing, so far as appears, either in the mind or heart of Mephibosheth to justify the attention and kindness which he received; but in Jonathan, his father, there was: and for the father's sake, a worthless, graceless son is often kindly remembered, when otherwise he would be left to perish in his own corruptions. There is a principle, underlying this subject, to which it becomes us to give earnest heed, and which is thus set down in the Divine testimony. "The mercy of the Lord is from everlasting to everlasting upon them that fear Him, and His righteousness upon children's children to such as keep His covenant." And this Jonathan appears to have done with heartiness and zeal, and hence the mercy of the Lord made a large provision for the wants of Mephibosheth. Yes, the good man does indeed leave an inheritance to his children's children. When he is dead, his influence lives—his prayers are a legacy of more value than all the gems of every earthly mine—than all the pearls in every ocean cave.

Christ the Head—the Church the Body.
By the Rev. A. T. CHESTER, D.D., Buffalo, N. Y.

"And gave Him to be the head over all things to the church, which is His body."—Eph. i. 22, 23.

THE church is not any one particular denomination. In the scriptural use of this name all are meant who have embraced the Lord Jesus Christ in the exercise of a saving faith, and who have professed attachment to Christ according to the forms of some evangelical communion; nay, if they have not made such open profession, because it has been impracticable, they are not on this account excluded from the fellowship of the Son of God. The church comprises all real Christians. It is this company of true believers that is called in the text the body of Christ. Of this company, considered as a body, Christ is the Head. The text exhibits an arrangement of Divine wisdom. God, Jehovah, gave His own Son to be head over all things to the church, which is His body. This passage is full of the most important instruction.

I. *We have in it a view of the exaltation of the church.*

II. *We have another truth taught in the text—the main instruction of the passage,—it is the superiority of Christ. He is the Head!*

III. *This passage also gives us light in respect to the nature of the present connection between Christ and His church.*

It is here represented by the connection of the head with the body.

IV. *One other distinct lesson is taught us in this passage, viz., the nature of the connection between the members of the church.*

It is the connection of the members of the same body.

There are two obvious reflections from this subject.

1. It is the duty of every member of this body to yield to the instructions of the exalted Head with which it is united. It is only as one can perceive the existence, and yield to the power of a sympathy with the Head, that there can be any assurance of that change which must take place in each child of earth, to fit him for the skies.

2. The other reflection has respect to the impenitent. They may learn from this subject where to look to obtain a correct view of religion,—the religion of Jesus. It is a system, like the complete framework of the human body,—the dwelling-place of the soul. But as we do not look at one's hands or feet, at his limbs or chest, to obtain a view of his character, but at his head—his brow, where mind holds its throne—his face, where moral traits are shown as in a mirror—so must those who would obtain a correct view of the system of religion, look, not at the body, but at the Head. This is a great mistake into which mankind are prone to fall; they look at the body of Christ, and because they detect some blemishes—for even true Christians are not yet perfect—they pronounce against it, and strengthen themselves in their unbelief and impiety. Oh, they should look on the Head!

But, Christian brethren, because the enemies of Christ will look at the body instead of the Head, and for the very purpose of finding fault, see to it that ye do all in your power to make the body agree with the Head. See that the vital union is preserved most carefully between every member and the Divine Head.

The Resurrection of Christ.

By Rev. E. F. ROCKWELL, North Carolina.

"And if Christ be not raised, your faith is vain; ye are yet in your sins."
—1 Cor. xv. 17.

THE death of Christ is the great central fact in the history of the world. To this the saints of old, for the space of four thousand years, looked forward, through the dim shadows of rites and offerings. For this Lamb, slain in the purpose of God, prophets, priests, and kings waited long, and died without the sight. To Him hanging on the cross as a sacrifice for sin, have all believers since that day looked back for comfort and peace. As the sun is the centre of the universe, so the Cross of Christ is the centre to which the hearts of all men that would attain blessedness must be directed. All the ends of the earth, and all ages of times, must look unto Him for salvation. No historical fact, since the world began, can have the importance of this; or needs more certain proof than this, whether Christ not only died, but rose again. No question can be raised that involves the interests of a greater number of persons, or for a longer time: for, as He is the only Saviour, if He be not raised, our faith in Him is ineffectual, and we are still in our sins.

I. *Christ undoubtedly died on the cross.*

II. *The dead body was laid in the tomb of Joseph.*

III. *This was a new tomb, hewn out of solid rock, and in which no other body had been deposited.*

IV. *This tomb was closed up by a door of solid rock, sealed up by authority, and a guard of Roman soldiers detailed to watch it.*

V. *But, to the confusion of those who had compassed His death, the body was gone on the Sabbath morning.*

All parties testify to this fact. The women who hastened to the tomb very early in the morning,—the disciples who also went,—the soldiers on guard reported the body missing; and how can its absence be accounted for? There are only four suppositions possible.

1. That the soldiers of the guard removed it.

2. That the Chief Priests and Pharisees caused its withdrawal.

3. That the disciples removed it.

4. No other supposition remains but that the body was removed without hands. He, by His own power, burst the gates of the grave, and took up that life that He had laid down. This would be the necessary consequence had no one seen Him afterward—had he immediately, on that Sabbath morning, ascended to heaven without manifesting Himself to men. But the angels that appeared to the women declared that He "was risen." Mary Magdalen first saw Him. Two other disciples, as they walked and went into the country, saw him next, "in another form," with a different dress, or a changed countenance. Afterwards He appeared to the eleven as they sat at meat, and "did eat before them."

On another occasion, at the sea of Galilee, "He showed Himself unto them." Paul informs us that He was seen by above five hundred brethren at once, which was probably on the mountain in Galilee, where He had appointed to meet them.

And so, after eating, and drinking, and familiarly conversing with His disciples for forty days, and appearing to none else, He ascended to heaven in the sight of them all. After His ascension He appeared, first, to the martyr Stephen, "standing at the right hand of God." He appeared to Paul on the way to Damascus, "as to one born out of due time," who refers often to this fact as important—" that he had seen the Lord," after His resurrection.

And though other persons saw the Saviour repeatedly after His resurrection, the eleven disciples were the chosen witnesses to testify concerning it to the world through all ages. And as so much is depending on their testimony, we may examine a little into their character. We may say that a competent witness must have three qualifications,—1, Capacity; 2, Opportunity; 3, Integrity.

1. Then, the disciples were capable of observing and judging of facts.

2. They had abundant opportunity to witness that about which they were to bear testimony.

(a.) By sense of hearing.
(b.) By sense of sight.
(c.) By sense of touch.

Just as Christ directed them,—"Behold my hands and my feet that it is I, myself; handle me and see; for a spirit hath not flesh and bones as ye see me have." And then, to give them full confirmation, took a fish and honey-comb, and ate before them. "To whom He showed Himself alive after His passion, by many infallible proofs, being seen of them forty days," proving to them that He had a real body of flesh and bones, by His eating, drinking, walking, and conversing with them.

3. They related faithfully what they had witnessed; we can put confidence in their integrity.

(a.) They gave their testimony there on the spot, and when the transactions were recent, and where they could easily be convicted of falsehood, if guilty of it, and by those strongly interested to do so: why was it not done?

(b.) Every motive of a temporal nature operated upon them to favour the Jews.

(c.) They attested their sincerity by enduring the greatest sufferings.

4. But that is not all; they had the unequivocal testimony of Him that cannot lie, in their favour to confirm their words; just as much as if He had spoken, as in reference to Christ, by word of mouth from heaven.

Hence they were not to leave Jerusalem to begin their testimony till they were endued with power from on high.

"And then they went forth and preached everywhere, the Lord working with them, and confirming the word with signs following." "Who gave testimony unto the word of His grace, and granted signs and wonders to be done by their hands."

5. We have a monument commemorating this great fact, and confirming the testimony of the witnesses, in the holy Sabbath. Immediately after the resurrection they set apart the first day of the week, and called it the Lord's Day, for this very reason, that on it He had risen,—they made it their day of religious worship.

6. We have one argument more bearing on this point, and that is,—The coming of Christ in power to destroy Jerusalem, and put an end both to the Church and State. His foretelling this is no ordinary prophecy,—His fulfilment of it no ordinary miracle. In the 24th chapter of Matthew, after giving a great variety of signs that are to precede, He says, "Then shall appear the sign of the Son of man in heaven;" and soon after He

says, "This generation shall not pass away till all these things be fulfilled."

We remark, in closing, then—

1. It is vastly easier to believe in the resurrection of Christ than to disbelieve it.

2. We have here a most convincing proof of the Divinity of Christ. He has the keys of hell and of death. He laid down His life voluntarily, and took it up again. "He was declared to be the Son of God, with power according to the Spirit of holiness by the resurrection from the dead."

3. We see that He finished the work for which He came into the world, made an atonement for sin, introduced everlasting righteousness, and is every way qualified to be the Saviour of the world, for He ever liveth to make intercession.

4. We have, in the resurrection of Christ, a pledge of the resurrection of His people. "Because I live, ye shall live also." He is the first-fruits, they are the full harvest.

5. But, finally, though it is true that if Christ be not risen, you may be still in your sins; yet it does not follow of course when it is proved that He has risen, that you are not in your sins. Without personal application to Him, and faith in Him as your Saviour, you cannot be saved. He was delivered for our offences, and raised again for our justification; but we are justified by faith in His name; and faith is an operative assent to His word.

Lydia's Conversion and its Consequences.

By Rev. TERTIUS S. CLARKE, D.D., Franklin, N Y.

"And on the Sabbath we went out of the city by a river side, where prayer was wont to be made, and we sat down and spake unto the women which resorted thither," &c.—Acts xvi. 13-15.

MAY it not be that many fail to be converted by reason of incorrect notions of what conversion is? May they not be unaware of the fact, that ignorance of the truth on this subject will be just as fatal to the soul as poison, taken by mistake, will be to the body? Is there not a sense of security here that ought to be alarmed? There are many that hear the gospel, to whom, as yet, it is far enough from being a savour of life unto life. May not one reason be, that they do not rightly apprehend it? They have, indeed, certain ideas about conversion; but whether right or not, how few of them take the trouble to inquire! My impression is, that many from this cause live and die unconverted,—their dim and cloudy views filling up the avenue through which truth, with its stirring realities, enters the soul.

It is, then, with unfeigned pleasure that I am able to give you an instance of real conversion, together with the circumstances and feelings which accompanied and followed it, and all endorsed by the spirit of truth; so that every one may see what it is—what is essential to it—what its effects are, and what he himself must be and do in order to be saved.

This instance is that of Lydia; and without adverting to all its instructive points, these, which will be illustrated in their order, will be sufficient for my purpose.

I. *What the impediment in the way of her conversion was, is seen in the statement, "Whose heart the Lord opened." Till then it was shut—it did not admit the truth which pressed from without.*

This was the impediment. There are many things which contribute to shut the heart against the gospel, and to keep it closed,—such as deeply-rooted prejudices, erroneous views of the truth, and especially habits of vice and licentiousness,—but then these things would not very seriously endanger one's salvation if they did not close up his heart to the impressions of guilt and the powers of the world to come. Yes, here is the impediment; and, what is worse, it is placed by sinners themselves across the path to life, and obstinately kept there.

II. *And here we naturally ask, "By whom was this impediment removed?*

"Whose heart the LORD opened." It was not effected by any charm in that prayer-meeting, nor by the power of human persuasion, nor by the unusual thoughtfulness and effort of Lydia herself. It was the work of God. Not that means are useless, nor that Lydia had no control over her own heart—but simply that as she had shut it against the claims of God, and would never of her own accord remove the barricade, so the opening depended on the mercy of God.

III. *But another important fact appears in this history of Lydia's conversion, relating to the circumstances in which this opening of closed hearts is effected.*

When this is declared to be the work of God, it is regarded by some as justifying the inference that human effort in the case is useless; and that the opening, as it depends on God, can be made in one place as well as another. But this is the language of a thoughtless, if not a bitter caviller. Where was it that her heart was opened?—and by what means? It was at a prayer-meeting, and by means of the truth that Paul preached there. In all this can you discover any violation of the laws of free agency, or anything justifying the inference in regard to the uselessness of means?

Still God is not confined to one method of operation. In Lydia's case, the means seemed like the gentle rain—in Paul's, there was the sterner voice of the storm—in the Jailor's at Philippi, the earthquake that shook the prison combined its voice with the truth that shook his soul. In every conversion recorded in the Bible, there was an apprehension of danger, great seriousness, and earnest inquiry after the way to be saved. It was thus with Lydia.

IV. *And now we come to the consequences of this opening of her heart.*

1. The *first* noticeable effect was, an earnest attention to the word.

2. The next effect of Lydia's conversion was her public profession of religion, and the baptism of herself and her household. She entered in due time into covenant with God and His people, and had the seal of the covenant applied to her children. Such an effect should follow in every case of conversion. The heart, which the Lord has opened, will pine if kept too long away from the ordinances of His house.

3. Another consequence of the opening of Lydia's heart to Christianity, was the manifestation of a benevolent, self-sacrificing spirit. "If ye have judged me to be faithful to the Lord," she said to Paul and his associate, "come into my house and

abide there." And the historian adds, "She constrained us." Yes, faithfulness to the Lord always brings with it largeness of heart.

And here I should close, were it not that two inferences are presented so clear, and at the same time so important, that I cannot forbear the statement, and a brief illustration of them.

1. The one is, that God moves in regeneration. Nothing is said as to the nature and source of the impulse that led Lydia to that prayer-meeting by the river's side. It may have been the force of early education—it may have been mere curiosity—and it may have been the persuasive, though unconscious influence of the Holy Spirit. So now God moves first in the regenerating process.

2. The other inference to which I alluded, as clearly springing from the history of Lydia, is, that it is not a matter of indifference, as is sometimes alleged, whether we attend religious meetings or not.

No Communications from the Dead to the Living.

By Rev. THOMAS L. SHIPMAN, Jewett City, Ct.

"It is not expedient for me doubtless to glory: I will come to visions and revelations of the Lord," &c.—2 Cor. xii. 1-4.

I HAVE not read this paragraph of scripture for the purpose of descanting upon the remarkable scene which it presents before us. We may not pry, with a vain curiosity, into things which the Apostle declares it was not lawful for him to utter. But why it was unlawful for him to communicate his "visions and revelations," may be both a proper and profitable inquiry. We may find in the sequel, that much practical truth stands connected with the solution of the inquiry.

We have an account of others, besides Paul, returning from the world of spirits. Lazarus was recalled from the dead. Many bodies of the saints which slept, arose and came out of their graves, after the resurrection of Christ, and went into the holy city, and appeared unto many. Dorcas was restored from the eternal world to earth. But there is no intimation that any of them made the slightest communication of what they had seen or heard in the world of spirits. Why this common and unbroken silence?

I. *It is the express will of God that we should derive our knowledge of the eternal world from the Bible.*

II. *Were such communications to be made, they would divert our minds from the Bible, our guide to eternal life.*

III. *Had Paul been permitted to utter his visions and revelations, it might have encouraged others to expect such communications, and dreams, and phantasms of the imagination been taken for heavenly visions.*

IV. *We have no reason to believe that messengers from the dead could give testimony more impressive than that we now have.*

God has "magnified His word above all His name." He is jealous for the honour of "the word." He will do nothing in His providence to disparage the preaching of "the word." "By the foolishness of preaching He saveth them that believe." You may look forward to some sudden, startling, overwhelming influence in the hour of death, but you will probably be disappointed. You will then be deprived of reason, or be so paralyzed by disease, as to look the grim messenger in the face, with the vacant stare of fatuity; or should you have "visions and revelations," not of "the third heaven," but of the lowest hell, "unspeakable," which you neither may nor can utter,— in the horror of your doom you will "give up the ghost." May God incline you to improve the passing hour as for your life!

III.—B.

A Faithful Saying.

By Rev. MARK TUCKER, D.D., Ellington, Ct.

"This is a faithful saying, and worthy of all acceptation, that Christ Jesus came into the world to save sinners, of whom I am chief."—1 Tim. 1. 15.

THERE have been many sayings current in the world, some of which were true and others false; some embodied important principles, others were only specious; some had been transmitted from generation to generation—from age to age—others have been forgotten; some have been practical, evincing great wisdom and knowledge of men and things, others have been unsound—have contained much error and false philosophy. The Apostle speaks of a saying which he affirms to be true and worthy of all attention. It refers to Jesus Christ and the object of His mission.

I. *We inquire what is implied in this saying?*

1. It is implied that men are *lost*. If it would be absurd to offer life to those who were not dead, it must be equally so to speak of saving those who were not perishing.

2. It is also implied that their salvation is a work of great difficulty. The names Christ Jesus, signify the Anointed One—One set apart for a particular work. If the work of salvation could have been achieved by any other being in the universe, God had not sent His only Son.

3. It is more than implied, it is affirmed, by the Apostle, that the chief of sinners may be saved.

4. We are also taught by this saying, the infinite grace and love of God. Christ Jesus came into the world to save sinners who deserved to die.

II. *We consider the propriety of accepting this saying, or, its claims to truth and general belief.*

1. It is a faithful saying; it is true. History substantiates the fact that more than eighteen centuries ago a stranger entered our world, asserting that He was the Son of God, the Messias who was to come.

It is proved by the fulfilment of prophecy. Predictions the most minute and convincing were accomplished—predictions which no human foresight could have suggested—which no human power could have brought about.

The truth of this saying is proved by the agreement of the types and antitype.

The truth of this saying is further attested by miracles.

Other witnesses have attested the truth of this saying. Thousands in every age who have been convinced of sin—of their lost condition—have trusted in Him for salvation.

2. It is worthy of all acceptation. A saying may be true, and still be unimportant. But this embodies the most interesting truth: to know and believe which is life eternal. It has as much interest and value at one time as another. In every part of this revolted world this report should be circulated and received.

It should be cordially received. The nature and claims of a report should decide the manner of its reception.

This saying is worthy of unqualified acceptation. Christ Jesus came to save sinners,—to turn away every one of us from our sins.

It is worthy of immediate acceptation. Danger cannot be too soon escaped,—the evil too soon averted. The message relates to a momentous concern—it deserves immediate attention.

I address multitudes to-day who have heard this saying ten thousand times, but it has been as an idle tale. Is it a true saying that Christ Jesus came into the world to save sinners? and how can you reject it? Gratitude should prompt to an acceptance. When guilt, like a heavy cloud, hung over the world, ready to burst upon us—when the wrath of God was kindled against us—when earth, smitten with the curse, gave signs that all was lost—then the Lord Jesus Christ came into our world, took upon Him our nature, obeyed the Divine law, endured its penalty, yielded up His life on the cross, that we might live. Are your hearts steeled against such love? "God commendeth His love toward us, in that while we were yet sinners, Christ died for us."

Religious Discipline of the Thoughts.

By Rev. RUFUS ANDERSON, D.D.

"Bringing into captivity every thought to the obedience of Christ."—2 Cor. x. 5.

PIOUS people often are wanting in control over their religious affections. They seem not to have the power of fixing them long on any object. Hence their religious feelings seldom rise into an elevated devotional frame.

Now if the nature of the difficulty in this case is not well understood, mistaken remedies may be applied, and disappointment be the consequence. The chief difficulty generally is in a want of due control over the thoughts,—for the thoughts and affections are most intimately connected. The heart is able to love only such objects as it sees; and it can look at them only through the medium of the understanding; that is, feeling is awakened, modified, influenced by means of thought. The inquiry suggested by the text, is therefore of great importance, viz. :—

How we may succeed in bringing every thought into captivity to the obedience of Christ; in other words, how we may acquire a religious control over our thoughts. And the inquiry is in the highest degree practical, because every one is more or less a thinking being, and has thoughts for which he is accountable, and which it is infinitely important for him to regulate by Christian principles.

I. *Let us first consider the nature of this discipline.*

This will be made best appear by some familiar illustrations. We will, then, suppose a pious man, but wanting in control over his thoughts, to be reading in the scriptures. He is really desirous of understanding what he reads, and, of course, makes an effort to read with attention, and for a short time his attention is fixed. But this is for a short time only.

The same man enters his closet for prayer. He assumes a reverent posture, and commences his petitions in an audible voice, as helping the attention. Meanwhile he discovers another train of ideas, or, more probably, successive, broken trains.

So in public prayer, in the house of God. One person leads in the prayer, and all in the congregation profess to offer up the same petitions. But suppose the heart-searching God were to put forth His finger, and write the prayer upon the wall; and that he were to write also, in parallel columns to it, the actual thoughts, meanwhile, of each professed worshipper. What a fearful exhibition there would be of thoughts foreign to the occasion.

Similar remarks might be made concerning other exercises of the house of God. Indeed, who of us would be willing to have the mere intellectual history of the hour he spends in this holy place (*i. e.* of his thoughts merely) written, by the omniscient God, for the perusal of his most intimate friend? I believe, not one.

One great reason why so little time is spent by Christians in solitary meditation on eternal things is, that they find these meditations so difficult and unprofitable for want of command over their thoughts.

One more illustration of the want of a religious government of the thoughts. It is, or should be, a grand question with every true Christian, how he should ensure the recurrence of religious thoughts in the intervals of his secular business, during the day. What I mean is substantially illustrated in the father of a family engaged in business in a foreign land. He does not think of the objects of his fond affection, now far away, merely morning and evening, but his thoughts revert to them whenever they can be spared from the business which called him away. And so it should be with the Christian, in respect to the objects and scenes of his heavenly home.

II. *Having considered the nature of this discipline, let us direct our attention to its importance.*

1. In the daily reading of the scriptures. Evidently we cannot expect the enlightening influences of the Holy Spirit on the thoughtless reading of the scriptures. How vain to expect it! The infinitely intelligent Being always knows where our thoughts are while we read His word, and cannot be deceived by mere words on a thoughtless tongue. But let the man who has subjected his thoughts to a thorough religious control, take the in-

spired volume. He opens it, and is at once prepared for an audience with the Most High.

With a mind thus under subjection, and even with no more than an ordinary share of intelligence, it is not necessary to read long portions of scripture at one time. For instance, if the reading be in the eighth chapter of the Epistle to the Romans, the first four verses might furnish full employment for an hour, or even a much longer period.

2. How important this control in the services of the sanctuary. We all come here professedly to worship God, and get religious benefit to our souls. But we must remember that "God is a spirit, and they that worship Him," to be acceptable, "must worship Him in spirit and in truth;" that is, with the sincere homage of the thoughts and affections. Suppose, now, that we had the power of self-control, and could say effectually to our worldly thoughts, as Christ to His disciples, "Sit ye here, while I go and pray yonder;" or as Abraham to his servants, "Abide ye here, and I will go yonder and worship." How holy, how heavenly God's earthly courts would then seem to us!

3. But nowhere is the indispensable necessity of control over our thoughts more clearly seen than in religious meditation. The very nature of such meditations supposes a fixed tendency of thought, a continuous train of reflections, in some one direction, on some one subject.

4. This control of the thoughts, is the indispensable means of attaining elevated spirituality and holiness. It is the indispensable means. For, what I now refer to is not a mere condition of the outward life. It is rather a state of mind, in which the soul having, through grace, acquired a new moral nature, the tide of its thoughts and feelings sets naturally and steadily heavenward. Now this state of mind is always produced by the agency of the Holy Spirit; but, at the same time, through the instrumentality of the truth, and never, in any eminent degree, by mere hasty glances, but by fixed and steady contemplations of the truth, and familiar acquaintance with it.

III. *The nature and importance of a religious discipline of the thoughts have been made sufficiently evident to permit us to pass to our last grand division of the subject, namely, How to acquire a religious control of the thoughts.*

This is to be done,—

1. By bringing our thoughts under the influence of a lively faith. A weak faith will never subdue the thoughts. There must be the "powers of the world to come."

2. By bringing the thoughts under the influence of love. We think most, and most easily, about that we most love. We must love the truth, if we would come under its controling influence.

3. By bringing the thoughts under the influence of hope. Hope is an "anchor of the soul." "We are saved by hope."

4. By bringing our thoughts under the influence of a fixed determination. Our thoughts will not be brought into captivity to the obedience of Christ by a slight effort, or in a single day. This is that earnest and protracted contest, which is called the Christian warfare. Many seem to regard that warfare as a conflict with outward objects, but it is a conflict within the soul. It is one of thoughts and feelings of opposite character, struggling for the ascendency in the soul.

5. By taking pains to prepare the mind for the performance of our religious duties, and to guard it against improper influences.

6. The last direction I would give for acquiring a religious control over our thoughts is, to erect mementos of spiritual things along the path of our daily business. An ancient heathen monarch is said to have had a servant cry out at his door every morning, "Remember that thou art mortal."

It only remains for each one to inquire, how far his own thoughts have been brought into this blessed captivity. Let us look for Divine aid, and not lose sight of the appropriate means, nor of the necessity for immediate and persevering effort. Think not that the heart can be kept, while the thoughts are uncontrollable. It cannot be. Our hearts will never be brought into full captivity to the obedience of Christ, unless our thoughts are. Both must be subdued, or neither will be.

A New Year Sermon.

By Rev. GEORGE B. CHEEVER, New York.

"And all the days of Methusaleh were nine hundred and sixty-nine years: and he died."—GEN. v. 26.

NINE hundred years! It almost covers the duration of the antediluvian world. When Noah began to build the ark Methusaleh was living, and was eight hundred and forty-nine years old; Lamech also was living, and was six hundred and sixty-two years old. Doubtless they were both pious, and probably some of their descendants also. Some of Methusaleh's brethren and sisters likewise, whom Enoch bore after him, and educated as such a man must have educated his children, were in all probability the subjects of Divine grace. Noah was not, therefore, entirely alone,—not entirely destitute of Christian sympathy and succour. His own father, Lamech, was alive until five years before the deluge, and his grandfather, Methusaleh, was living up to the very year that the deluge came. Nay, if he died a natural death, it could not have been more than a month, if so much, before the deluge. We do not know, indeed, that he did not perish *in* the deluge, but if not, then the funeral of Methusaleh must have been the very last thing that Noah attended.

In dwelling upon this interesting text, I shall first take a simple survey of the age and manners of the antediluvian world; and second, I shall draw some important lessons from such a survey.

I. *As to the age and manners of the antediluvian world.*

The youth of the world was the season of man's greatest age; perhaps, also, it was the season of man's greatest wickedness. Three things we know with certainty, amidst all the darkness that hangs over the life of the antediluvians; they lived to a great age, they rose to a great height of depravity, and except Enoch, they all died. The assurance of a very long life would be to any man either a great temptation to sin, or a great means of holiness; most likely the former. "Because sentence against an evil work is not executed speedily, therefore the heart of the sons of men is fully set in them to do evil." For more than seven antediluvian generations no death is recorded in the scriptures. For aught we know, the funeral of Adam was the first which his posterity attended for nearly a thousand years. There was, indeed, another funeral—the murdered Abel was buried,—but the parents were the only mourners.

When Methusaleh was born, Adam was six hundred and eighty-seven years of age. When Adam died Methusaleh was two hundred and eighty-two. The oldest man lived in the society of the first man two hundred and eighty-two years. Methusaleh was the grandfather of Noah; and when Noah was born Methusaleh was three hundred and sixty-nine years old. Methusaleh and Noah were therefore contemporaries during the long space of six hundred years. Noah had never seen Adam: the father of the second race of mortals had never seen the father of the first. But Lamech, Noah's father, and the first-born of Methusaleh, had lived while Adam was yet alive, ninety-five years; and he, as well as Methusaleh, could describe to Noah, from personal knowledge and recollection, the teachings and the venerable grandeur of the father of them all.

We cannot tell how many of the posterity of Seth were men of piety, we may hope that at least this was the case with the first-born, whose names are recorded in the scriptures. The generations so recorded are the first-born of the first-born: in that line came Enoch and Noah,—the first translated without seeing death, and the second preserved amidst the universal deluge to be the second father of the world.

As to that numerous progeny of the antediluvians undistinguished by name in the scriptures, but embraced in the general appellation of sons and daughters, it seems probable that but too many of them, from the earliest period, had corrupted their way before God.

II. *We may reduce the lessons to be gathered from this survey under several specifications.*

1. We may learn an appalling lesson as to the agglomerative tendencies of human depravity. In order to people the earth speedily, it was necessary that the life of the antediluvians should be extended over a period more than twelve times the limit of human existence afterwards assigned in the scriptures. It was also requisite for a full and fair experiment of human nature, and afforded scope and opportunity for the most rapid growth in knowledge and goodness. But the experiment resulted so miserably, that the destruction of the whole race proved necessary. Had it been much longer continued, the wickedness of human beings, in combination with the increase of their numbers, would have made earth well nigh a hell in all respects but its penal inflictions. Now, here is a lesson in human experience which, one would think, might silence for ever the advocates of the theory of human perfectibility.

2. I have spoken of the darkness that hangs over the life of the antediluvians. The extreme conciseness and paucity of detail in the sacred history concerning them are remarkable. We may draw from it a salutary lesson. Over all achievements of fame, all wonders of genius, all events of history, in which the actors anticipated an immortality of glory, the pen of inspira-

tion draws a blank. It is a parcel of insignificant rubbish—it is like the chaos of an unformed world—it is all passed over in forgetfulness, and the record of their life is comprehended in the merest affirmation of mortality—*he died.*

> Once in the flight of ages past,
> There lived a man:—and who was he?
> —Mortal! howe'er thy lot be cast,
> That man resembled thee.
>
> He saw whatever thou hast seen,
> Encountered all that troubles thee;
> He was—whatever thou hast been
> He is—what thou shalt be.
>
> The annals of the human race,
> Their ruins since the world began,
> Of him afford no other trace
> Than this,—THERE DIED A MAN.

Now, it is scarcely possible to read a more affecting and instructive lesson than the Holy Spirit has thus transmitted for our consideration, as to the worthlessness of all mere mortal grandeur in the eye of God. The pleasure, wealth, power, knowledge, glory, of ten centuries crowded into one life, with all the changes and shows of a human existence, continued through a period which with us suffices for the transit of nearly thirty generations, are just as unnoticed as if they had never had an existence. The only thing of absolute value is that which connects us with God, and makes us partakers of His holiness; all things else are baubles. Crowns are playthings, dukedoms and dominions of no more importance than the grains of sand that go to make up an ant hill.

3. The consideration of the great age of the antediluvians, and its effect upon their state on earth, might lead to some faint conception of what an Apostle calls the power of an endless life. It may do this in two ways,—first, the power of such a life for the increase of holiness; second, in the progressive accumulation of depravity. Enoch lived three hundred and sixty-five years,—as many years as there are days in the year,—an existence beyond the period of three centuries and a half,—and, by the faithful improvement of his privileges, through the grace of God, during this short period,—short in comparison with the ordinary antediluvian age, though long in comparison with our age, for a saint's earthly walk with God,—he became so holy, that in the strikingly simple and energetic language of the scriptures, "God took him." If this were the case in a world of sin, temptation, and opposition to holiness, what will be the rapidity of his increasing resemblance to God by the power of an endless

life, in that world where God, in the infinite perfection of His attributes, is all in all.

On the other hand, the whole race of antediluvians who lived in wickedness, became so wicked in the progress of less than a thousand years, that it was absolutely necessary for God to destroy them. This was a state of probation,—a limited period of human existence. Change time into eternity, remove restraint, and let despair take the place of hope, and you have simply human wickedness, endlessly progressive, without accompanying pleasure. In every age the wickedness of man needs only eternity to act in, and it constitutes hell.

4. We are all naturally as wicked as the race of mankind destroyed by the deluge. The great wickedness of the antediluvians was principally owing to the multiplication of their years; it was probably no greater than we ourselves should arrive at, if our life were as long as theirs. Doubtless it will be more tolerable for the antediluvian world at the day of judgment, than for the world of the ungodly, who, under the preaching of the gospel, reject the Saviour from their hearts, and die impenitent.

5. The mere duration of years does not constitute a long life, but the fulfilment of life's purposes. It was some distinction to have been the oldest man; it would have been a greater distinction still to have been the wisest man; but a greater than all to have been the holiest man. It is only a well spent life that can be enjoyed over again in the recollection. When Enoch was translated, he had lived longer in living to God, than the whole antediluvian race put together, who lived only for their own pleasure. No man lives long, who does not live to God's glory; but he who does that, LIVES ETERNALLY.

6. There was a time in the life of every ungodly antediluvian, in which his wickedness had reached such a point—his long habits of sin had gained such strength—that all hope of his salvation departed. At such a moment, though long before the close of his mortal career, it might have been said, with awful emphasis, *he died*. There is probably such a time in the life of every ungodly individual now; a time when man's evil habits have become so confirmed, and his heart so hardened by the deceitfulness of sin, that it is morally impossible he should ever after be converted.

7. Our subject teaches the danger of religious procrastination. At the beginning of the year, to which God in His mercy has spared us, this lesson comes with unusual solemnity. The habit of procrastination would be dreadfully dangerous, even if life were lengthened out to the farthest period of antediluvian existence; its indulgence would harden a man's heart, and carry

him, long before the day of his death, beyond the confines of his day of grace.

We should feel the value of our days, not so much by the rapidity with which they are passing—though that is a solemn consideration—as by what they are doing for us—what they are laying up in store before us. They are so many rapid messengers, whom we send into eternity before hand; and we are to meet our days again; we do not, cannot annihilate them. We have only sent them before us, to prepare us a mansion in heaven, or to make us a bed in hell. We shall meet them in eternity, for time is eternal, and even now is waiting in eternity to bear its testimony in regard to us. O, how solemn is this thought! The soul of time, if I may so speak, travels with our souls into eternity.

> Now! It is gone. Our brief hours travel past,
> Each with its thought or deed, its why or how:—
> But know each parting hour gives up a ghost,
> To dwell within thee, AN ETERNAL NOW!

The Great Separation.

By Rev. ALBERT BARNES, Philadelphia.

"I am come to set a man at variance against his father, and the daughter against her mother, and the daughter-in-law against her mother-in-law."—MATT. x. 35.

THE subject which is suggested by these words, is, the great separation which religion makes in families. The Saviour, in the text, simply states a fact. He does not say that he aimed at such a separation; or that it was in itself desirable; or that religion would be responsible for it; or that there would be no possibility of avoiding it: He states the fact simply as it would occur—evidently in His view a lamentable fact, and one that would be attended, sooner or later, with unhappy results. The union of families is desirable. It is such an object as the "Prince of peace" would seek. Endeavouring to keep the spirit of these words in view, and to pursue such a line of thought as shall best illustrate them, I shall invite your attention to two points.

I. *The union of families in religion is desirable; or, in other words, it is desirable that a family should be all united in the same faith, and in the same hope of heaven.*

Before suggesting the reasons for this—which indeed appear obvious almost without argument or illustration—I would observe, that in other subjects than religion, separations often occur in a family which create no evil, and which are, in fact, unavoidable. They are such as relate to the professions and callings in life, the daily avocations in the domestic circle, or the separation of a family when children advance to years of maturity. There is often much painfulness attending such separations, but there is no blame, and no injury is done to individual interests, or to society at large.

What is there in religion, it may be asked, which makes it so much more desirable that the members of a family should be united in that than in their professional pursuits? What is there that makes separation a subject of special regret? I shall submit a few considerations which are so obvious that they will probably at once occur to your own minds; at any rate they will commend themselves to you as true. They are these:—

1. Union in a family on the subject of religion is desirable, because all its members have the same interests at stake. It is not here as it is in regard to worldly matters. The same great object, substantially, may be obtained in a family in worldly matters, in separate callings in life. Happiness, health, property, respectability, may be secured though one be a farmer, another a merchant, another a mechanic, another connected with one of the liberal professions. In reference to religion, all the members of a family have substantially the same interest at stake. The soul of one is of the same value as that of another, and is to be saved, if saved at all, in the same way. Each one has been redeemed by the same blood; and each one is advancing to the same judgment-bar. Pardon, needed equally by all, is to be obtained by each in the same manner; and being obtained will confer the same peace on all.

2. It is desirable, because they are all under substantially the same obligation. That obligation may be slightly varied by age, or capacity, or the relation sustained, but it rests substantially on all.

3. Such union is desirable, in order to promote the happiness of a family; for religion enters more deeply into the things that

promote or mar domestic enjoyment than anything else. All the father's hopes are identified with his religion, and all his expectations that his children will ever be happy are identified with that also; and when there is not reason for that hope in regard to the child, there must be anxiety in proportion to the sense which the parent has of the value and importance of religion. Besides, religion is as needful to the happiness of one member of a family as another.

4. In like manner, unity in religion in a family is desirable to promote the happiness of those who are Christians. In most of the families that compose the congregations associated for public worship, there is one or more who is a sincere Christian. The happiness of such is in religion. If a child desired to pour into the bosom of a tender parent the purest, sweetest, most enduring joy, he would become a Christian. If a husband so loved the partner of his bosom as to desire to promote her happiness in the highest degree, he would become a Christian.

5. Unity in religion in a family is desirable, in order to give consolation in times of affliction. Nothing is more common than the breaking up of a family circle. Death comes. A husband, a father, a mother, a child is removed, and the survivors go forth and weep together. Now, religion would have made all that weeping circle calm and submissive. It would have met their common sorrows by common joys, and though afflicted here together, yet they could have looked forward to a world where they would rejoice together, where all tears shall be wiped from every face.

6. Once more. Unity in religion in a family is desirable, in order to promote the eternal welfare of all. There is no reason to believe that one can be saved in one way and another in another. There is but one path that leads to heaven, and that is a "straight and narrow" one. If anything is clear from the Bible, and from all the deductions of reason, it is, that they who have different characters in this world must meet a different doom in the next, and that this great principle cannot be set aside by all the tenderness of ties in the domestic relation. Is there any one of our children on whom we can look but with overwhelming emotions of horror with the anticipation that he will be at the left hand of the Judge, and is to "dwell with devouring fire" for ever? Christian fathers, mothers, ye who hope in the mercy of the Lord, the affairs of this world are trifles light as air when this thought enters the soul. What think ye of the gaiety and vanity, of the worldliness and want of religion, of the neglect of prayer in your closets and in your families, which may be the means of separating a child from your side at the bar of

God; which may unclinch your hand from the hand of a son there; which may sunder the embrace of mother and daughter there for ever, that the daughter and the son may "go away into everlasting punishment!"

II. *My second object was to show that religion does in fact make a separation in families.*

I design, under this head, merely to suggest some of the circumstances where religion makes such a separation.

1. It divides families at the communion table. Now, I will not say that in all cases it is true religion which makes this separation at the communion table. I will not venture to affirm that all who come to the Lord's Supper in the churches are true Christians; nor will I say that all who do not have no evidence of piety. On these points my subject requires me to make no affirmation, and I would not dare to do it, for it is not given to man to search the heart. But there are two considerations which may, without impropriety, be suggested here, and which demand the attention of all who do not make a profession of religion.

(1.) The first is, that so far as the evidence goes in the observance of the Lord's Supper, it is, that true religion makes the difference between those who commune and those who do not.

(2.) The second thing is, that your neglecting or refusing to make a profession of religion, is a public proof of the same kind, and of the same force, that you are not Christians. This may not, I admit, be infallible.

2. There will be less doubt in regard to a second separation which religion makes in families. It is in reference to the grave. It requires the exercise of large charity to believe that all families in the tomb sleep there with the same prospect of future glory. They may occupy the same dark house, and be arranged side by side, close to each other as they were when living. But what shall make us believe that they all sleep there with the same prospect of heaven? Religion made a difference while living: it made a difference in their plans of life, in their principles of action, in their conversation and deportment, in times of temptation and affliction, and on the bed of death, and why does it not perpetuate that difference in the grave? There might be much, could we see all, that would be melancholy in looking on a family burying-place besides what meets the eye.

3. There is less doubt still in regard to a third separation which religion makes. If there is not absolute certainty in regard to the effect of religion in causing the division at the communion table—if there is still uncertainty of increasingly painful

character in regard to the separation in the grave, there can be none of the agency of religion in the divisions of the day of judgment and of the future world. Here there is no room for conjecture, none for doubt. If the line run at the communion table be not the true line—if we are deceived about the dead, and hope when there is no ground for hope, and fear when there was really no reason to fear—yet the line will be drawn at the judgment-bar with unerring accuracy. That line will be so drawn that the universe will see and approve the reason why it is done, and it is a line which will be run wholly by religion. On this point the scriptures leave us no room to doubt; and the account in the Bible is one that wholly accords with our own reason, that it is religion that is to make the separation there—makes THE GREAT SEPARATION FOREVER. It makes a division there in such a manner that there shall be no future union. It places at the one hand of the Judge a father, and at the other a son; at the one hand a mother, and at the other a daughter; in one world a parent who sought the conversion and salvation of his children, and in the other those children, neglectful, impenitent, unbelieving.

My object will be gained if it secures two or three results which I will now state in the conclusion of the discourse.

1. If it leads Christians here to feel more deeply, and to pray more fervently, for their impenitent children, partners in life, parents, and friends.

2. If the subject leads those who are not now Christians, to similar reflections, it will accomplish another object which I wish. Children of pious parents, parents of pious children, husbands of pious wives, how can you bear the thought of an eternal separation from your friends?

3. A third result to which our subject should lead should be to cause us to look forward to the future world, and to contemplate the possibility that a family should be united in heaven. It is possible that there should be such an eternal union. It is not necessary that religion should make an eternal separation. The blood which has been sprinkled on one heart may cleanse all; the same Spirit that has renewed and sanctified the father or mother is able to renew and sanctify each child.

Why should it not be? A whole family united in religion—what a spectacle of beauty on earth! A family lying side by side in their graves, to be united again in the same blessed resurrection; what a spectacle for angels to look down upon with interest! A whole family united in heaven—who can describe their everlasting joys? Not one is absent. Nor father, nor mother, nor son, nor daughter are away. God grant of His infinite mercy that every family in this assembly may thus be united in religion in all the joys and sorrows of this life; united when they lie down in the grave in the hope of the same resurrection, and united on the banks of the river of life, to drink of the streams of salvation for ever! Amen.

The Sea giving up its Dead.
By Rev. WILLIAM R. WILLIAMS, New York.

"And the sea gave up the dead which were in it."—Rev. xx. 13.

THE resurrection was a favourite theme with the Apostles. The fact of Christ's having risen, was with them the crowning miracle of His earthly course, and an irrefragable argument of His divine mission. The resurrection of all mankind by Christ's power, to be judged at Christ's bar, was one of the truths upon which the first ministers of the gospel sought to turn the eyes of all their hearers. Peter preached this doctrine to the scribes of Jerusalem, and Paul proclaimed it amid the philosophers of Athens. And what thoughts struggle within us, as we look forward to such a change! We are prone, perhaps, to think too much of these perishable tabernacles of clay. But we do not, my beloved hearers, think enough of them, unless we think of them often and vividly, as bodies that are one day to rise again, endued with an indestructible existence, and capacitated for the endless bliss of heaven, or the eternal misery of hell.

I. *This great doctrine, the resurrection of the body, seems yet better fitted than the kindred truth of the immortality of the soul, to make a powerful impression on the mind of man, when receiving the gospel for the first time.*

The thoughts of the man,—his fears, his hopes, and his plans,—have had reference chiefly to the body. Bring him to look upon it as possible, that this,—the material frame-work in which he has enjoyed or suffered, by which he has laboured and acquired, which he has clothed and fed, and in which he has sinned,—this body, which in most of his thoughts, has been regarded as the whole of himself,—is to live again beyond the grave, and he is startled. Talk to him of the inward man of the soul, and he listens, as if you spoke of a stranger. But bring your statements home to the outward man of his body, and he feels that it is he himself, who is to be happy or to be wretched in that eternity of which you tell him.

In what glorious and terrific imagery does the scripture before us array the scenes of the resurrection. In the heavens, thronged by angels in all their glory, is seen the descending throne. Upon it, in His own and His Father's glory, sits the Son of Man, the crucified Nazarene, now the Judge of quick and dead. Before Him the material heavens are rolled together as a scroll, and the elements melt with fervent heat.

It will be a scene of solemn interest, not only as the meeting of man with his Redeemer and Judge, but from the meeting of mankind together. The scriptural accounts of the judgment represent it as an occasion when we shall know ourselves at least. From their descriptions of that day, as a day of disclosures, when the secrets of all hearts shall be made manifest, they seem also to imply that we shall know others, and be known by them. Without our consciousness of our own identity, there could evidently be no sense of guilt; and without our knowledge of the identity of our fellow-sinners, it seems to us, there could be no disclosures, such as the Bible predicts. Man then, in that gathering, will not only know himself, and know his God, but he will know his race. And this, to the sinner, will add inconceivably to the terrors of that assembling.

The meetings of the resurrection will form, then, no small portion of its terrors. This is the truth, upon which we would chiefly insist, from the part of scripture now before us. We have considered, generally, the resurrection of the dead. Let us next consider,—

II. *The sea giving up its dead.*

The sea will be found thickly peopled with the mortal remains of mankind. It is the great highway of traffic,—a highway on which the builder cannot encroach, and no monarch possesses the power of closing the path, or engrossing the travel. Thus continually traversed, the ocean has become to many of its adventurous voyagers, the place of burial. But it has been also the scene of battle, as well as the highway of commerce. Upon it have been decided many of those conflicts which determined the dynasty or the race, to whom for a time should be committed the empire of the world. All these have served to gorge the deep with the carcases of men. It has had, again, its shipwrecks. Though man may talk of his power to bridle the elements, and of the triumphs of art, compelling all nature to do his work, yet there are scenes on the sea in which he feels his proper impotence. And when God lets loose His winds, and calls up His billows, man becomes sensible of his dependence. Even in our own times, with all our improvements in the art of navigation, and with all the expenditures that are incurred to increase the mariner's security, it has been calculated by some, that each year one thousand ships are lost at sea.

The sea, then, has its dead. And when the trump is blown, the archangel's summons to the judgment, the sea shall give up these its long buried treasures. No relic that has formed part of the corpse of a child of Adam will be left unclaimed or unsurrendered in that hour. All, all shall be there.

III. *The meeting of the dead of the sea with the dead of the land.*

1. There must be, then, in this resurrection from the sea, much to awaken feeling in the others of the risen dead, from this, if from no other cause; these, the dead of the sea, will be the kindred and near connections of those who died upon the land.

2. Let it be remembered, again, that a very large proportion of those who have thus perished on the ocean, will appear to have perished in the service of the landsman.

3. Others of those buried in the waters have lost their lives in defence of those upon the shore.

4. Let us reflect, also, on the fact, that many of those who have perished on the waters will be found to have perished through the neglect of those living on shore.

5. Many of the dead of the sea will be found to have been victims to the sins of those upon shore. Those who have perished in unjust wars waged upon that element, will they have no quarrel of blood against the rulers that sent them forth?

The meeting, then, of the dead of the land with the dead of the sea will be one of dread solemnity, because of the ties of kindred and influence that bound them together, and because multitudes of those buried in the deep died in the service of the landsman, or in his defence,—many by his neglect, and many as the victims of the varied wickedness in which he had instructed, hardened, or employed them. Those who have been allied in sin, and accomplices in transgression, will find it one of the elements of their future torment, to be associated together in the scenes of the last judgment, and in those scenes which lie beyond that day.

In conclusion, let us dwell on some of the practical results of the theme we have considered.

1. The dead shall rise,—all shall rise,—and together. From the land and from the sea, wherever the hand of violence, or the rage of the elements have scattered human dust, shall it be reclaimed. And we rise to give account. We rise to be judged.

2. If the re-appearance from the seas of the sinner, who perished in his sins, be a thought full of terror, is there not, on the other hand, joy in the anticipation of greeting those who have fallen asleep in Christ.

3. This community especially owes a debt to that class of men, who go down to the sea in ships, and do business in the great waters.

4. It is, again, by no means the policy of the church to overlook so influential a class as is that of our sea-faring brethren. They are in the path of our missionaries to the heathen.

5. While humbled in the review of her past negligence, and in the sense of present deficiencies, as to her labours for the seamen, the church has yet cause for devout thankfulness in the much that has recently been done for the souls of those who go down to the sea in ships.

6. And now we ask each of you,—In that day, when earth and sea shall meet heaven in the judgment, where do you propose to stand? Among the saved or the lost—the holy or the sinful—at the right hand of the Judge, or at His left?

Religion our Life.

By Rev. BARON STOW, Boston.

"It is not a vain thing for you, because it is your life."—Deut. xxxii. 47

NOTHING is more common than for men to insist upon the superlative importance of their own particular theory, business, or profession. Whatsoever is connected with ourselves, we are very apt to overrate, while the interests and affairs of others, we are likely in the same proportion to undervalue. This is the spirit of the world—this is human nature *as it is.*

In a great multitude of minds, this principle is made the basis of judgment respecting the work of the Christian minister. We are often considered as acting professionally—consistently enough, perhaps—and yet only professionally—and as, therefore, liable to over-estimate the value of our avowed object. But if the Bible be true—and it remains to be proved that it is not true—then personal religion is the one thing needful, and our reasonings, and pleadings, and beseechings, and warnings, come not under the head of overheated enthusiasm; and the strongest language we can utter, and the most vigorous action we can employ, are not only justified but imperiously demanded.

This is the language of a man who stood, and who knew that he stood, on the border of two worlds. He understood and felt what he said. He spoke of the value of religion; and as he looked back on time, and forward into eternity, he testified to its importance as beyond all comparison,—" It is not a vain thing for you, because it is your life."

I. *It is not a vain thing.*

This it would be very easy to show, for its truth is confirmed by the testimony of all scripture and of all Christian experience. But the very terms of the negative imply a strong affirmation.

II. *It is your life.*

Strong as is the implication of the negative, the affirmative is infinitely stronger. How significant and emphatic the expression —*It is your life.*

When we say that personal religion is not a vain thing for you, because it is your life, we mean that it is essential
 1. To your peace of mind.
 2. To your support under the trials of life.
 3. To your fitness for the eternal world.

I speak as to wise men. Is a religion that can do all this for you a vain thing? Is that a vain thing which alone can give you peace of conscience; which alone can support you under the trials of life; which alone can light up the valley over which death stretches his gloomy shadow; which alone can fit you for a place in the paradise above, and raise you to happy and eternal companionship with saints, and seraphs, and God? *It is your life.* Without it you are undone now and for ever.

Fathers Invited into the Ark.
By Rev. MILTON BADGER.

"Come thou and all thy house into the ark."—GENESIS vii. 1.

THUS spake God to the patriarch Noah, at a most interesting and solemn crisis. For one hundred and twenty years, the inhabitants of the earth had been warned of coming wrath. Noah, by Divine direction, had been engaged in preparing an ark for the salvation of all who would believe. His work was now completed, and but seven days yet remained, ere the Lord would break up the fountains of the great deep, and open the windows of heaven, and sweep away every living thing from the face of all the earth.

At this moment of deep and solemn interest, when all things were fast preparing for the revelation of the righteous judgment of God, a voice from heaven breaks upon the patriarch's ear, saying, "Come thou and all thy house into the ark."

The command was addressed to the FATHER OF A FAMILY, and on the manner in which he received and treated it, depended his own salvation for time and for eternity, and on it, too, might depend the endless destiny of all his house.

The ark which Noah built is an emblem of the ark which God has provided in the person of His Son, for the salvation of men from another deluge predicted in His word—a deluge, not of water, but of fire. And I shall consider the text as the voice of God to every father of a family who has not entered the ark, Christ Jesus, saying unto him, "Come thou and all thy house into the ark." And I shall offer some considerations to induce every such father to obey, immediately, this voice of God.

I. *There is provision in the ark for thee and for all thy house.*

You are not required, like Noah, to devote years of labour and sacrifice to preparing for yourself a refuge. The labour has been laid upon God's only Son. The sacrifice has been paid in streams of His precious blood. The ark is built and furnished—all things are ready—the door thereof is yet open, and the Spirit and the bride say, Come. Myriads of households have already entered. There are the families of the patriarchs, and of the martyrs, and of the whole army of the faithful. And thou, father, who art now without, and thy children with thee, there is yet room for thee and for all thine. This day the Saviour calls, "Come, come thou and all thy house."

II. *There is no safety for you or for your children out of the ark.*

As God liveth, there is a storm coming which will empty the earth of all her inhabitants. Not one, of all the race of men, can abide the day of its coming, or flee from before its fury. No cavern so deep—no mountain top so high—no island of the ocean so remote as to afford a shelter. No combination of human power—no mighty effort of all the angels of heaven could avert its desolation. There is no safety from it but in the ark of God. With the children of your love around you, you may now feel that you are happy, although you and they are yet without the ark. But your happiness is imperfect; it is of short duration; and it is all at the mercy of God's forbearance. Let the heavens grow dark, the rains descend and the floods come, and it vanisheth like a bubble.

You may be the most kind-hearted and affectionate of earthly parents, and yet, if you are remaining with your children out of the ark which God has prepared for you, you are doing them an injury which, it may be, nothing you can hereafter do will be able to repair. Out of Christ they are unsafe. O, there is reason why God out of heaven should call to thee to-day, saying, "Come thou and all thy house into the ark," for out of it there is no safety for thee or thine.

III. *You should enter the ark of God, and seek to bring all your children in with you, not only because your salvation depends upon it, but because it may be indispensable to theirs.*

1. Your children, that are out of the ark of God, are unwilling to believe that there is a storm gathering, or that the ground on which they stand will be swept by the overwhelming tide. They are unwilling to believe that the ark is a place of safety, or that there are not other plans equally safe, and altogether more desirable. Now, who could convince them of their error, like you, their father? What teacher could reason with them so irresistibly? What minister plead with them so affectionately? You, they respect. You, they love. To you they are bound by cords which bind them to none else. Your counsels they will not utterly disregard. Your persuasions they cannot absolutely resist.

Have you ever told your children that they had sinned against God—that they were justly condemned to eternal death—that they must repent of all their sins, and believe in the Lord Jesus Christ, or perish for ever? Have you done this, and done it repeatedly, and done it in all the fervour of parental affection? We wish you to enter the ark to-day, that you may teach your children to enter it also. We wish you to seek the Lord while He may be found, that your children may find Him also.

2. Your children need an Almighty arm thrown around them, to gather them out of the snares and temptations of the world, into the kingdom of God's dear Son. They need to have the Holy Spirit poured out upon them, that they may be convinced of sin and of a judgment to come, and be humbled at the foot of the cross. And who shall come with strong supplications and with tears to the mercy-seat for this blessing, if not their father? If a child of yours were condemned to be executed on the morrow, who could be expected to plead with the executive of the state in his behalf like his own father? And who can be expected to wrestle at the throne of grace for the endless life of your offspring, like him whose image they bear, and to whom they are dearer than his own heart's blood? O, it is parental prayer that has had such power with God in perpetuating the blessings of His grace upon the seed of the righteous. It is parental prayer that has brought multitudes of children and youth to the feet of Jesus.

3. Your children need the influence of example, as well as of instruction and prayer, to induce them to seek first the kingdom

of heaven. And whose example can exert such an influence upon them as that of their father?

And wilt thou, who art a father, in view of these considerations, hesitate whether thou shalt enter the ark of God? If thou hast no mercy upon thine own soul, wilt thou have none upon the souls of thy children? They are bone of thy bone, and flesh of thy flesh. They are entrusted to thy care. Their Maker and thine has enjoined it upon thee, to take care of their souls. They need your most faithful instructions. They need your most fervent prayers. They need the influence of your pious example. And will you not regard their necessities? You would not deny them the meat that perisheth; will you deny them that which endureth unto everlasting life?

What must be the distress of a father, summoned to the death-bed of an unconverted son, there to feel that his neglected duties, and his ruinous example, have hardened his own son in impenitency, and blotted out his hope of heaven! Or, think of an unconverted father laid, at an unexpected moment, on his dying bed. His children come around him. The morning and the evening incense has never gone up from his dwelling to God, and now it is too late. But there are scenes more heart-rending than these—scenes beyond a death-bed. The unfaithful father must meet his ruined children at the bar of God. O, what an interview that!

Or turn, for a moment, to a different scene. Methinks I see, at the right hand of the eternal throne, a father in glory, and all his children are glorified spirits around him. They rise up, and with united voice call him blessed. What tongue can describe, what heart conceive the blessedness of such a father? Would you make that blessedness your own, begin, O, begin every duty which you owe to your own soul and to the souls of your offspring to-day. Come thou and all thy house into the ark. Fathers, I speak to you; and I speak in behalf of your own soul and the souls of your dear children. Judge ye what I say.

Why should the Work Cease?

BY REV. WILLIAM B. LEWIS, BROOKLYN, NEW YORK.

"And I sent messengers unto them, saying, I am doing a great work, so that I cannot come down; why should the work cease, whilst I leave it, and come down to you?"—NEHEMIAH vi. 3.

AS Nehemiah, with his faithful Jews, "builded the wall of the city," he was invited by Sanballat and others, to a consultation upon public matters. Their designs, he had occasion to know, were unfriendly. Perhaps they intended, after alluring him into the plain, to lay violent hands upon him. They certainly meant to put a stop to the repairs. And the very least evil that could result, would be the suspension of the work during his absence.

So he declines a conference. At once Sanballat repeats the proposal, but with as little success. Four different times messengers come soliciting an interview, and in each instance Nehemiah replies, I am doing a great work, so that I cannot come down; why should the work cease, whilst I leave it, and come down to you?

In applying the text to ourselves, as engaged in a revival of religion, I propose the following inquiries.

I. *In what respects is this a great work?*

It is such, as it requires great effort—demands the power of God—is carried on against great opposition, a mighty adversary, with his servants and abettors—reaps blessed results, the quickening of Christians, the conversion of sinners, and the praise of Divine grace—and, because perverted or unimproved, contributes to painful results, the hardening of the hearts, and the aggravated ruin of multitudes.

II. *In what respects are we doing this great work?*

We are not to forget that the efficiency is God's. "Not by might, nor by power, but by my Spirit, saith the Lord of hosts." It is one of the chief delights of the Christian in a revival, to feel and to say, "Lo, this is our God!" To exalt the Holy Spirit! To magnify His office and His work.

Yet, in some important respects, we do this work. For, we use the means of its advancement.

We preach the word—frequently, plainly, and with adaptation to the season, and to the numerous classes which the season occasions. In the inquiry meeting, and from house to house, we confer with the troubled soul,—explain to him the way of God more fully.

We bring the unconverted to the house of God.

We pray for them.

III. *What, in the course of a revival, is to be guarded against, as likely to cause the work to cease.*

Past success. Christians count the converted; pronounce on the power and extent of the work; congratulate themselves and each other; and are satisfied.

Unbelief. The idea obtains, that God will not save many in so small a congregation; or in a congregation where the proportion of the unconverted is so small.

Discouragement from the character of those who remain unconverted.

Weariness,—from continuing in an uniform and absorbing work.

A diminution of attendance upon the house of God. The influence of the mere presence of each member of the church, is mighty. The influence of his absence, mightier still.

Worldly business. It is a hard lesson for Christians to learn that their business is God's, if such that they have a right to pursue it; and that God's work is theirs.

Worldly company. When Christians go again, for their happiness, into circles where religion is not ascendant, or court or admit the attentions of the irreligious and the gay—it is saying decisively that we have no further occasion for the company of the Holy Spirit.

Habitual and easily besetting sins. The first step, on engaging in a revival, is to part with these.

Our selfish ends answered. Numbers and strength have been added to the church. My own house has shared in the blessing.

A vague impression that the work will go on. If the idea obtains, that the preaching is good; the preacher wise and successful; the church humble and prayerful; the congregation deeply moved; the Spirit powerfully operating,—and therefore, irrespectively of the part individuals may act, the work will advance,—it is likely to cease.

Prayer intermitted. Exalt God less; recognize, realize less, your entire dependence on the Almighty Spirit; let prayer flag in the closet, prayer meetings become thin and lifeless, and the conviction less fixed and less felt, that this work advances only as God is here,—and the work will cease : it has ceased.

IV. *Why should this work not cease ?*

The work honours God.
The presence of God.
The promises of God.
The number already converted.

The establishing of converts.
It is a delightful work.
The influence of this work on other churches.
The worth of the soul.
The number of the unconverted.
The character of the unconverted.
The nearness of many to ourselves.
The influence that the conversion of a soul may set in motion.

Finally, if the work ceases, it is that we " go down " again into carelessness and sin. The close of a revival is as sad, as its commencement is happy. The church laying down their watch, and relaxing their effort and prayer, and the irreligious falling into indifference, must compensate the adversary, it would seem, for the inroads he has suffered. Shall this be? Can we bear the thought?

V. *How may we secure the continuance of the work?*

Continue all that we have done, to invite the presence of the Spirit, and to promote the work. Abandon all that may have hindered its more powerful progress. Cherish your interest in the revival. Be present amid its moving scenes. Learn within those walls how little is the world, how valuable is the soul, how great is God! Be humble; be watchful; be solemn; be prayerful.

If you have withheld your presence, and your hearty co-operation, repent. Now throw yourself into the work. Show that you have enough religion, enough sympathy with the Saviour, enough regard for the souls of men, to concur in the saving operations of the Spirit.

If you cannot show this—if it is not so—then inquire into your own standing before God. Inquire whether there is not the first and best of reasons, why you, YOU should enter into this work; whether this revival may not have been sent to rescue *one* at least from a state as fearful as avowed impenitence!

The Tokens of Perdition.

BY THE REV. GEORGE B. IDE, PHILADELPHIA.

"Which is to them an evident token of perdition."—PHILIPPIANS i. 28.

WE all know what is meant by a token. When we hear the thunder rolling at a distance, and see the clouds collecting among the hills, and becoming every moment darker and more heavy, we know that a tempest is approaching. When we witness the workings of disease,—behold it consuming the beauty of youth, and the vigour of manhood,—imparting a feverish bloom to the cheek, and a preternatural lustre to the eye,—we know that these are the auguries of death.

These are tokens in the natural world. But the moral world has also its tokens. Most men exhibit certain *religious* phenomena, from which, viewed in connection with the known influence of moral causes, we may estimate their prospects for eternity, and forecast the probabilities of their salvation.

Some of these are tokens for good. But I cannot be insensible to the fact, that multitudes present appearances of a far different character,—appearances which to the spiritually instructed eye, are ominous of approaching ruin, and which fill the pious observer with emotions like those of the benevolent physician, when he discovers in the symptoms of his patient the certain presage of dissolution.

But as those in whom these tokens are most clear and numerous, are usually least conscious of their existence, it will be my object distinctly to describe them.

Before entering upon this subject, however, I would wish to guard against misapprehension, by stating explicitly what we mean when we affirm that particular classes of unconverted men exhibit the omens of destruction. We do *not* mean that the salvation of such persons is *impossible.* If, indeed, they would repent and believe the gospel, they would undoubtedly be saved ; for all who thus comply with the overtures of mercy, however aggravated their guilt or desperate their condition, are delivered from the curse of the violated law, and become heirs of eternal life. But such is the strength of the barriers which their own conduct has thrown in the way of their repentance and submission to Christ, as to produce a fearful improbability that they will ever exercise these affections, and thus obtain a preparation for the world of glory. That this improbability may and does exist in specific cases, is evident, not merely from the deductions of reason, and the known connection between cause and effect, but also from the unerring testimony of revelation.

With these preliminary remarks, I proceed to describe those features in the character and condition of particular classes of unregenerate men, which render their conversion improbable, and, in the fearful language of the text, are "to them an evident token of perdition."

I. *The first is a false hope of piety.*

The scriptures expressly declare that those only who possess the Spirit and obey the commands of Christ, are His true disciples. They teach us that all the subjects of saving grace experience a moral renovation, in consequence of which they renounce their sins, separate themselves from the world, live as the inheritors of immortality, and manifest an intense and unremitted devotion to the cause of their God and Saviour. And yet we see multitudes in the enclosure of the church whose conduct is widely at variance with this inspired description. In their temper and habits they appear but little different from the irreligious around them. They betray an addiction to the vanities of earth, and a disregard of eternal interests, as gross and prevailing, as if this narrow round of months and years were the whole of their existence. They evince no solicitude for the prosperity of Zion; make no exertions for the salvation of sinners; and by their inconsistency and unfaithfulness, "crucify the Son of God afresh, and put Him to an open shame." And is it possible that such are real Christians? "By their fruits ye shall know them." Judging by this infallible rule, we can form no other opinion of their state than that, beguiled by an egregious self-deception, they have laid the "flattering unction" to their souls that they are converted and pardoned, while they are still "in the gall of bitterness and in the bond of iniquity." Well, then, may it be said, that a fallacious persuasion of piety is, to those who indulge it, "an evident token of perdition."

II. *Another token, equally fearful, is a premature depravity.*

By this expression it is not my design to imply that all men are not naturally corrupt, but simply to indicate the development of that corruption. It is seldom, for example, that we see a youth of confirmed and incorrigible profligacy. But I see before me such a youth. Though scarcely arrived at manhood, he is a veteran in guilt. With remorseless audacity, he tramples on every thing sacred and holy, makes a jest of his early convictions, sneers at moral principle, derides the solemn sanctions of inspiration, and defies the vengeance of the Eternal. And can we, while contemplating the immortal destiny of such an individual, perceive in it a single ray of hope? Must not the fact, that one so young in years is so old in sin, be deemed a mournful presage of reprobation? He has placed himself within the verge of a whirlpool that rarely gives back its prey; and though it is still in the compass of Omnipotence to draw him from its fatal power, there is far more cause to fear that, after a few rapid and giddy circles, he will go down the yawning vortex into the abyss of despair.

III. *Another token, of similar import, is an inveteracy in transgression.*

The almost invincible force of habit is a subject of universal remark. Small must be his acquaintance with men, who does not know that to relinquish what has become familiar to them by custom or association, is an effort of the highest difficulty. "Can the Ethiopian change his skin, or the leopard his spots? Then may he, who is accustomed to do evil, learn to do well." Miserable man! by his own suicidal presumption he has flung himself into a torrent, whose black and swollen waters are rapidly hurrying him to destruction. He may resolve, and strive, and shriek for help, and make convulsive efforts to escape, but the impetuous stream still bears him onward. And now, as the roar of the cataract strikes louder on his ear, and the wild waves foam and toss around him, he buffets the current with feebler stroke and waining resolution, till despair flashes on his soul, and with a cry of horror that pierces the heavens, he is swept over the dizzy brink, and disappears.

IV. *Another token of perdition is a confirmed belief of destructive error.*

The confidence which the votaries of error repose in its delusions, is widely different in different persons. With some, it is little more than a cherished wish that their system were true and an anxious endeavour to make it appear so, combined with many secret fears that it will prove to be false. Others manifest a more settled credence. By the constant repetition of sophistical arguments, they have so perverted their moral sense, as to "call evil good, and good evil," to "put darkness for light, and light for darkness," to confound the distinctions between sin and holiness, and to pursue the downward road to the pit, with an unfaltering trust that it will end amid the glories of the upper world. It is to this class that we refer, when we affirm that an establishment in fundamental error is the precursor of ruin. "God has sent a strong delusion, that they should believe a lie, and be damned, because they believe not the truth, but have pleasure in unrighteousness." How dreadful, then, is a fixed reliance on the doctrine, that there is nothing for the ungodly to fear in a coming world! It is a placid but treacherous river, down which the credulous voyager glides serenely, lulled by the music of its waters, charmed by the beauty of its shores, and praising the smoothness of the current, which he fondly imagines is wafting him to the port of heaven,—till death dispels the hallucination, and he awakes in "the lake of fire."

V. *Another token of perdition is an unsanctified, worldly prosperity.*

Irreligious men, in their blindness and infatuation, eagerly covet such prosperity, and deem it a signal proof of the Divine regard. But no mistake can be greater. A fulness of sublunary good, when unaccompanied by piety, is to be considered a curse rather than a blessing, inasmuch as it presents an almost insuperable obstacle to the spiritual welfare of those who possess it. In every age of the Church, instances of conversion among the fortunate devotees of wealth and honour have been "like angel's visits, few and far between." While the lowly children of poverty and sorrow have repaired, in crowds, to the arms of that compassionate Redeemer who invites the weary and heavy laden to find rest in His bosom; the vast majority of the prosperous, the opulent, and the great, despising His salvation, have continued to bask in splendour, to riot in affluence, and to live at ease in their possessions, till their pomp, and luxury, and pleasure have been exchanged for the woes of hell.

VI. *Another token of perdition is apathy of mind under divine chastisement.*

Their infliction is the highest effort of infinite compassion—

the reserved agency to which it applies, when all the resources of goodness and forbearance have been expended in vain. And yet how many are there, on whom even this instrument has been employed without effect, and in whose unrelenting bosoms the rebuke of Jehovah has produced no compunction. What hope, then, is there, that any thing in the whole circle of moral influences, will ever bring them into cordial obedience to the cross of Christ? What can impress and soften hearts on which the rod of the Almighty has fallen and left no scar? Though it is not for us to foretel their fate, but to leave them to the disposal of that God whose love they have slighted, and whose judgments they have despised; still we cannot avoid the apprehension that in them the terrific threatening of insulted mercy will be verified, "He that being often reproved, hardeneth his neck, shall suddenly be destroyed, and that without remedy."

VII. *Another token of perdition is a return to insensibility after serious impressions.*

There are multitudes who exhibit this characteristic. During some revival of religion, or under the searching expostulations of some pungent sermon, they have been awakened from their natural state of thoughtless security. Their sins have been set in order before them. They have been made to see the importance of an interest in Christ to their present and eternal happiness. They have felt something of the power of the world to come, have shuddered in view of their approaching condemnation, and, in anguish of soul, resolved to attend to their immortal welfare. But their convictions are now effaced, and their resolutions forgotten. How improbable, then, is their salvation! Every view, which can be taken of their state, conspires to prove that their peril must be extreme. Their very tranquility is the harbinger of destruction. It is the ease of the expiring patient when raging inflamation terminates in gangrene. It is the repose of the sleeping volcano—the calm which precedes the hurricane—the stupor into which conscience sinks when the palsy of spiritual death begins to settle upon the soul. To all the applications of truth and strivings of the Spirit they are impregnable. Nothing, therefore, but a miraculous interposition of sovereign grace can pluck them from the precipice on which they stand. It is an indubitable fact, that very few of those who, from a state of religious solicitude, decline into apathy, are ever truly converted.

VIII. *The last token of perdition, which I shall notice, is an impenitent old age.*

III.—T

The young, I am well aware, are often encouraged to postpone repentance, from a persuasion that they shall become pious in the decline of life, and that that period is more favourable to the attainment of religion than any other. But no expectation can be more delusive. Among the innumerable situations of guilt and danger, in which infatuated mortals place themselves, there are none so forlorn of hope, so destitute of every cheering promise, as an irreligious old age. The physical powers, at that season, are enfeebled and bowed down with the weight of years. With this decay of the body there is a sympathetic and equal decay of mind. Nor is this all. The corrosion of time is still more visible in the moral faculties. They have long ceased to have any anxiety about their spiritual welfare. They seem scarcely to consider that the soul can be lost, that an eternity of bliss or of woe is before them, or that the hour for their departure for it is near. Oh, it is enough to break the benevolent heart to see a hoary-headed transgressor tottering on the verge of the fathomless gulf, and yet reckless of his impending doom, till his feet slide, and he vanishes in the depths of despair!

Thus have I endeavoured to set before you some of those traits in the character of several classes of unregenerate men which render their salvation improbable. In this enumeration, I have by no means included all which might, with propriety, have been embraced in it. But those which have been mentioned are surely sufficient to prove that the spiritual circumstances of vast numbers among the unconverted are solemnly critical.

It is not from any love of such a theme, or from any delight in harrowing up your feelings, that I have been induced to present this topic. God is my witness, that every part of it has been prepared and delivered with a bleeding heart. At the description of each fearful token, I could have sat down and wept, in anguish of spirit, over those who exhibit it. No; it is not because I, a guilty sinner, find pleasure in portraying the perils of my fellow-sinners, that I have called your attention to this subject; but because I, a pardoned sinner,—a sinner from whom numberless marks of perdition have been washed away by the blood of Christ,— would urge you, by the terrors of an impenitent state, to repair to that wondrous fountain, of which I know the efficacy.

I can only sit down beside you, and watch your moral symptoms, and weep as I contemplate their increasing violence, and breathe forth my earnest prayers to that Great Physician who alone can remove them. To Him I invite you. Seek Him while He may be found. Seek Him, ere yet the distemper of sin shall be beyond remedy, and mercy shall depart, and hope shall expire, and the "recording angel," with a pen dipped in "the wine of the wrath of God," shall write on your foreheads, "INCURABLE."

The Triumph of the Cross; as opposed to the modern theory of Second Adventism.

BY THE REV. HUBBARD WINSLOW, BOSTON.

"And I, if I be lifted up from the earth, will draw all men unto me."—JOHN xii. 32.

WE have fallen on strange times. And yet not entirely strange; for ever since the melancholy disaster in Paradise, man has been prone to morbid excitements. The present is one of the points, in the wheels of revolution, at which this weakness of our fallen nature is very strongly developed. Not on one subject only, but on all, there is an impetuous rush of feeling, in which passion overleaps reason, and a fiery haste to *do*, prevents the calm pause to *think*. At such a time, how cheering to hear the familiar voice of that well-tried and glorious Friend, speaking from a higher world, "And I, if I be lifted up from the earth, will draw all men unto me." This is none other than our Divine Saviour.

The sentiment is clearly this,—The cross of Christ is to gain a moral triumph over all the world.

I here announce this as an antagonist doctrine to the recent second-advent theory. The former teaches that God is to purify the world from sin by the power of the *cross*, the latter that He is to do it by the power of *fire*. The one is a moral agency, and a moral result; the other a physical agency, and a physical result. In the latter case moral government is virtually, as connected with the cross, abandoned; in the former, it is carried on to glorious consummation. If God must needs interpose fire, to do what the cross was to do—purify the world from sin—then the cross is defeated. In the drawing of men to Christ, as lifted up upon the cross, the following facts are to be distinctly noticed.

I. *There was to be no miraculous agency.*

Miracles were interposed to put the seal of God upon His holy religion, but not to extend its dominions from age to age; for a perpetual miracle would defeat itself. It would cease to be a miracle.

II. *This drawing to Christ was to be effected through the agency of those heavenly truths which cluster about the cross.*

The bright development of the character of God, as a being of infinite justice, mercy, and truth; the awful malignity of sin, as illustrated in the agonies of Jesus; the amazing value of the soul, as seen in the price paid for its redemption; the immortality of man; and the endless destinies of weal or woe pending on his relation to God,—these are the truths which, radiating from the cross, were to seize on the hearts of men and draw them to Christ.

III. *These truths were to be made effectual by the Holy Ghost, whose influence is secured and sent down to men by virtue of the cross.*

Accordingly the Holy Ghost was given, in greater measure after the ascension than ever before, and has through all ages accompanied the gospel, and drawn men to Christ.

IV. *This was to be a gradual work.*

Our Saviour compares it to the operation of leaven, which a woman hid in three measures of meal till all was leavened. He also compares it to the process by which the mustard seed rises from the smallest beginning to a stately tree.

V. *In this drawing to Christ, no other than moral means were to be employed.*

It was for Mahomet to take the sword, for the Brahmin to wield the terrors of caste, and for the Roman pontiff to light the fires of the stake; but it was for the heralds of the cross, unarmed with carnal weapons and with carnal sophistries, to proclaim Christ crucified,—the wisdom and the power of God for salvation. And never have they swerved from this course, but they have brought reproach on the cross, and evil on their own heads.

VI. *This drawing to Christ was to be effected in a calm and noiseless way.*

How like this are all God's other works of blessing. How noiselessly does the sun rise, and pour his beams over the world—how calmly do the wheels of nature move round—how gently does the acorn start from the earth, and rise in spreading branches to heaven. Such is the modesty, so to speak, of God's way,—such the beautiful "hiding of His power." And how unlike this, are the noisy and disorderly movements of second adventism.

VII. *This drawing to Christ was to be effectual, and, ultimately, universal.*

My word shall not return unto me void, saith Jehovah, it shall accomplish the end for which I sent it. Jehovah even takes His most solemn oath on this subject,—As I live, saith the Lord, every knee shall bow, and every tongue shall confess. All people, and kindred, and tongues shall come and worship, and bow down before Him. The knowledge of the Lord shall fill the whole earth, as the waters fill the seas. None shall have occasion to say unto another, Know ye the Lord; for all shall know Him from the greatest unto the least. The Lord shall make bare His holy arm in the eyes of all the nations, and all the ends of the earth shall see the salvation of our God.

Now every student of history must know that these prophecies have not been fulfilled. Hence, if the Bible be God's book—if the doctrine of the cross be true—the modern theory of second adventism cannot possibly be true.

That theory is in direct contradiction to the scriptural doctrine of the cross, which we have been exhibiting. It is equally in contradiction to the whole course of Providence. All things, in the course of Providence, perfectly harmonize with the views we have taken of the gradual conquest and ultimate triumph of the cross. The great law of God's kingdom, both in the natural and moral world, is one of gradual progression.

Nor is this all. To have the mind so intensely absorbed with the single idea of the speedy destruction of the world, is to divert it from the essential duties of religion, as well as of social life. The single point comes to be, to believe this theory,—there is no repentance of sin, no regeneration of heart, no drawing of men to the cross of Christ. The great and beneficent design of the gospel is defeated. The cross is set aside, and another agent is looked to.

Death by Spiritual Blindness.

By Rev. T. E. VERMILYE, D.D., New York.

"But if our gospel be hid, it is hid to them that are lost"—2 Cor. iv. 3.

WE can scarcely conceive of a more affecting commission or a more terrible doom than that which Isaiah was commanded to bear against rebellious Israel, when God was about to give them up to the blindness of their minds and the hardness of their hearts. "Go and tell this people, Hear ye indeed, but understand not; and see ye indeed, but perceive not. Make the heart of this people fat, and make their ears heavy, and shut their eyes; lest they see with their eyes, and hear with their ears, and understand with their hearts, and convert and be healed." With what feelings must the prophet have borne such a commission, which seemed to leave no avenue for mercy,—which, by its very terms, cut off all hope from His people. And yet, have we ever reflected, that under the government of the same God the same principles must still exist: that with clearer light and more impressive sanctions, the guilt and danger of rejecting the claims of the gospel cannot be less? Have we ever thought of the solemn inference, "If our gospel be hid, it is hid to them that are lost?"

Let me ask your attention to the scope and meaning of this declaration, and your personal concern with it.

I. *Inquire what is comprehended in the subject here spoken of, " our gospel."*

The term, as you are well aware, signifies, "glad tidings," and in its technical use the good news of salvation to a perishing world; the revelation of free pardon and the promise of eternal life to sons and daughters of apostacy and guilt. It finds its necessity in the fact of human depravity, and comprehends all those doctrines of grace and truth which flow from God, and through Jesus Christ result in the complete salvation of sinners. The Apostle styles it "our gospel," not, however, with any feeling of pride and selfish appropriation, which the whole scope of the passage disproves, but in contradistinction to the schemes of philosophic teachers, and especially in distinction from the instrumentality employed under the Old Testament. It was committed to him and his fellow-labourers, to make it known among men; and with respect to their ministry of the truth, there was one fact which set it above all other means of instruction, the Holy Spirit wrought with them in the dispensation committed to their hands, imparting strength to their own hearts, and sealing the truth on the hearts of their hearers. Hence it is called the ministration of the Spirit.

II. *We call your attention to the intimation that this gospel and all its benefits may be hid, is hid from the minds of some.*

The Apostle makes mention of two veils which concealed from the minds of the Jews the true import of their law, and with these he contrasts the gospel, in our text. The first veil rested on the law itself; it arose from the obscurity of the types and figures of that economy which were the symbols of those spiritual things the Jews were not ready to apprehend. But the second veil was on their hearts; it was that their perverse prejudices and corrupt affections blinded their minds to the purity of the truth, and the import of those shadows of good things to come, of which the substance was Christ, and redemption through Him. And the Apostle would intimate, that if under the former dispensation there might have existed some excuse for the Jews, under the gospel there could be none; there was no impenetrable veil resting on its pages; it was fully authenticated and plainly preached. Neither in the Gospel, nor yet in the method of its promulgation, was to be found the difficulty. Nothing but the veil on their hearts could shut out its light from any minds, and render them insensible to its claims. If any did not discern its truth, their own prejudices, their pride, their sinful lusts intervened to obscure its lustre, and preclude them from its blessings. And where the same conduct is indulged among us, the same consequences must ensue. Among the various classes who are thus blinded to the sacred oracles, there are indeed different modes by which the god of this world accomplishes his fatal purpose, though all may be traced finally to the depravity of the human heart.

1. The gospel is hid to those who deny its divine origin, and who, impelled by the pride or the lusts of the mind, embrace instead a cold and cheerless infidelity.

2. It is hid to those who make no personal application of its

doctrines, and in whom it exerts no experimental power. There is a large class of persons who professedly accredit its divinity, and in words acknowledge the truth and even the importance of its doctrines, whose belief and concern seem there to end. They have no conception of its spiritual design, nor do they seek to attain it. As to personal, practical religion, a personal acceptance of Christ by faith, a personal renovation of the heart, they do not seek it, perhaps do not believe in it. Compare, then, the large portion of gospel hearers with this standard, and how lamentably, even by their own professions, do they fall short. One professes to believe that a good moral life, a decent attention to the relative duties of his station, or perhaps doing no harm to any, is enough. On such ground he rests his hopes. Another, without venturing the infidel's creed, yet feels a repugnance to what is termed the strictness of the gospel, and makes this an excuse for not complying with its practical demands. With another again, making, perhaps, high pretensions to reverence for religion, it becomes a matter of mere sentimentalism, and the preaching of the gospel a mere gratification of the taste, while the heart is still unrenewed, and Christ is rejected. Of intellectual hearers there are not a few such.

III. *Notice the consequence.* "*If our gospel be hid, it is hid to them that are lost.*"

The Apostle, by this emphatic expression, evidently intends to refer to the final award which they will meet in the presence of the Judge. Then "the wicked shall be driven away in his wickedness."

1. We are taught by this subject the entire sufficiency of the gospel and its ministration for all the purposes of instruction, conviction, and conversion. Such is very clearly the thought in the mind of the Apostle, and the point of the text; for the benevolence of Deity has provided this scheme, and if it fail, men are lost. "If they hear not Moses and the prophets, neither will they be persuaded though one rose from the dead." Wisely and justly are we shut up unto the faith of the gospel.

2. We learn the consequences that must necessarily ensue upon our neglect or rejection of the gospel. It is left with you, as moral and accountable agents, to embrace or refuse it. Means and motives, light and authority are employed, and if all these fail, "if our gospel is still hid, they to whom it is hid are lost."

Tubbs and Brook, Printers, 11, Market Street, Manchester.

The Open Door.

By Rev. EDWARD N. KIRK, DD., Boston.

"BEHOLD, I have set before thee an open door, and no man can shut it: for thou hast a little strength, and hast kept my word, and hast not denied my name."—REV. 3 : 8.

THE description of this local church is a just description of the Protestant Church viewed as one. And the promise, therefore, once verified to that local church, remains, in every age, a promise to every other to which the description is applicable. Where there is fidelity to Christ, and a desire to advance his kingdom, there he promises to open an effectual door that no power, human or Satanic, can shut.

I. *What is the appropriate work of the Protestant Church, or the true Church of God?*
 1. A defence of the Gospel.
 2. She must proclaim the Gospel to every creature.

II. *What is that open door? It is such as was given to Paul in Philippi, when he first carried the Gospel across the frontier of Europe; an opportunity to get into prison, to work hard, suffer much; but also to get the Gospel there, and plant a Christian church.*
 1. Rome is earnestly striving to reconquer the world.
 The most earnest and unwearied efforts are now on foot to bring England, Russia, and the United States, under Catholic control, and thus to shut the door.
 2. But Christ is opening it. Let us turn the glass, and look at the other side of the case. Rome has, in fact, reached her climax.
 This is the age of science, of a free press, of free discussion, of the open struggle for mastery between truth and error. Rome's method of treating error is obsolete.
 What, then, comes of all this? Two results. The Protestant churches have but little of the strength inspired by zeal and faith. And yet he that hath the keys of David hath set before them an open door. Mighty barriers have been removed within this century. They have unlimited access to the Catholic people of the world, and the motives calling them to carry the Gospel are mighty.
 One of the strangest phenomena of our age is the comparative indifference of Protestant Christians. It is in vain we exhibit the open door to those who have no desire to enter it.

The Transfiguration of Christ.
By Rev. Mr. F———.

"He was transfigured before them."—Mark 9 : 2.

THE narrative given by the different evangelists of this remarkable event in the life of our Saviour is both interesting and instructive.

Let us review the narrative, as gathered from the sacred records, and consider some of the lessons taught by it.

I. *We are taught the future glory of Christ. His appearance on the Mount of Transfiguration was a representation of the glory with which he will be invested, when, at the end of the world, he shall a second time appear upon the earth.*

II. *We are taught the doctrine of a general resurrection. The transfiguration of Christ points forward to the completion of his work, namely, his resurrection.*

III. *The transfiguration of Christ teaches another truth intimately connected with what we have been considering, namely, the doctrine of a future retribution.*

IV. *We learn from the transfiguration of Christ the abrogation of the Mosaical, and the establishment of the Evangelical, dispensation. On the mount there appeared in the persons of Moses, Elias, and Christ, the representatives of the law, the prophets, and the Gospel.*

There are several inferences, which flow naturally from the subject discussed, to which, in conclusion, I call your attention.

1. How diversified are the states of God's people upon earth! Though the three disciples were exalted to the very heavens in point of privilege, in being permitted to witness the unveiling of Christ's glory on the mount, yet this exaltation was of brief dura-

tion, for soon they had to descend into the valley again, and to go "through much tribulation in their way to the kingdom." Thus is it with all the people of God. Their life is at best a chequered scene; joy is quickly followed by sorrow.

2. If Moses and Elias left heaven to converse with Christ in regard to the decease which he should accomplish at Jerusalem, surely that subject is of the greatest importance. And if it occupied their thoughts and attention, surely it should occupy ours.

3. If we would have our bodies made like unto the glorious body of Christ, we must be like him in the spirit and temper of our minds.

Strength against Temptation.

By Rev. E. H. GILLETT, New York.

"Be strong in the Lord.—Eph. 6 : 10."

ON the eve of one of one of the most eventful of England's naval conflicts, Nelson hung aloft from the mast-head that inspiring admonition, which was read with a thrill of heroic feeling by his fleet : "England expects every man to do his duty." Not less startling and inspiring, as addressed to the young men of our land, should be the stirring admonition that comes to us from a greater leader, and at a crisis more momentous, Be strong in the Lord.

I. *The strength required.*

1. It is not primarily physical strength. The time was when this was a prime element in the estimate of a man, nor can we doubt that it is undervalued now.

2. Neither does the direction of the text apply specifically to intellectual strength. This is not without its importance, although without moral aims it is a blind giant, and with perverted aims it is a wilful giant.

3. But far more important than this is moral strength. Here, too, something depends upon original endowment. There are some whose moral natures seem made of wax. Most unfortunately there is nothing in them like flint to strike fire from. The

devil shapes them at will, as a woman kneads her dough. A strong temptation bears them away, as a whirlwind does the down of a thistle.

Yet sometimes where we witness this, it is not all due to nature. It would be a libel upon her to say so.

There is a moral greatness, not necessarily religious, which we admire, for it is strong. It may be heathen greatness, it may be a Pagan strength, but it rests upon the basis of strong character, and the moral element of it forces our applause. There was strength, when Socrates scorned to escape from prison, and chose rather to drink the fatal hemlock. There was strength, when Joseph Reed, of Revolutionary memory, approached by bribes of British gold, nobly replied: " I am poor, very poor, but poor as I am, the King of Great Britain is not rich enough to buy me."

But how much more noble and enviable than this is the strength of religious principle, strength in God. It is not strong necessarily in muscle, in intellect, in strategy; but it is strong in resistance to moral assault, to temptations that, in winning guise and in more than carnal strength, would draw the soul to perdition. The real battle of life is with Satan and his arts and followers, and the real hero is he who wins in this conflict. Strength here is real strength —it is the strength of angels, the strength of God. It lays hold upon the arm of Jehovah. It plants itself upon the rock of ages, and then it defies the world. Assaulted by bribes, it scorns them. Threatened by power, it despises its terrors. Lured by honours, it tramples them under foot. Charmed by pleasures, it stops its ear to their syren song.

II. *But whence is this strength to come? Be strong in the Lord, is the reply.*

The strength that alone is stronger than the world, is strength from above, strength in the Lord. Many a time, without this, all other energy has shown itself to be pitiably weak.

It is he who looks to an eternal crown, who can afford to spurn the poor rewards of earth's ambitions, he who feels that God's eye is on him, who cares not for the averted looks or the scrutinizing glance of men.

Where is the secret of his strength? Follow him to the cross, where he goes to gaze and meditate—follow him to the place of solitary communing with God in prayer, and you shall see. He went there overburdened, consciously weak. He comes back strong, a spiritual giant.

The shield of faith quenches all the fiery darts of the devil. He stands his ground. Tell him there is a fortune for a lie. He will show you that the lie would leave its leprosy behind it to taint the fortune. Tell him of the pleasures of gay society and of the mazy dance. He calmly looks upward, exclaiming, There they sing the new song. Vex him with taunts, and reproaches, and ridicule, and studied contempt; how firmly he replies with his eye on Calvary, I will not shrink to tread the path my Master trod.

Surely the strength of a true life is in God and from God.

The Omnipresence of God.

By Rev. JAMES W. ALEXANDER, D.D., New York.

"WHITHER shall I flee from thy presence."—PSALM 139 : 7.

THERE is a mystery about the Divine Omnipresence, which we do not learn to solve, after years of meditation. As God is a simple spirit, without dimensions, parts, or susceptibility of division, he is equally, that is, fully, present at all times in all places.

His attribute of essential presence were the same if universal matter were blotted out. Only by a figure can God be said to be in the universe; for the universe is comprehended by him.

Such Omnipresence as we have predicated of the Most High is absolutely incomprehensible. Yet we have to believe it, because the reverse would be absurd.

And it seems to me that we shall succeed in bringing this vital and precious doctrine more near to our apprehensions if we so revolve it on its axis as to present to us some of the several perfections of God as concerned in his Omnipresence. As the idea of God is the idea of his collected attributes, the omnipresence of God is the presence everywhere and at all times of all these attributes.

I. *It is the Omnipotent God who is omnipresent.*

II. *God is Omnipresent as the Allwise.*

III. *He who is Omnipresent is the Holy One of Israel.*

IV. *Divine Justice is Omnipresent.*

V. *He who is Omnipresent is infinite in goodness.*

The doctrine, I trust, has been applying itself to our hearts. Its practical lesson is one and simple. Walk in the power of truth which you know. Live in the deep conviction that God, as thus apprehended, is everywhere present, and is with you. Hail the tokens of his holy, loving presence on every side; in heaven, in nature, in the word. God is here; he filleth all things; he seeks your heart as his temple. Know this; believe it; recall it a thousand times; live in it; act on it. Give yourselves up, again and again, every moment, in every act, to this glorious All-present One.

The Wise Reckoning of Time.

BY REV. ALBERT BARNES, PHILADELPHIA.

"So teach us to number our days, that we may apply our hearts unto wisdom."—PSALM 90 : 12.

THE meaning of the prayer it is not difficult to understand. It is, that God would teach us to take such an estimate of life that we may be led to act AS IF we saw its close—AS IF we saw the number of days that we are to live. For wise, and not unobvious reasons, God has concealed the end of life from us. (1) Because if sinners knew the exact hour when they were to die, they would defer preparation to the last day or hour, knowing that they would have time then to attend to it; or (2) because, if men knew the exact time when they were to die, the world would be filled with gloom, and our houses become like the cells of condemned malefactors, for what would be the effect on the families that compose this congregation, to understand precisely the names of those among us who are to die this year? What sadness would be in our dwellings as we looked upon the child dear to us destined to death, as the day drew near! Or (3) because the kind of uncertainty which now hangs over the awful subject, is best adapted to lead us without delay to prepare for our departure. The two settled things are all that is needful for us—first, the event is not far distant; and, second, it *may* occur at any year, any month, any hour.

What would be the answer to this prayer, if it were answered? What views of life would it enable us to take? What plans would it lead us to form? These questions will direct our meditations, and in a series of observations I shall aim to answer them.

I. *We should obtain a practical view of life as exceedingly short.*

II. *We should obtain a view of our fast-fleeing days and years as a precious part of probation.*

III. *We should be led to act as if life were soon to close.*

IV. *It would lead to the change of many plans which we are now forming, and which are far from the wisdom which would be suggested by the proper numbering of our days.*

V. *Such an answer to the prayer would show the propriety of an immediate attention to whatever is necessary to prepare to die.*

To die—dreaded, repulsive, chilling word; I know you will

think of it as little as you can ; but I know also that the time is not far distant when it *must* be thought of ; and I know too, that, by the help of the Almighty Spirit, I could show you how that word would lose almost all its terrors ; perhaps become a subject of delightful contemplation. Pleasant or unpleasant, however, it is a word and a thing that pertains to you and me—and we are equally interested in knowing what is a proper preparation for it. I am drawing near to the close of my remarks, and I would finish what I have to say by pressing this point on your attention. What is to be done ? How ?

With some of you, my hearers, everything is to be done. To this day, in some instances, in a life already somewhat protracted, you have done literally *nothing* to prepare for the eternity which is before you.

Unpardoned, unrenewed, unsanctified, worldly, ambitious, vain, unreconciled to God, and designing to remain thus, I admonish you, with the fidelity of a pastor, and the tenderness of a friend, that for such a purpose you must soon give account to God.

And ye Christians, friends of the Redeemer, heirs of glory, who have been taught by the Eternal Spirit that your days are like the weaver's shuttle, will you not to-day in sincerity breathe forth this prayer, and open your bosoms to the heavenly answer ? So teach us to number our days, that we may apply our hearts to wisdom.

Carried into Abraham's Bosom.

By Rev. O. P. CONKLIN, New York.

"AND was carried by the angels into Abraham's bosom."—LUKE 16 : 22.

THERE is much that is great and godlike in the human mind, even though debased by the fall. And it is a redeeming feature of our fallen nature that so much of sympathy and tenderness and affection are left. Seldom is the dying man destitute of some one to cling to while life lasts. But what then, Is the soul left alone, then—left to wing its way in solitude ? By no means. Just here comes in one of the most interesting revelations of the Bible, and one of the prominent revelations of my text—to wit that as soon as the redeemed and sanctified soul leaves the body it enters into immediate and conscious fellowship with angels. But, beautiful and interesting as is this first revelation of our text, it is by no means its main or most important revelation. Nor is it the one for which I have selected it. This main revelation may be considered and treated as threefold, involving,—

I. *There are chief places of bliss in heaven.*

Among the Jews, festivals, and religious festivals too, were common. Very many of their ideas of happiness and of religious enjoyment would concentrate' therefore, around the festival. Hence it would not be unnutural for a Jew to conceive of heaven as a great and interminable religious festival. That the Jews did so conceive of it, is evident enough from several of the representations of the New Testament. Our Lord himself spoke of heaven as his Father's house, in which there are many mansions. Such a house would be perfectly adapted for social, festive, and religious intercourse. Abraham was the father of the Jewish Church, as indeed he is the father of true believers under the Christian dispensation. Abraham would preside at that festival, in order that the figure may be consistently carried out according to Jewish apprehensions; for, as at a family festival, the father of the family would preside, so at the heavenly festival the father of the faithful would of course preside. Now the place of honour at any festival was next to the master of the feast, and the expression of our text, "Into Abraham's bosom," shows that Lazarus had this place of honour.

II. *The second thought is, that these chief places are occupied by those whose mortal lives were full of sickness and suffering.*

Lazarus was carried to Abraham's bosom, that is, to a chief place in heaven. Why was it so? If the declaration had been made of Paul, we should not so much have wondered at it. He could see that he was not toiling and suffering in vain. He could see the kingdom of the Lord extending, could see churches springing up and flourishing in the midst of heathen abominations; could see multitudes turning to God, through his instrumentality, and preparing to shine as stars for ever and ever in the crown of his rejoicing. There was also much in his very activity, and the constant change of scene and incident, to divert his mind from cares and sorrows, and restore it to a healthful and elastic state; and the same is true of all who, like Paul, are permitted to spend their lives in the active service of their Master. But how different with those who serve the Lord by a meek submission to his will, through a life of sickness. All such must walk by faith alone. They can see no good results to others from their lives. The dull monotony of the sick chamber, the frequent necessity of avoiding company, the lack of occupation, the corroding effects of pain, the long and dismal nights, and the cheerless days. Whosoever, therefore, resists all these evil influences and tendencies, and still keeps up faith and hope—still serves God by meekness, submission, and fear—still hushes every murmur, and kisses the rod, does, to a certainty, more to magnify religion, and exhibit its glories and triumphs, than could possibly be done in the brilliant career of Paul. Now this was manifestly just what Lazarus did, and this was just the reason why he was carried by angels into Abraham's bosom.

III. *That such lives are not to be esteemed mainly useless : nor are they to occasion one murmuring or repining thought.*

In our day, the call for action is so loud, as to seem almost the only call upon the follower of Christ. And when one is debarred from active effort, he seems to himself almost shut out from usefulness. But the revelations of our text show us that this is a false view. Religion does as much need passive, suffering exemplifiers, as it does active, flaming exemplifiers. The service of the sufferer is a more difficult, and therefore a higher, service than that of the labourer. Not every one is qualified for the higher service. God, therefore, sometimes takes those who promised to be the most effective labourers, and transforms them into sufferers; and we, in the lowness and narrowness of our views, stand by and look on wondering.

God appoints some to be bright and shining lights in the pathway of suffering, while others are spared, simply because such are better fitted to honour him, and illustrate the soul-sustaining power of the Gospel in this most difficult sphere. To our limited view, their lives seem incomplete, and the dealings of God mysterious, perhaps severe.

God is his own interpreter, and all shall hereafter be made clear, consistent and glorious.

Alpha and Omega.

By Rev. J. M. SHERWOOD, Bloomfield, New Jersey.

"I am Alpha and Omega, the beginning and the end, the first and the last."—Rev. 22 : 13.

CHRISTIANITY is older than the creation, and will outlive it. It is not an after-thought, but the first in the Divine mind, the pervading spirit and genius of all its out-goings. It is not an arrangement lying on the surface of things; but it is radical and all-comprehensive in its relations to the Government of God. It penetrates to the foundation of the eternal mind, it guides the counsels of the Godhead, it gives direction to all creative and administrative power. It is itself the brightest and the crowning manifestation of God to his creatures.

I. *Jesus Christ is the real Alpha and Omega of the present order of things.*

By the present order of things, I mean the entire creation of God as it now is, the infinite number of worlds and systems which are in being, with the various orders of intelligences which people them, together with the Power which governs and disposes of this entire material and spiritual universe.

Now, in an absolute sense, Christ is the Alpha and Omega of this whole creation. He is over it all, and in it all, and the life of it all, and the genius of it all, and the substance and end of it all—The Fountain of being, the Source of Power, the absolute Ruler, the efficient Life, and the final Cause. Creative power begins with and ends in him. Providence is the executor of his will. Redemption underlies all the arrangements, counsels, and purposes of God. Christ in his person and office is the real centre of the universe. The Cross is the symbol of the power which is evolving, directing, shaping, and consummating the everlasting kingdom of Jehovah.

II. *Jesus Christ is the Alpha and Omega of all the divine manifestations made to the creatures of God.*

God is a spirit, having no visible form or sensible quantities. Before he can be known or contemplated by us, there must be some manifestation of himself.

We have in the material universe a most wonderful manifestation of God. All his natural attributes are thereby brought to light, and we are confronted with Deity.

But the light of nature affords but an imperfect and uncertain idea of God.

It is the plan and work of human redemption which most clearly and signally makes God known to man, and even to angels. This work has Christ's mediation for its basis, Christ's atonement for its grand expression, and the Holy Spirit as its efficient agent.

We know nothing of God save as Christ has revealed him in his own person and work.

It is in Christ only that God speaks, shines forth, acts. The glory of the Godhead shines for us only in the face of Jesus Christ. We see in him God's moral perfections as well as his natural attributes. The goodness, and mercy, and holiness, and justice of God find fearful expression in the person and work of the incarnated One.

The material universe is not studied aright by us till it is made radiant in the light of the cross. Divine Providence is a sealed book till the Lion of the Tribe of Judah breaks the seal and interprets it to us.

III. *Christ is the Alpha and Omega of the Holy Scriptures.*

He is the central character, the life, the essence, the burden, and the substance of them. To set forth Jesus Christ as the way, the truth, and the life, is their chief end. He is not lost sight of from Genesis to the Revelation. He is the first promise of mercy made to man, and equally the last. His office-work, and history are blended and interwoven with the whole structure of Revelation. His coming in the flesh was the central fact around which clustered all the promises and prophecies, the expectations and economies of the Old Testament dispensations. His sacrificial sufferings were symbolized on Jewish altars till the Sacrifice of nobler name appeared. He was the one Hope of the patriarchs, the Burden of the prophets, the End of the Law, the Substance of the Jewish faith, the Matter of the evangelists, the Doctrine of the epistles, and the Glory of the apocalyptic visions. He is both the matter and spirit, the genius and life, the glory and the end of that Divine Revelation which is our only guide to eternity.

IV. *Christ is the Alpha and Omega of man's salvation*

This work is his from first to last. His mediation underlies it all. His death has made it possible and practicable. His blood is both the ransom and the remedy for sin. His intercession is the procuring cause of pardon. His righteousness is our only defence. His spirit awakens, converts, and sanctifies the heirs of grace. His power rules, protects, nourishes, and raises to the heavenly kingdom his chosen people.

There is no salvation for a solitary sinner aside from Christ. Salvation begins with and ends in him. No man can save himself. All the world united, and all the angels in heaven, could not deliver a solitary sinner from the curse of God's violated law.

This mighty work the Father has intrusted to his Son.

V. *Christ is the Alpha and Omega of the life of God in the soul of the believer.*

By nature we are dead in sin, and no will or power of man can give us life.

Christ is the Life of God in the soul; in its feeblest beginnings, in all its growth and development, and in its final completion. Every virtue and every grace of the Spirit is from him. Every holy exercise, every gracious affection, every acceptable service, every victory over sin and the devil, every enjoyment in God, every attainment in grace, and every hope of glory—all come from Christ as the Fountain, or procuring Cause, or efficient Agent.

And being the Alpha of this new life, he will not fail to be the Omega of it also.

VI. *Christ is the Alpha and Omega of the saints' final glory.*

Heaven is the culmination of Christ's power and of Gospel blessedness.

Christ is the Head, the central Life, the great Attraction, and the chief Glory of that exalted and everlasting kingdom. He is the Theme of that one song in which the glorified will give expression to their eternal gratitude and felicity.

Christ is now in every believer's soul "the hope of glory;" then he will be our glory consummated and realized. Grace began with him, and eternal glory shall be completed in him.

1. We infer from this subject that Jesus Christ is an indispensable necessity to every one of us. Talent, genius, wealth, power, influence, life itself, all are vain and useless unless consecrated to Jesus Christ.

Yes! this Christ whom we preach to you to-day, dying sinner, is the one great want of your nature. Your heart wants his love. Your life wants his blessing. Your soul wants his atoning and cleansing blood. Your eternity wants his glorious presence.

2. How real and how fearful is the sin of living away life and probation aside from the service and glory of Jesus Christ.

It is true that some of my hearers live as regardless of Jesus Christ as if there was not such a being in all the universe. You have never prayed to him. You have not entered his service. You have not consulted his glory in a solitary act of your life. You have not sought his pardoning mercy. His love has not blessed you. His Gospel has brought no life and peace to your soul. You have no interest in him. You have laid up no portion in his kingdom. Life hastens to its end, and probation wears away, and yet Christ has received no glory from you; and without him your eternity will be one of woe and wrath.

Jesus the Mediator.

By Rev. WALTER CLARKE, DD., New York.

"For there is one God, and one mediator between God and men, the man Christ Jesus."—1 Timothy 2; 5.

NOT till we understand that our Lord is the mediator, can we comprehend any of his subordinate offices or explain any of his dependent and secondary names. And this is our topic this morning—Jesus the mediator between God and men.

A mediator is a person adjusting certain affairs which are at issue between the parties for whom he deliberates and acts. He may derive his office from the mutual choice of the parties, or from his own natural relations and rights, or by appointment from one having authority in the premises. What shall be his particular task, and what his official powers, will be determined in every instance by the case in hand.

I. *My first point shall designate the parties between whom Christ is set to negotiate and act.*

Our text says He is the mediator between God and men. Observe: not between God and some men; God and the Israelites;

God and the saints; God and the elect. The language is universal. There is one God; for all nations, ages, and people, one and but one God. Between these two universal parties, then—between the everlasting God on one side, and his human children on the other—between him and each particular tribe, household, and person of the race, stands Jesus Christ the appointed and actual mediator.

II. *But what was there in the circumstances and relations of God, or of men, or of the moral universe, to make it necessary or advisable to introduce a mediator, and delegate divine and human interests to his charge?*

To this question Scripture and Reason give the like sufficient answer. The apostacy of Adam had taken place under an admistration of law. That open revolt of our humanity had thrown the moral constitution of the world into utter disorder. Here, then, was our sad and pitiable condition. During a brief and disastrous probation under a government of divine law, we had transgressed and fallen. That government of law held us as prisoners; it could allow us no reprieve, no new trial, no forgiveness, no favour. In such circumstances, if God, yielding to his paternal compassion, could do anything for our recovery, the first act of mercy must be to transfer us from this now vindictive economy of law into another realm and another covenant, where we could enjoy temporary exemption from the penalty of sin, and have a new probation under conditions of lenity and grace. Fix distinctly in mind, my hearers, the difference between these two systems of divine administration. They are called in the Scriptures covenants. Our race rebelled and fell in the former scheme, in the dispensation and under the reign of law. If they should remain in that economy, Reason and Scripture declare alike the inevitable consequences. They can have no second probation, no momentary reprieve, no forgiveness, no relief, no [restoration, no escape. Mercy said, Let something be done for this perishing race. And since the first thing to be done was to remove them out of that ruinous scheme of law into a new dispensation of grace. Mercy said, Make the transfer; put these perishing souls under that better covenant into that better economy. Who, then, shall take charge of them? Here is a new kingdom to be set up, a new government to be administered. Who shall represent the supreme authority? Who fill the waiting throne? And as he is not the father, but the Father's deputy, this new king must be mediator between God and men. Here was the state of things and here the emergency, in God's universal government, which called for a mediator. Thus are we and all the children of Adam in new relations to Jesus Christ.

III. *It remains that we should now inquire as to the extent of Christ's authorized mediation.*

Certain matters lying between God and us have gone now into the hands of Jesus Christ. Upon all these matters we are to have dealing not with the Father: he refuses—he says to us, Treat with my Son—hear him. What are these questions?

For example: The race through disobedience of the divine law, had fallen into utter apostacy and ruin. But God would give them an opportunity of pardon and restoration; would give them, that is, a new trial under a new system, and with the aid of sufficient helps, and remedies, and means. Before they could be removed terms must be made with the divine government; the execution of the law staid; a truce procured; a reprieve granted. Justice must be so satisfied that she shall yield to the solicitations of Mercy, and surrender her captives. If men are released from impending wrath, it must be as prisoners are sometimes allowed to go forth from confinement, on suitable bail and sufficient security. And if Christ will be our mediator, he must instantly step into this gap, and stand in this breach, and become responsible for us. The Father proposed, and Christ accepted, this most responsible post of mediator. Accordingly the Scriptures tell us that through all the universe of God, Jesus Christ is known and trusted as the surety of this new covenant.

Again: when this transfer is effected, and the race is removed from the domain of law into that of mercy, it will devolve upon their mediator to have exclusive charge of them there. The Scriptures tell us, therefore, that accepting the office of mediator, Jesus became at once the superintendent and Lord of the whole human race.

And then, if the race is to have a new probation in a new economy, and under a new king, there must be instituted and administered among them a new Providential government.

But more: The race had lost the knowledge of their Maker. If they were to have a new probation, and under a new economy, there must be a new revelation of the now unknown God. For the must be set forth now as God in Christ. Here, therefore, was a fourth work which the mediator must take in hand. Men were to be pupils for a time in this new school of mercy.

Further than this: If the race is to have a new trial, and that with a view to final restoration, there must be conditions of acceptance, and terms of pardon.

Once more: There must be introduced into this new scheme of mercy a great system of renovation, in the use of which penitent men shall be regenerated, and trained, and sanctified more and more, till they are restored to perfect holiness and made meet to be admitted among the sons of God in heaven. This work, therefore, must be delivered into the hands of the mediator. And since this is the appropriate work of the Holy Spirit, the Spirit and all those instruments and helps, which he uses in sanctifying our fallen manhood, must be given to Christ, that he may employ and impart and administer them as he shall find reason or need in his mediatorial reign. It was not without a meaning, therefore, that the Saviour directly on his return to heaven, sent the Holy Spirit to reside among men.

We must not omit in this rapid enumeration of the objects of God's convenant of mercy, the fact that the plan of redemption required the establishment in our world of the Christian Church. Our Lord is the appointed Head of the Church. Finally the plan of grace requires that there should be in this system of mercy a tribunal of judgment, that they who submit to the terms of redemption may be formally accepted and saved, and they who remain obdurate and disobedient be openly cast off and condemned. Christ has explicitly informed us that this concluding work of judgment has been deputed entirely to him. The Father judgeth no man, but hath committed all judgment to the Son.

This account of Christ's mediatorial office shows us, first, and by way of application,

1. Why it is that the Saviour so uniformly calls to us to come to him.

2. The sufficiency, propriety, and perfect safety of the way of salvation by faith in Crist.

3. The precise nature of Christian justification.

4. That this mediatorial scheme in which we are having present probation, is only a brief episode in the divine government, and must, therefore, soon come to an end. The plan was to give the race one more opportunity and one new trial. And so soon as it has been fully proved that the rejectors of mercy are resolute and incorrigible, they will be removed from this realm of mercy into the prison house of woe in the Father's empire of law. Then Jesus will surrender his throne, deliver up his kingdom, and enter with his saints into the house and presence of the Father.

The Providence of God.

By Rev. ELIAS NASON, MEDFORD, MASS.

"FOR we know that all things work together for good to them that love God."—ROM. 8 : 28.

THE declarations of Scripture in respect to the destiny of the true Christian, are such as to fill his heart with the liveliest gratitude.

They assure him that a far-seeing intellect is planning for him; that a mighty, unseen hand is guiding him; that a shield of celestial temper is protecting him; and that blessings greater than his mind is able to conceive, are in reserve for him.

I. *In the development of this heart-cheering thought, I would observe, that God deals with his children after a fixed and definite plan.*

II. *That God not only carries on his great designs by a preëstablished plan; but that the minutest concerns of human life are also comprehended in it.*

It stands revealed to us, that not a sparrow falleth unobserved by him; that the very hairs of our head are numbered by him; that he is present every where and knoweth all things.

Now we observe in the course of nature, as of Providence, that the most signal events do often hinge and hang upon what seem to us the most minute and trifling circumstance—

"A pebble in a streamlet scant
  Has turned the course of many a river;
A dew-drop on the tiny plant
  Has warped the giant oak for ever."

III. *But God has a plan; that plan extends to the minutest circumstances in the Christian's life; and by that plan God makes every thing work together for his good.*

It *is* a blessed privilege to be a Christian; and I would to God that every one who hears me would renounce his sins, come to the Lord and *be* one!

It *is* a blessed thing to be a Christian. All things are turning and labouring and conspiring to bless him.

The rudest blocks God's cunning hand works in to build the temple; and all becomes resplendent by the grace of Jesus Christ.

(1.) Then let me say, if God be working so for us, my brother, we ought not to be too solicitous about results.

(2.) Let us also suppress our murmurings at the allotments of providence.

(3.) If all things are working together for our good, what reason have we to envy the wicked in their riches and prosperity?

(4.) If all things be working together for good, let us cast away our fears and press onward.

(5.) And if all things are working together for our good, let us praise with livelier gratitude that crucified Redeemer who by the shedding of his blood and by his intercession at the throne has turned the streams of anger into streams of mercy, and has made our cups run over.

(6.) But while all things work together for good to those that love the Lord, we are told upon the same authority, "the way of the ungodly shall perish!"

Running all along under human plans and undertakings are the great plans and undertakings of God; and whatever schemes conflict with his, must eventually come to nought.

Is it not the hightest wisdom, then, for you that lay such plans, to come to God; open your heart to God; make your plans tally with his plans; give yourself up to his guidance; put your expectations in him, love him, and thus have all things—here—hereafter work together for your good?

The Great Preacher.

By Rev. ELIHU P. MARVIN, MEDFORD, MASS.

"AND there shall come forth a rod out of the stem of Jesse, and a Branch shall grow out of his roots: and the Spirit of the Lord shall rest upon him, the spirit of wisdom and understanding, the spirit of counsel and might, the spirit of knowledge and of the fear of the Lord; and shall make him of quick understanding in the fear of the Lord: and he shall not judge after the sight of his eyes, neither reprove after the hearing of his ears: but with righteousness shall he judge the poor, and reprove with equity for the meek of the earth: and he shall smite the earth with the rod of his mouth, and with the breath of his lips shall he slay the wicked."—Isaiah 11 : 1-4.

HERE it is distinctly prophesied that our Saviour, when he should come into the world, would be peculiarly endowed, by the Holy Spirit, with wisdom, discernment, and might in speech, such as should make him a remarkable preacher.

It was thus that he himself recognized his mission: "And he said unto them, Let us go into the next towns, that I may preach there also : *for therefore came I forth.* And he preached in their synagogues throughout all Galillee."

I. *Notice what a consummate master Jesus was of real eloquence.*

Of course I do not refer to the petty arts and studied rules of the professional orator and actor. He needed none of these to aid him ; he was infinitely above them all.

Our Saviour, being omniscient, might well surpass in power all the speakers and orators of the world. He "knew all men, and needed not that any should testify of man." Aside from earnestness and naturalness, his great power of eloquence consisted, first, in the clearness and completeness of his views ; and secondly, in his perfect command through language of all the powers and passions of the human soul.

II. *Consider how plainly and forcibly our Saviour preached the great doctrines or fundamental facts of the Gospel system.*

All his teachings have their foundation, manifestly, in the few first principles of the Gospel. His object in every conversation, every sermon, every trope, every figure and parable, was to set forth doctrine, and through it, duty, more and more distinctly and vividly.

Wherever we turned for illustrations of his eloquence, we found the distinguishing doctrines dropping naturally and copiously as the rain in vernal showers, which must so surely precede the bloom of summer and the fruits of autumn. And we shall meet them, on every hand, as we turn now,

III. *To the peculiar manner and amazing power of the Saviour's preaching.*

And here, we find the field opening so widely before us, that we can only indicate a few of his various and vast resources. We may begin with mentioning his strange faculty of holding the minds of his hearers steadily to the one simple truth which he was urging.

(*Instance Nicodemus and the Woman of Samaria.*)

Again there seems to be this striking difference between the Lord Jesus and all other preachers: *They* receive the truth by revelation, and seek to demonstrate it by reason and argument. *He* announces it by direct knowledge and authority. It requires no effort on his part to make it real. The spiritual world is all unveiled to him: he sees what he represents. Hence there is a vividness in his delineations which is often startling,

A few examples will make very plain this peculiar manner and astonishing power of The Great Teacher.

(*Parables, &c.*)

Treasures of a Well-spent Life.

By Rev. JOEL HAWES, D.D., Hartford, Ct.

"Laying up in store for themselves a good foundation against the time to come, that they may lay hold on eternal life."—1 Timothy 6 : 19.

THESE words, viewed in their connection, inculcate the duty of living and acting with a wise reference to our future good ; or of so spending life, as it passes, that we may lay for ourselves an abiding foundation of happiness against a coming time of need, and so lay hold on eternal life.

But I do not propose to dwell on this duty now, just in the form here expressed, but to bring before you a subject obviously enough suggested by the text, and which, I hope, may be useful as the theme of the present discourse. It is this—the treasures of a well-spent life.

I. *Let us first endeavour to form a just idea of what is meant by such a life.*

A brief answer is—a well-spent life is a life so spent as to secure the great end of living. And what is that end? The answer in the Catechism cannot be bettered—"It is to glorify God and enjoy him for ever." No life is well spent which disregards or fails of this great ultimate end of human existence.

In a single sentence, a well-spent life is a life early imbued with the principles of piety, and unfolds itself under the influence of the truth and grace of God. It is virtuous, diligent, frugal; it is kind, benevolent, generous; it is animated with love to God and love to man, and as age comes on, it keeps itself warm and living by keeping itself in contact with the living, moving world around.

II. *Treasures of which I am now to speak—the treasures of a well-spent life. What are they?*

1. The first item in the inventory which I mention is health and cheerfulness, especially in the decline of life. These, we all know, are blessings of inestimable value; and though not the invariable, they certainly are the usual attendants of a life spent as just described.

2. Pleasant reflections on the past.

It is a fact not enough thought of by many, that life reproduces itself in its decline, or is lived over again in advanced age.

3. Sustaining consolations in the present, and joyful anticipations in the future.

4. A rich inheritance to be transmitted to children, and other near relatives and friends.

It is a treasure of Christian example, of holy influence, of heavenly teaching, of prevailing prayer, including covenant promises of God's favour here and of his eternal friendship and love hereafter.

5. The rewards of heaven must be taken into the account, if we would estimate aright the treasures of a well-spent life. Such a life does not terminate in itself or at the grave. It gathers up the results of its entire course on earth, and sends them forward to enhance its joy and blessedness in the future world.

I close with two remarks, suggested by the subject:

1. The poorest sincere Christian on earth is richer than the rich-

est worldling. Take an illustration from the parable of Dives and Lazarus, in the 16th chapter of Luke.

2. Or subject reminds us of the heritage of poverty and misery which an ill-spent life is sure to gather to itself in the latter end.

Are any of wou, my hearers, living such a life ; a life of estrangement from God, and of all due preparation for the coming time of need ? This may seem a light matter to you now ; but not so when life's courseis run, and the results ef it gather around the closing scene, and you are called, as death draws near, to reflect on the past, to consider the present, and look to the future with all its solemn issues before you.

Let all, then, begin right who would spend life right. Begin with God ; enthrone him over the heart and life ; take His will as the rule and His glory as the end of your being, looking to both worlds, fully determind to make the most of your existence, whether it be now or never so many myriads of ages hence.

The Future State of the Heathen.

By Rev. ENOCH POND, D.D., Bangor, Maine.

"The end of these things is death."—Rom. 6 : 21.

THE Apostle Paul in this verse, and in those which precede it, is addressing those who had recently been converted from heathenism to the faith of the Gospel. He reminds them that, in their former heathen state, they had been "the servants of sin." They had "yielded their members servants to uncleanness, and to iniquity unto iniquity." But in the text he assures them that "the end of these things is death." "For," he immediately adds, "the wages of sin is death ; but the gift of God is eternal life, through Jesus Christ our Lord." The death here spoken of stands in immediate contrast with eternal life. Consequently, it must be eternal death.

In contemplating the future state and prospects of the heathen, it is proposed to show—

I. *That the heathen are sinners against God.*

II. *That being sinners, they are justly exposed to the penalty of the divine law.*

III. *That from this penalty they can not be delivered without repentance and reformation.*

IV. *That the heathen in general exhibit no satisfactory evidence of repentance, but the contrary.* And

V. *The Scriptures teach directly, and not by mere inference, that the end of heathenism is eternal death.*

There is a remedy for all this evil; a remedy sovereign and effectual! and this we have in our own hands. It is the Gospel. This offers peace and pardon to those who are guilty and ready to perish. This bears on its wings of love the messages of light and salvation to those who sit in darkness, and in the region and shadow of death. Let the Gospel be universally diffused and embraced, and the broad road to ruin is no longer frequented.

Divine Instrumentalities.

By Rev. SAMUEL W. FISHER, D.D., New York.

"Thus saith the Lord to his anointed, to Cyrus, whose right hand I have holden, to subdue nations before him; and I will loose the loins of kings, to open before him the two-leaved gates; and the gates shall not be shut."—Isaiah 45 : 1-6.

IT is an obvious fact that, for the enlargement of his Church, God often selects special instruments. In setting into motion a whole system of agencies this is almost uniformly the case. We recognize the fact all along the history of the Church. We see men raised up with peculiar gifts and clothed with peculiar powers to effect certain great works. The text gives us a remarkable illustration of this method of divine procedure. Cyrus was a heathen; but there was that in his character, training, and circumstances that preeminently fitted him for the special work he was to perform as the restorer of the Church.

In the bosom of the Church itself there are two still more remarkable examples of this law; the two men who bore the largest part in the inauguration and establishment of the chief dispensations. Moses and Paul, instance also Luther, Calvin, and Whitfield.

It is just as certain that the great Sovereign chooses *particular nations* to effect certain parts of his work in the final triumph of the Gospel. " *This people have I* FORMED *for myself; they shall show forth my praise.*"

This nation, to whom the passage before us refers, is a marked illustration of this thought. The Jew was designed to be the *conservator* of the word of God. He was chosen for this purpose.

At every step of the progress of Christianity since, illustrations multiply of the truth contained in our text, that God forms nations to his work, and chooses them because of their fitness to accomplish certain parts of that work.

Other nations have contributed some of the finest influences that have moulded us; our position has modified our character; but the vitality, the commanding energy that has given birth to such great results, is directly traceable to the Anglo-Saxon. The nation which has brought forth Whitefield and Wesley, and Wilberforce, and Newton, and Carey, and Morrison, and Williams, and hundreds like them, has done vastly more for us than all the world besides. We glory in this filial relationship, not because it allies to earthly greatness, but to the piety which, clothed in the radiant panoply of a consecrated learning, has entered, with unconquerable zeal, into the work of preaching the Gospel to every creature.

To this point, therefore, let us direct attention; let us trace out some of those things which indicate *that God has formed us as a nation to exert a special and vast influence in the evangelization of other nations.*

I. *If you look at the natural constitution of this race, you will see in it an admirable fitness for this work.*

The Anglo-Saxon inheriting, in common with the Northern races, strong intellectual powers, conjoins with these a hardy, persistent, energetic nature. It has the constitution which bears up under the severest toils of body and mind; it conjoins with this an energy springing from the fulness of natural vigour, that delights in action and perpetually impels to progress.

The multitudes, that from other races unite with it, are quickly subdued by its all controlling energy.

A race like this is formed of God to be a vast power for good in this world. He combined in it the finest qualities of half a dozen nations, that it might impress itself upon others. Not for itself, nor for any merely temporal object has he created it; but to diffuse the truth, to be a plastic power among the nations, in the hand of Jesus, in hastening his final triumph.

II. *Let us look now at the peculiar training which God has given to this race—a training all in harmony with this great object.*

Just as the education of Cyrus and Moses and Paul gave them a special preparation for their missions towards and in the Church, so the divine Providence has given scope and stimulus to the original endowments of the Anglo-Saxon fitting him for the offensive work of missions among the nations.

His home was on that little Isle of a few thousand square miles. The sea, the open, the boundless, the free, mingled the music of its surges with the harvest song of its reapers, and the anthems of his Sabbath worship. His ships traversed all oceans, visited all shores; round and through the world they carried the spirit and the power of the little Isle. They became the carriers for all nations, gathering peaceful tribute from all peoples.

From this adventurous spirit three results followed. The *first* was reflexive; this people who could thus take must also give. Hence sprang up the artisan; manufactories rose on all sides; villages of yesterday swelled into vast cities crowded with earnest workers. The Island became a work-shop for the world.

Associated with this was a *second* grand result. Undesigned on his part, seeking at first only a field whereon his peaceful energies could develop themselves, this Anglo-Saxon seats himself upon what was once the richest throne of the past.

India to which he went as a trader, becomes his vassal.

But in addition to this there is a *third* result of this education of the Anglo-Saxon which bears more directly upon us—a result which, more than all the others, has reacted on the race, fitting it to be God's chosen instrument for the evangelization of the world. This spirit peopled this continent. The spirit of enterprise was interpenetrated by the spirit of vital Christianity; it was guided by the practical wisdom which sought here to create the home of a free, God-fearing people.

In this process of national culture, you see the development of just those qualities which, when consecrated by the Spirit of the Gospel, are to constitute the finest missionary race in the world.

III. *Intimately connected with, and constituting part of, the method in which God is forming this people for the aggressive work of missions, are that individual freedom and the settlement of governmental difficulties and constitutional principles which have given such a peculiar form to our civilization.*

Now you are to mark this thing in this connection. These great results have been reached through protracted struggles. They are not the sudden achievement of a race, all at once casting off the disabilities and burdens of absolute power. They are the outgrowth of centuries. The blood of martyrs, the tears and prayers of confessors, revolutions now peaceful, now sanguinary, now moving forward under the impulse of deep religious conviction, then struggling into life as the result of the native love of freedom, reforms, experiments, crises and eras of vast significance, succeeding each other for nearly two centuries, have consecrated, watered and developed these principles. It is the long process through which a race has been unfolding the noblest energies of humanity.

IV. The providence which has thus been training us, has given us large material possessions, and the power to develop and use them.

In the material elements of national wealth, coal, iron, the precious metals, and a soil of great variety and richness, no country surpasses this. In productive power and inventive genius, this nation, by the confession of the ablest foreign writers, has no superior.

All this has a direct, logical connection with our work as a people, who are to propagate the Gospel aggressively through the world. Capital is one of the means God uses to convert the world.

V. It is admitted that if this devotion to material interest stood alone, it would soon exhaust itself, producing wealth and consequent luxury, it would conduct us speedily to a corrupt and effete civilization. But this is not the case; it is largely animated and guided by a high literary, as well as religious, culture. Education diffused through the masses has become an essential characteristic of this race.

Nor are we to pass lightly by, in this connection, the language which this race employs for the expression of its intelligence. Of all living tongues, where is there another so copious, versatile, sinewy; another that, like the race it represents, is so composite and cosmopolitan, absorbing into itself the energy and the life of all dead and living tongues?

VI. The character and position of the Protestantism we possess constitutes our most vital, substantive efficiency.

At the very beginning there was a marked distinction between the races from which we sprung and others. Christianity was always foreign to the peculiar life of the Roman and Grecian. But in the Anglo-Saxon and cognate German races, it had a different reception. And as in the Anglo-Saxon the development of the principles of the Common Law advanced, Christianity went hand in hand with it. Every step towards the establishment of individual freedom was consecrated by the higher principles of religion. When the Reformation came, asserting the right of private judgment, exalting the Bible and conscience above the authority of kings and emperors, the Anglo-Saxon, long trained in the line of civil freedom, at once grasped them and fought for them with wonderful energy. Henceforth the two were indissolubly united. No matter what was the specific object to be attained, whether political or religious, underneath the great struggle, deep in the heart of the Briton, these twin powers were the ever-present, animating forces.

The transfer of the contest to this land was only an advance in the same direction. The Protestants of Europe have a mighty conflict yet before them. They can not propagate the truth abroad over the world, until they have mastered the evil influences that settle down upon their own lands. But we have fought and won this battle.

The diversities of belief, the breaking up of the outward form of the Church into various denominations, against which Erastianism and the Papacy protest so vehemently, are securities for the perpetuity of the truth, and sources of vast efforts towards the conversion of men. They give to our Protestantism, what has been the boast of the Papacy, a place where men of every temperament and education can labour in harmony with themselves; they enlist all kinds of good and natural influences; they suit the broad aspect of society; they push themselves into new fields. What is lost from the concentration of a vast organism, is more than gained by the augmented power of individuals.

VII. *Whoever shall write the history of the American Church, will be obliged to notice the remarkable character given to it by revivals of religion.*

These have not been, as in many other churches, an occasional incident; they have entered into its life; they have given character to its development; they have marked its progress. Since the days of the Apostles, the Christian Church, in any other of its branches, has never witnessed displays of God's converting power so wonderful, numerous and extensive, as this church has enjoyed during the last sixty years.

VIII. *One thought still remains, to give completeness to our discussion. For full half a century, God has been organizing the American Church for the work of foreign missions, and training it, in actual service, for this great object.*

Early in our history, the apostolic Eliot, and a century after, the no less devoted Brainerd, illustrated and kept alive the smouldering fire. But the time had not come for the inauguration of this spirit as the all-animating life of the Church. The homework overtasked all her energies. She built her homes, and cleared her forests, and reared her sanctuaries with the rifle at her side. Then came the *great contest*. She had to win peace and freedom along the path of trial, and in garments rolled in blood. When freedom came, civil institutions were to be settled; the foundations for the highest civilization of unborn millions must be laid. And now *the hour* has come; the trains of influence from various sources converge to a point.

The conversion of the world was in itself no new idea. It was as old as the grand predictions of the prophets; it flamed forth on the apostolic banner; it had stirred the heart of the Church, in every age since Jesus ascended, to achieve her noblest victories; it floated up to heaven on the wings of sacred song; it gave strength to martyrs and confessors when the sword of persecution was unsheathed. But in its relation to us as a nation set to bear a great part in making it a reality, it was new, bold, almost presumptuous. As yet the nation had hardly won a name, much less influence among the sovereignties of the world; as yet these sovereignties held fast the doors of entrance to their benighted populations, as sternly as the eternal ice closed up the north-west passage; at, such an hour, in such circumstances, the Church heard the clarion voice summoning her to gird herself for the conversion of the world.

I take my stand at that not distant day—a day which some in this house, in a green old age, shall live to see; I behold the preparations of centuries revealing their ultimate purpose and rushing on to the grand conclusion; nations into whose languages your missionaries have translated this living truth, cast away their idols and receive it to their hearts; the Koran is a relic of the past, while mosque and minaret are consecrated to the Great Prophet; the Shastérs are powerless, while the ancient temples of Budha and Vishnu, purged from their foul and bloody incarnations, resound with the praise of the incarnate Son of God; the Tartar throne, in the kingdom of the children of the sun, is known only to history, while their crowded cities welcome the children of Him whose light shall lighten the world; Ethiopia ascends from the mephitic darkness of ages, and with her passionate heart steadied, and her feeble intellect enlarged by Christian culture sends heavenward the song of a rapturous thanksgiving; the nations that have drunk the blood of Christ's martyrs, passing through their baptism of blood, wounded and bruised hasten to the feet of Him whose sceptre is full of mercy, and whose touch alone can heal; the man of sin is broken, despairing of conquest, prays only for existence; clinging to the skirts of this vast army of Gentiles, the sons of

Abraham—the dreadful imprecation of their fathers, "His blood be upon us," expiated—read with purged vision the glowing predictions of their prophets of Jesus the Son of God ; while over ten thousand towns and cities floats the peaceful banner of the Anglo-Saxon and American Church.

Let us with one heart circle his throne with anthems of praise. " Now to the King immortal, invisible, the only wise God, and to Jesus Christ, the lamb slain from the foundation of the world, be honour, and power, and glory. for ever and ever." AMEN.

The Manifestation of Love.

By Rev. ROBERT R. BOOTH, Connecticut.

"HEREIN is love, not that we loved God, but that he loved us, and sent His Son to be the propitiation for our sins."—1 JOHN 4 : 10.

TO the consideration of this *highest love*, let me direct your thoughts. I know the majesty and glory of the theme. It is the great matter of angelic praise and wonder. It would seem to be the theme, almost the only the theme, which befits such a Sabbath as Jehovah-Jesus has permitted us to welcome, in this land remote from home, in which we assemble and spread the table of our Lord in the very place where the sacramental ordinance was first instituted, and where our Lord and Saviour yielded up his life, a ransom for us all. As we fix our thoughts upon this "love divine, all love excelling," the text suggests the following points,—

I. *In whom this wondrous love originated.*

The language of the text emphasizes and impresses this: "Herein is love, not that we loved God, but that He loved us."

II. *To whom it was displayed.*

Of this the text also teaches, in declaring that "He loved *us*." It thus concentrates the workings of this transcendant, divine love upon a *single province* in God's mighty empire, and upon a *single race* in the vast range of potentates and principalities and powers which God has created.

III. By what a sacrifice it was revealed.

Notwithstanding all that is impressive in the *origin* and the *objects* of this love of God, it is when we reach the climax in the teaching of the text that we are really humbled and hushed in awe: "He sent his Son to be the propitiation for our sins." This is the announcement which unfolds the fulness of this love ; this is the unequaled revelation of the heart of God, which constitutes the crowning glory among his infinite perfections.

1. With such a love before you, can you not trust your God, and come to him in the spirit of adoption? I ask this of believers.

2. Is there nothing in this love to touch your hard and impenitent heart, and bring you to the attitude and utterance of the Prodigal? I ask this of those who are not yet reconciled to God.

Check Out More Titles From HardPress Classics Series In this collection we are offering thousands of classic and hard to find books. This series spans a vast array of subjects – so you are bound to find something of interest to enjoy reading and learning about.

Subjects:
Architecture
Art
Biography & Autobiography
Body, Mind &Spirit
Children & Young Adult
Dramas
Education
Fiction
History
Language Arts & Disciplines
Law
Literary Collections
Music
Poetry
Psychology
Science
…and many more.

Visit us at www.hardpress.net

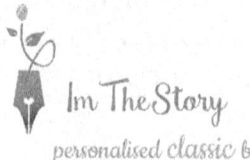

personalised classic books

"Beautiful gift.. lovely finish.
My Niece loves it, so precious!"

Helen R Brumfieldon

UNIQUE GIFT

FOR KIDS, PARTNERS AND FRIENDS

Timeless books such as:

Alice in Wonderland • The Jungle Book • The Wonderful Wizard of Oz
Peter and Wendy • Robin Hood • The Prince and The Pauper
The Railway Children • Treasure Island • A Christmas Carol

Romeo and Juliet • Dracula

Visit
ImTheStory.com
and order yours today!